FROM GERMAN
PRISONER OF WAR
TO AMERICAN CITIZEN

FROM GERMAN PRISONER OF WAR TO AMERICAN CITIZEN

A Social History with 35 Interviews

Barbara Schmitter Heisler

McFarland & Company, Inc., Publishers
Jefferson, North Carolina, and London

LIBRARY OF CONGRESS CATALOGUING-IN-PUBLICATION DATA

Heisler, Barbara Schmitter.
    From German prisoner of war to American citizen : a
social history with 35 interviews / Barbara Schmitter Heisler.
        p.   cm.
    Includes bibliographical references and index.

    ISBN 978-0-7864-7311-3
    softcover : acid free paper ∞

    1. World War, 1939–1945 — Prisoners and prisons, American.
2. Prisoners of war — United States— Interviews.   3. Prisoners
of war — Germany — Interviews.   4. Germans— United States.
5. Immigrants— United States— Interviews.   I. Title.
D805.U5H47 2013
940.54'7 — dc23   2013026684

BRITISH LIBRARY CATALOGUING DATA ARE AVAILABLE

Front cover: Several thousand German prisoners en route to their
new camps in the United States come up on deck for a few hours
of ocean air (U.S. Army Photograph)

Manufactured in the United States of America

McFarland & Company, Inc., Publishers
  Box 611, Jefferson, North Carolina 28640
  www.mcfarlandpub.com

For my father

Table of Contents

Preface

The research and writing of this book took almost ten years to complete. Its conceptual history goes back to a 1997 article in the *Washington Post* entitled "Enemies Among Us: German POWs in America" (Farquhar). The article reminded me of a remark my father had made when I was a teenager in the 1950s in Germany. While going to visit an acquaintance he had casually remarked that the man had been a prisoner of war in America. More important for the genesis of this book, Michael Farquhar's article not only provided general information on the internment of German prisoners of war on American soil, but also noted that thousands of former prisoners had returned to the United States as immigrants.

Growing up in postwar Germany, I remember well the horror stories I heard about German prisoners of war who had been held in Russia — some of whom did not return to Germany until 1956. In the 1960s and 1970s, after I had immigrated to the United States, I encountered stories about American prisoners held in Vietnam. I was immediately fascinated by what seemed unusual in the context of these stories, not only that the German prisoners in the U.S. were well treated, and even "enjoyed their stay," but that thousands wanted to return to America. As a sociologist with an abiding interest in international migration and as a German immigrant whose father — drafted into the Wehrmacht before I was born — spent a few months as a Russian prisoner of war, I found my interest piqued by the events surrounding the internment of German prisoners of war on American soil and their eventual return to the country of their captivity. I was curious to learn more about these unusual immigrants.

Given my research and teaching obligations, I had to postpone work on this subject for several years, until a sabbatical in 2002. During that time I began researching the available literature on German prisoners of war in the United States and on German postwar immigration, and I spent

1

many days in the National Archives in College Park, Maryland, looking through the accumulated files of the Provost Marshal General's Office and related records such as those of the War Manpower Commission and the Secretary of State. Much of that research provides the background information for this book.

While the literature on German prisoners of war and on German immigration in the postwar period includes some references to former prisoners of war who immigrated, my research revealed little systematic information about the men who had come as "Hitler's soldiers" and returned as immigrants. There was little on their backgrounds, their experiences as prisoners of war, their return to their war-ravaged homeland and their eventual immigration to the United States. To gather such information I set out to interview as many men as I could locate. I was keenly aware of the fact that by the time I began the research many potential respondents might be elderly and infirm or no longer be alive. This made the urgency of my project even greater. In the end, I was able to interview 35 men and I collected information on many others from published and unpublished memoirs, wives and children of men who had died, and unpublished interviews conducted by students of oral history. I only regret not having been able to start this project ten years earlier.

Although the topic is historical, this study is timely. Since the publication of Arnold Krammer's pathbreaking book *Nazi Prisoners of War in America*, first published in 1979, the subject has received renewed attention in recent years. In addition to some scholarly works, this newer literature includes a growing number of memoirs, attesting to a strong interest in the personal experiences of the men who participated in the war. At a time when our images of prisoners of war have been dominated by the excesses found at Guantánamo and Abu Ghraib, it is important to remember the very different treatment accorded to "Hitler's soldiers" on American soil. Although they were initially feared as "treacherous Nazis" bent on sabotaging the home front, their stories are reminders that even hated enemies can become friends and citizens.

This book is about the experiences of former German prisoners of war who immigrated, but it is also about postwar German immigration and the multiple hurdles confronting Germans who sought to leave Germany behind. Finally, it briefly explores the broader connections between captivity and migration, which has received little or no attention in the literature. While the events depicted in this book are relatively unusual, they are not unique. Former German prisoners of war interned in Canada also returned, as did some Italian prisoners held in the United States; and some German prisoners of war remained in France and the United Kingdom after the war. What sets this case apart are the sheer numbers involved.

I thank my respondents for giving of their time and sharing their life stories with me. Without them this book would not have been possible. My deepest gratitude goes to Hermann Kurthen, who patiently read several versions of the manuscript and whose thoughtful comments and suggestions have contributed significantly to improving the final product. All remaining mistakes are my own. I also thank Gettysburg College for providing me with travel funds necessary to conduct the interviews. Several individuals were helpful in suggesting names of possible respondents: Betty Cowley, Anita Buck, Lewis Carlson, Tom Buecker, Robert Billinger, Catherine Bell, Mary Bess Paluzzi, Kent Powell, Arnold Krammer, Michael Waters, Michael Luick-Thrams and Dietrich Kohl. Finally, special thanks go to my husband, Martin Heisler, who patiently supported my obsession with this project.

Introduction

Between 1947 and 1960 more than half a million Germans immigrated to the United States.[1] Among them were several thousand men who had been in America before. They had been part of an earlier "migration of captives" (Billinger 2000, xiv)—some 380,000 German soldiers who had been prisoners of war on American soil.[2]

Few Americans are aware of the fact that more than 400,000 enemy prisoners of war were interned on American soil during World War II. The vast majority, 380,000, were members of the Wehrmacht who had been captured by Allied forces on the battlefields of North Africa, Italy and Normandy. Transported to the United States on returning liberty ships, troop transporters and ocean liners, they were interned in some 500 camps located throughout the continental United States. The first contingent of prisoners, all members of the Heeresgruppe Afrika (Field Marshal Rommel's famed Afrika Korps), arrived on American soil in November 1942; the last able-bodied prisoners returned to Europe in July 1946. Depending on when they arrived and returned, these involuntary migrants spent between one and three and a half years on American soil.

Who were these men who were forced to "migrate" to the land of the enemy and who voluntarily returned there as immigrants and future citizens? What experiences during their captivity drew them back? From their limited perspectives as prisoners of war, what images and perceptions did they have of America and the American people? How did these perspectives and experiences influence their perceptions of their home country and their decisions to return? Did their prisoner of war experience help or hinder their eventual return to "the place where we had the good life" (Rudolf Velte quoted in Dell'Angela 1996)—procuring a visa, finding a sponsor, paying for and finding transatlantic transportation—and their eventual settlement in the United States?

5

Seeking some initial answers to these questions, I discovered that there was little systematic information on the men who came as "Hitler's soldiers" and returned as immigrants. While statistics on the numbers of German prisoners of war held on American soil and of postwar German immigrants to the United States are readily available, we do not know exactly how many former prisoners returned after the war. The American government, or more specifically, the Immigration and Naturalization Service, did not collect relevant data. Returning former prisoners of war were simply counted among all German immigrants. Consequently it is impossible to know precisely how many former prisoners returned. An estimate of 5,000 by a former POW was first reported by Arnold Krammer and frequently repeated in the literature. It is plausible, but unreliable.[3]

Perhaps not surprisingly, the existing literature on these "return migrants" is sketchy. A relatively large and diverse literature on German prisoners of war in the United States is rather narrowly focused on "prisoner of war history" (Moore and Federowich 1996). As such it provides rich and detailed information on all aspects of the prisoner of war program on American soil: the conditions and circumstances surrounding the establishment and administration of camps, the daily life in the camps, the labor program, the relations between captives and captors, and the efforts made by the Americans to reeducate several thousand men in the principles of democracy. While this literature makes some references to prisoners who immigrated, these tend to be sketchy and anecdotal.[4]

The literature on post–World War II German immigration provides even less information.[5] While it may mention that former prisoners of war were among the hundreds of thousands of Germans who were seeking a new life abroad, they are simply included in the larger stream of German immigrants (Freund 2004, Nerger-Focke 1995, Steinert 1995). In short, as Robert Billigmeier observed almost thirty years ago, there is no "systematic study" of "these immigrants drawn back to the country of their imprisonment, or of their occupations, destinations, or measures of integration" (1982, 125).

To be sure, the former German POWs who left their devastated homeland to begin a new life abroad represent a small percentage of postwar German immigrants to the United States, and while it is not unusual for individual former prisoners of war to visit the places of their internment many years after the war, the return migration and settlement of large numbers of former prisoners to the land of their captivity is unusual. It deserves more systematic attention than it has received.

Research and Theory

While the subjects are prisoners of war, the primary focus of this study is on the conditions and circumstances that shaped their unusual journey from prisoner of war to immigrant. At a time when few Germans traveled abroad and most ordinary people had led a relatively isolated life in Nazi Germany,[6] they had been in America before. Unlike other temporary visitors (tourists, students, migrant workers), their sojourn was unexpected and involuntary. They were enemy soldiers who were forcibly transported to American soil where they were confined to prisoner of war camps.

Yet, while their movements were restricted, the conditions and circumstances that defined their captivity afforded them with considerable opportunities "to travel" through the American countryside, to interact with Americans, both military and civilian, to observe many aspects of everyday life, and "to see the differences between Germany and the United States" (Pelz 1985, 42–55).

For thousands of ordinary German soldiers, "captivity was a form of *Bildungsreise*" (Lagrou 2005, 5), and for many of the young men who "had been impressionable boys when drafted into the German army, the time as prisoners of war was formative" (Billinger 2000, xv). Many among them liked what they saw and while still in captivity expressed an interest in "staying or returning to America" (ibid.).[7] After one to three years of having led a relatively peaceful life far away from the death and destruction of the war in Europe, they were released from American captivity. When they returned to Germany, they found a devastated, bombed-out homeland. Families were scattered, prewar social networks had been severely fractured and the population in the four occupation zones was highly mobile and uprooted (Krause 1997). Not surprisingly, the desire to leave Germany behind was widespread among the population (Freund 2004).[8] Yet for most Germans the dream of seeking a new life abroad remained unfulfilled.

As recent research and theorizing in this field have demonstrated, transnational migration is a complex and multivariate process. In addition to objective socioeconomic and political conditions and prospects in the home country (so-called push factors) and perceptions of conditions and opportunities in the country of destination and expectations about a better life (so called pull factors), migration does not take place in a social and political vacuum. It is deeply embedded in social and political structures and institutions, and social networks that connect migrants and nonmigrants across time and space (Boyd 1989, Fawcett 1989, Morawska 2007, Portes 1995, Portes and Böröcs 1989, Tilly 1990).

Since the beginning of the 19th century, Germany had been an important part of a transatlantic migration system. Between 1820 and 1930 some 5.9 million Germans immigrated to the United States (Rössler 1992). Although the system weakened considerably in the wake of American restrictions on European immigration in the 1920s, and the Great Depression of the 1930s, over half a million were able to immigrate after the First World War and throughout the 1920s. In the mid-1930s the stream had become a trickle, and with the exception of select refugees from Nazi Germany, it came to a virtual halt with the outbreak of war.

Given its long history, transatlantic migrations were deeply embedded in the German collective conscience, and the networks of relatives of many Germans extended to the United States.[9] Yet while individuals and families considering emigration in the aftermath of World War II could activate these networks to seek information and to secure the sponsorship necessary for successful immigration, most ordinary Germans, including former POWs, confronted significant political and legal hurdles.

In the immediate aftermath of the war, the Allied military governments imposed severe travel restrictions on the German population which made it exceedingly difficult for most Germans to leave the occupied territories.[10] Even after exit restrictions were lifted in July 1949, prevailing American immigration policies posed formidable obstacles well into the 1950s. Although the quota of 25,957 individuals yearly was officially reopened in March 1946,[11] until September 1948, visas available under the quota were restricted to special groups, including victims of National Socialism and close relatives of American citizens, in particular children, and husbands of American women who had been married before July 1932. Even in 1950, half of the German quota was filled by ethnic Germans (people of German ethnicity but without German citizenship), displaced persons, and close relatives of American citizens (e.g., husbands, parents and children), leaving few spaces available for ordinary Germans who did not fall into these categories.[12]

The oversubscribed quota system was not the only hurdle confronting would-be immigrants. To insure that newcomers would not become a burden to the welfare system, immigrants were required to have an American sponsor. Potential sponsors (individuals such as relatives or voluntary organizations, including churches) were required to demonstrate that they were in a financial position to support the immigrant (military personnel did not qualify as sponsors). An affidavit from the sponsor pledging support for the newcomer had to accompany the visa application submitted to American consulates. Until the passage of the McCarran-Walter Act in 1952, labor contracts from American employers were not acceptable.[13]

Like the the vast majority of their countrymen, and unlike individuals who could immigrate outside the quota system (most notably, rocket scientists and war brides), or who received preferential treatment as close relatives of American citizens (spouses, parents, siblings), the former POWs seeking to return to "the place where we had the good life" (Otto Fernholz referring to Camp Ruston[14]) had to negotiate these hurdles. Like their compatriots, they could activate their existing networks of American relatives to secure the sponsorship necessary for obtaining the coveted visa. However, their previous sojourn on American soil had provided them with material and immaterial resources that were not available to their compatriots. Their American networks were not restricted to relatives but included individuals and families they had befriended during their captivity, and such networks could serve as a source for additional sponsors. While the vast majority of German immigrants' information about the United States was based on secondary sources (books, movies, letters from relatives), the information and images that guided the former POWs were based primarily on personal observations and experiences. In addition to the English-language skills they had acquired as POWs, these personal experiences provided them with a certain confidence about their destination. For them, immigration to the United States was less a voyage into the unknown and more of a "homecoming."

This book takes up the challenges posed by the questions raised above. At the empirical level it seeks to provide more detailed and systematic information about these immigrants, information that is central to answering these questions. The answers to these questions tell us much about the backgrounds and experiences of the men who were propelled "to settle in the country of the enemy" (*Leader and Signal*, December 28, 1949). Placing their experiences in the context of the conditions and circumstances that defined the captivity of German POWs on American soil, the conditions they found on their return to Germany and the economic, social and legal complexities of postwar German immigration to the United States, I explore the connections between their dual experiences as "Hitler's soldiers" and as immigrants and American citizens. Beyond the particular historical events of this case, this study concludes by exploring some broader theoretical issues of war and migration.

Sources and Methods

In addition to the secondary literature — scholarly and popular books and articles, autobiographies, newspaper and magazine articles — this study is based on archival sources and in-depth interviews with former prisoners of war who immigrated. Archival sources include the records of the Provost Marshal General's Office (RG 389), the War Department (RG 107), the War Manpower Commission (RG 211), the Department of State (RG 59), the Immigration and Naturalization Service (RG85), and Displaced Persons/Office of Military Government for Germany (RG 260) at the National Archives in Washington, D.C., and College Park, Maryland. I also consulted the collection of American and POW *Zeitzeugen* in the archives of the New Mexico Farm and Heritage Museum and archival material at Weber State University in Ogden, Utah, and at the Historische Institut, Munich. The centerpiece of my research, however, is the in-depth interviews I conducted with thirty-five former prisoners of war interned on American soil who immigrated to the United States between 1948 and 1961.

LOCATING RESPONDENTS

Given the lack of available data and the fact that the potential subjects for this study were elderly and many had probably died before I started this research in 2002, finding potential respondents proved challenging and circuitous. I began the process by searching for names and references in published materials (books, articles in local history journals, magazine and newspaper articles), names in local museums and on websites of former prisoner of war camps and other websites devoted to the Second World War, and autobiographies. Together, these sources originally yielded the names of sixty-four potential respondents: former POWs held on American soil who immigrated after the war.

I was unable to find addresses for nine individuals originally identified and discovered that nine additional men had died before or shortly after I began the research, leaving names and addresses of forty-six men. I then contacted each by mail, explaining the purpose of my research, asking for an interview and enclosing a self-addressed stamped envelope.

Of the forty-six men originally contacted, eight did not respond or my letters were returned by the post office as undeliverable with no forwarding address. Attempts to reach these individuals by phone or to find different addresses proved unsuccessful, as phone numbers had been disconnected or were simply not available in the public record.[15] Two additional individuals responded to my letter but indicated that they were too ill to be interviewed (one had poor hearing, the other Parkinson's disease). I also received responses from the spouses of two individuals informing me that their husbands had passed away recently and learned from another source that a third man had died a few years earlier. Another man who had originally responded to my letter indicating his willingness to be interviewed could not be reached by phone to set up the appointment for the interview. After repeated attempts to reach him I found the phone disconnected. This left thirty-two possible respondents.

All thirty-two eventually agreed to an interview. A third of these promptly returned the self-addressed stamped envelope indicating their willingness to be interviewed. Four weeks after I mailed the letters, I contacted the remaining men by phone, learning that they had not responded to my initial letter for a variety of reasons. In addition to their natural suspiciousness concerning my motives, these included having misplaced my original letter, having been on vacation, or personal or family illness. Once contacted by phone, they agreed to an interview. After I had begun to write the manuscript, I found the names of eight additional men. Attempting to contact them, I found that three were still alive. All three agreed to an interview.

Unfortunately, three of the original respondents who had agreed to an interview died by the time I could arrange travel, and I decided to conduct interviews with their wives. One of these interviews did not yield sufficient information because the wife (the second wife, an American woman) had little knowledge of her husband's time as a POW and his immigration. I decided not to include the interview, but I included the interviews with other wives. They had immigrated with their husbands and had extensive knowledge of their POW experiences as well as substantial documentation (personal letters, newspaper articles). Including these interviews, I interviewed thirty-five respondents. When appropriate I collected information from newspaper accounts and interviews conducted by other scholars and students about additional prisoners of war who had died before I started this research.

The interviews were conducted between 2002 and 2010.[16] With the exceptions of two men whom I interviewed in their offices and three men I interviewed in my hotel, the in-person interviews took place in the homes of the respondents. Four men were interviewed by telephone. One declined to meet in person; another man whose wife had recently had a stroke was not comfortable with an in-person interview at the time, and two of the men I discovered in 2008 and 2010 lived too far from my home, making a telephone interview a reasonable option.

The in-person interviews typically lasted between two and three hours. Telephone interviews were somewhat shorter and in all cases included follow-ups. In addition to getting basic biographical information and life histories, the interviews focused on three segments of the respondent's life experience: the prisoner of war experience, the postwar return experience, immigration to the United Sates and post-immigration experience. In many cases I would follow up with a telephone call and sometimes e-mail. Interviews were conducted in German or English, depending on the respondent's preference, and frequently in a combination of both languages.

SAMPLE CHARACTERISTICS

The final sample of thirty-five respondents is a convenience sample. While it is not statistically representative of German POWs who immigrated (such a sample is impossible), my sample includes a fair distribution of respondents from different socioeconomic backgrounds, geographic origins, and war experiences. Their life stories reveal both their shared experiences and the complexities and diversity of their individual experiences as prisoners of war and later as immigrants. In particular, they provide considerable insight into the paths that defined their journeys from "Nazi" prisoner of war to voluntary immigrant and American citizen.

My sample includes eighteen members of the Afrika Korps, five men captured during the Italian Campaign, and twelve *Westfrontgefangenen*, captured after the Normandy invasion in France and on German soil by the advancing Allies. It includes men who had volunteered and men who had been drafted. Although most were enlisted men, my sample also includes three officers (all members of the Afrika Korps) and four NCOs.

While the Afrika Korps most likely included more individuals committed to the German imperialist war goals and the myth of Aryan superiority (Reiss 2005), the men captured during the Normandy invasion were mostly disillusioned and many had recognized that the war was lost for Germany. While two of my respondents told me that they had been convinced National Socialists at the time of their capture and several could probably be classified as "nationalistic," the majority of my respondents, including most members of the Afrika Korps, were lukewarm supporters of the regime, or *Mitläufer*, "ordinary guys caught in the uniform" (Tom Kocher quoted in Dell'Angela 1996).[17]

Depending on the time of their capture and release, my respondents spent between one and three years on American soil, where they were interned in camps and on army bases located throughout the continental United States, the South and Southwest, Midwest, East and West. Except for the three officers and one NCO, all worked inside the camps or outside the camps in agriculture and related industries. During their captivity, the vast majority were transferred several times to different camps, often located at great distances and in different states. With the exception of three men who claimed that they had no contact or "kept their distance" from Americans, all respondents reported that they had some contact with Americans. The duration and intensity of the contact varied considerably from relatively intensive and prolonged to fleeting and short.

The men I interviewed were overwhelmingly young, between 17 and 26 years old, when they became prisoners of war, representing the birth cohorts 1916 to 1927.[18] They had grown up within the national socialist state and its institutions: Hitlerjugend, *Arbeitsdienst* and Wehrmacht (Hitler Youth, work service and military service) were their dominant experiences (Lehman 1984). With a few exceptions they had never thought much about America, and their images of the United States were mostly limited to those of cowboys and Indians portrayed by the popular German writer Karl May, skyscrapers in New York, gangsters in Chicago, and prewar Hollywood movies. Although a few men had relatives who had immigrated to the United States in the 1920s, and with the exception of one man who married an American woman in 1940, my respondents had never met an American before their captivity. Like the vast majority of their countrymen, they "did not know about everyday life" in America (Freund 2004, 100).[19]

Although a handful of my respondents expressed some criticism of some aspects of their captivity, including complaints about picking cotton, excessive heat, food restrictions imposed after V-E Day in 1945, and in two cases poor treatment by farmers, all indicated that they had been pleasantly surprised by what they saw and experienced. Based on rumors and Nazi propaganda, they expected to be treated badly (several men even said that they had heard they might be castrated). Instead they traveled in luxurious Pullman rail-cars, their camps were more comfortable and better equipped than the Wehrmacht barracks, food was plentiful and they had good medical care. Although they were not free to move around and although they worried about their families back home, they were lucky to be alive, and given the fact that they were prisoners of war in an enemy country, their lives were rather comfortable. Most of my respondents indicated that they tried to "take advantage" of their time on American soil, taking courses offered in many camps in a variety of subjects, learning English, keeping busy with sports, cultural activities and artistic pursuits, and just observing the world around them.

Four men (all born between 1916 and 1920) were married before they became POWs. Given the young age of my respondents, most were not married. Except for three men, all married after returning to Germany and most had children before immigrating to the United States. Slightly more than half of the men I interviewed had not completed their education before they had volunteered or were drafted into the Wehrmacht and did not have fixed civilian occupations to which they could return after the war.

My respondents came from different parts of the former Reich, including seven men from the eastern provinces of Silesia and Pomerania, and one Austrian. They had grown up in small towns and rural settings as well as large and medium-sized cities, such as Berlin, Leipzig, Hamburg, Bremen, Munich, Stuttgart, Braunschweig and Saarbrücken. Most came from working-class backgrounds, their education limited to the *Volksschule* (the basic German compulsory education) and in some cases, the completion of an apprenticeship in a trade. My sample also included nine men from middle-class backgrounds and two individuals from upper-middle-class background with more advanced education. The latter two were officers who incidentally married American women; one having married in 1940 before American entry into the war, the other after returning from captivity in 1947. The demographic characteristics of my sample (age, family status and place of origin) is similar to that of German emigrants in the 1950s: compared to the population overall, they were younger and included many families and refugees (Freund 2004, 44).

All respondents were repatriated to Europe by U.S. government decree, leaving American soil between 1945 and 1946. Half did not return directly to Germany, but served between one and two years as forced laborers in the United Kingdom or France, eventually returning to Germany between 1947and 1948. These transfers (sometimes ironically referred to as "slave-trades") were highly controversial (Jung 1972, 242–48; Reiss 2002, 307–08).[20] Although respondents who spent additional time in England agreed that they were treated well, most expressed some resentment about their fate. The men who ended up in France confronted a more difficult time than those in Britain (Billinger 2008).[21] Only three of my respondents ended up in France. One of these men had a good experience. He got along well with the farmer for whom he worked and even considered staying longer than required. The other two had a more difficult time.

My respondents returned to the United States as legal immigrants between 1948 and 1962, with the majority arriving in the mid-1950s, when migration from Germany to the United States became easier for Germans not belonging to a special visa category.[22] With the exception of the two men who were single, they immigrated with their wives (in two cases wives would follow a year later) and in most cases with children born in Germany. Unable to get a visa for the United States, four men first immigrated to Canada but were able to move to the United States a few years later.[23]

Like other immigrants to the United States, my respondents initially settled in the city or town where their sponsors lived (Freund 2004). In cases where the sponsor was someone they had met as a prisoner of war, they often returned to familiar places. In cases where the sponsor was a relative, they ended up in the hometown of the relative, a place that was usually different from the places they had known from their time as a prisoner of war. In cases where the sponsors were churches, most immigrants requested to return to the places they had known as prisoners of war.

Although their knowledge of English varied at the time of their captivity, with three exceptions all respondents learned some English. After returning to Germany, several men were able to use their linguistic skills to find employment with British or American occupation forces and three respondents were able to immigrate with the sponsorship of Americans they befriended while working for the occupation forces.

Like most immigrants, many of my respondents initially took unskilled jobs at the bottom of the American occupational structure. Eventually, all were able to get better jobs, frequently in their occupational field, especially if they were skilled craftsmen. Several men also took advantage of educational opportunities in the United States to get additional education or training. Three men completed college and received more advanced degrees. Two men studied medicine and became physicians. One man became a college professor of European history, and another became a social worker who founded a successful international adoption agency. All became American citizens within a relatively short time span (usually after the five minimum years of residence) and all became successful members of the broad American middle class.

Plan of the Book and Chapter Outline

Drawing on archival research and the existing secondary literature, the first chapter outlines the salient conditions and characteristics of the prisoner of war program on American soil that defined the experiences of German prisoners of war. These conditions differed significantly from those experienced by POWs held in Europe or Asia.[24] They provided unusual opportunities for German POWs to observe and (in an albeit limited way) participate in some aspects of everyday American life. At the same time, many Americans who had been initially wary of the "enemy among us" (Fielder 2003) came to see these visitors as "folks like us." This largely unintended consequence made "enemies human" (Pabel 1955).

In the second chapter, I turn to the empirical heart of this study, the interviews. While my respondents' experiences reflect the broad themes described in the previous chapter (i.e., that, with very few exceptions, prisoners were treated well, that they had plenty of food, access to sports and entertainment, and that they had contact with Americans while working in agriculture or on army bases), the interviews provide more detailed information on their backgrounds and experiences as "Hitler's soldiers" than previously available. Although they came from different backgrounds and their wartime experiences varied, the vast majority of the men I interviewed had personal contacts with Americans working in camps and on army bases or as contract workers in agriculture and related industries. With the exception of three respondents, all acquired some knowledge of English. They returned to Europe with positive personal experiences and, in some cases, a desire to return as soon as possible.

The men I interviewed returned to Europe between 1945 and 1948.[25] Although most did not return in the immediate aftermath of German surrender (*die Stunde Null*— the zero hour), thus avoiding the most dire conditions suffered by the German civilian population, they returned to a devastated homeland (Wedekind 2006). Following a brief summary of the social, economic and political conditions in postwar Germany, the third chapter focuses on the multiple political and economic hurdles, foremost among them American immigration policies, that confronted German would-be immigrants, including the former POWs, to the United States in the ten years following the war.

In the fourth chapter, I use the interview data to analyze my respondents' personal experiences: their return home, and their quest to return as immigrants. Like the thousands of Germans seeking a new life abroad, my respondents' quest to return to America was doubtless influenced by the devastation they found and the difficulties of reintegrating into civilian life, finding a job, securing housing. These difficulties were clearly magnified for the men from the eastern provinces who could not return to their homes, and who ended up as refugees in the four allied occupation zones. At the same time their previous sojourn in America had left an indelible impression of the country and the American people, an impression that added momentum to their desire to return. While several respondents indicated that they had made up their mind to return when still on American soil or immediately after returning to Germany, others took a more pragmatic and deliberate approach.

No matter how strong their desire to return "to the place where we had the good life," my respondents had to overcome the hurdles imposed by American immigration policies (in particular an oversubscribed quota system and the need to have a sponsor). At the same time, their previous sojourn had provided them with material and immaterial resources that helped them navigate these hurdles. The chapter concludes with a brief exploration of my respondents' lives as immigrants and citizens. Depending on their human capital and the timing of their arrival, some of the men experienced some initial difficulties finding a job, while others were able to hit the ground running. All were happy that they had been able to return and all joined the broad American middle class.

In the context of Guantánamo and the notorious abuses of Abu Ghraib, the stories of the German POWs who were initially seen as "a brutal, treacherous group" of "Nazi Supermen" (Smith 1944), but who became friends and future citizens, seems almost quaint, belonging to a different time and place. Yet, while they are unusual, the events depicted in this book are not unique. Although their numbers are smaller, Italian POWs also returned to the U.S. and so did an unknown number of German POWs held in Canada; and some remained in Britain and even in France. Although students of international migration have long recognized that war and the effects of war are major forces in international migration, the connections between war, captivity and migration have not received much attention. In the final chapter I use this case study to reflect on some of these larger connections.

1

The Germans Are Coming

Like other wars before and since, the Second World War generated a large number of prisoners on both sides of the conflict.[1] German prisoners of war were held in British, French, and Russian camps; American, British, French and Russian soldiers were held in German, Italian, Rumanian and Hungarian camps. Of the estimated two and a half million German soldiers who ended up in American captivity by the end of the war, about fifteen percent were transported to the United States.[2] It is important to note that this percentage is three times greater than the total number of Americans taken prisoner in Europe and the Pacific (Doyle 1978).

Although 1,346 German naval officers and crewmen who had been captured on surface ships in American ports after the onset of hostilities had been held on American soil during the First World War (Lewis and Mewha 1955, 57, 63), there was no historical precedent for transporting hundreds of thousands of enemy soldiers captured abroad and interning them on American soil. Thus, when Hitler declared war on the United States in December 1941, the American government had not anticipated or planned to intern thousands of enemy prisoners of war on American soil. Giving in to pressures from the British government, the U.S. Joint Chiefs of Staff agreed on an emergency basis to intern some 50,000 German soldiers captured in the North Africa campaign in August 1942 (Hörner and Powell 1991). The War Department was hardly prepared to accommodate them and hastily organized a system to deal with the new arrivals. Responsibility for the prisoners of war was placed in the hand of the commanding general of the Army Service Forces (ASF), and the newly created Provost Marshal General's Office (PMGO) was put in charge of organizing and administering the prisoner of war program (Jung 1972, Pluth 1970).

The first 2,000 German prisoners captured in North Africa arrived on American soil in fall 1942. In the absence of existing prisoner of war camps, they were interned in makeshift camps on military installations and in former Civilian Conservation Corps (CCC) camps. The number of prisoners increased rapidly in the final months of the North Africa campaign which culminated in German defeat in spring 1943. It soon exceeding the 50,000 men originally agreed upon, and the Office of the Provost Marshal General embarked on a large-scale project, constructing dozens of large prisoner of war camps on American soil.[3]

The prisoner of war program put in place in fall 1942 was guided by two concerns: the security of the American public and the humane treatment of the prisoners according to the 1929 Geneva Convention on the Treatment of Prisoners of War.[4] To insure maximum security and to protect the American public from what one officer referred to as "a brutal, treacherous group," (quoted in Lewis and Mewha 1955, 110) bent on escaping and sabotaging the American home front, the newly constructed camps were large compounds, usually accommodating several thousand prisoners (3,000 to 6,000), and they were heavily guarded.

The layout of the camps followed a standard pattern. A camp usually consisted of four compounds, each housing 500 to 700 prisoners. Each compound consisted of four barracks, a mess hall and an infirmary. Camps were located away from large cities and far from the East and West Coasts in relatively isolated areas in the South and Southwest, with the largest number in Texas.[5] In addition to the relative isolation, a southern location was favored for its relatively mild climate, which allowed for cheaper construction so that barracks did not have to be heated in the winter, although no one considered the oppressive heat in the summer. In addition, many of the army posts that served as initial camps were located in the South.

To insure the humane treatment of prisoners, the United States carefully followed the mandates of the 1929 Geneva Convention on the Treatment of Prisoners of War.[6] Accordingly, enlisted men and NCOs were separated from commissioned officers and the latter were placed in special officer camps. Following the convention's mandate that prisoners of war be treated humanely, and that their accommodation and food be the same as that of the captors' own armed forces, the camps were well appointed with army cots and blankets, showers, and plenty of food, including meat, milk and vegetables. They included canteens where prisoners could purchase incidentals such as chocolate bars, soft drinks and cigarettes. Medical and dental care was provided by army medical officers. There were opportunities for leisure pursuits, including sports (especially soccer), music performances and theaters, and many camps developed impressive theater and musical performances attended by prisoners and frequently by American military officers and their families.

Prisoners had access to books, and newspapers (albeit censored), and musical instruments were provided by the YMCA. Many camps eventually developed camp newspapers edited and written by the prisoners. Opportunities to learn English and take courses in other fields of study (e.g., geography, history, science) offered by fellow prisoners who had been teachers in civilian life were abundant and some camps even offered university-level courses through nearby university extension services. Prisoners were permitted to write two letters and one postcard per week and receive unlimited mail from home. All mail was censored. Men who had close relatives in the United States—grandparents, parents, siblings, aunts or uncles—were allowed to correspond with them, and at the discretion of the camp commander, they could receive visits from such relatives (Waters 2004, 62–63).[7] It was also possible for brothers or fathers and sons initially held in separate camps to petition the commander of the camp that they be united in the same camp (Fiedler 2003, Hennes 2008).

The interests of prisoners were represented by a camp spokesman whom they elected from among their ranks to voice grievances and requests of the camp community (Article 43 of the Geneva Convention) to the camp commanding officers and to represent prisoners with members of the Swiss Legation, the International Red Cross Committee and the YMCA, which oversaw the humanitarian treatment of prisoners in accordance with the Geneva Convention (Krammer 1991, 36–42).

While it seemed reasonable to fear that large numbers of German POWs would want to escape or engage in sabotage, the initial fear of "thousands of escaped Nazi prisoners sabotaging and raping their way across the United States" (Krammer 1991, 114) was not borne out. Escapes turned out to be relatively infrequent (with most large camps experiencing no more than three or four during the entire war) and most escapees were captured within three days. Of the total of 2,222 escapees, only seventeen were still at large when the War Department announced its final tally in 1947 (Krammer 1991, 136), and by 1951 only six remained at large and these were captured or came forward between 1953 and 1985.[8]

In his comprehensive overview of the German prisoner of war experience in the United States, Krammer lists three reasons for the relatively low rate of escapes: (1) the German military was a tightly obedient unit in which each rank was responsible for its actions to its superior; (2) the extensive recreational opportunities and programs occupied much of the prisoners' free time; (3) the realization that there was simply no place to go and that they could not rely upon help from American civilians. The documented cases of attempted escapes clearly illustrate the geographic and social difficulties confronting would-be escapists: the vastness of the country and the fact that, unlike in Europe, where American prisoners of war might be able to cross the border into France where they might get help from the French underground, the borders to Mexico and Canada were far and the terrain was not hospitable (Heisler, B. 2007).

A spectacular but foiled attempt to escape by a group of twenty-five German navy men interned at Camp Papago Park, Arizona, illustrates these difficulties. They were led by Captain Jürgen Wattenberg who was according to a report of the escape in *Newsweek*, "one of the shrewdest and most reckless Nazi officers in or out of captivity" (January 8, 1945). The men dug a tunnel out of the camp, hoping to escape to Mexico. All were caught within a few days (Moore 1978). In addition, the vast majority of German POWs had little interest in escaping. After all, they had escaped the fighting and bloodshed of the war and while they worried about their families back home, they were secure, well fed and generally well treated. For them the war was over (Heisler, B. 2007).

Although security issues turned out to be less worrisome than originally expected, the interment of German POWs on American soil was not without problems. Two problems in particular stand out: (1) the early domination of many camps by Nazi elements who did not allow the expression of opposing opinions, and (2) the rationing of food for POWs after German capitulation in 1945.

Lacking experience and adequate, well-trained guards, and recognizing the tightly controlled discipline of German forces, the American authorities initially left much of the prisoners' organization and the internal control of camp discipline in the hands of the prisoners themselves, in particular the selection of camp spokesmen required by the Geneva Convention. Since the more convinced Nazis were better organized, they often came to dominate the camps and frequently threatened and intimidated those who disagreed. Prisoners accused of disloyalty were occasionally dragged out of their beds and beaten senseless,[9] and while the number is not precise, several prisoners were murdered by their fellow POWs.[10]

Although the Provost Marshal General's Office was aware of these problems, American authorities initially turned a blind eye as long as there was discipline in the camps; or, believing that all Germans were Nazis, they belittled the dangers posed to those who thought differently, or they simply felt powerless to change them. It was only after the American press publicly acknowledged the political struggles within the camps (Krammer

1991, 164), that the Provost Marshal General addressed the increasing complaints by journalists and anti–Nazi prisoners of war who were bullied and felt threatened by their fellow prisoners.

The eventual solution, the segregation of anti–Nazis into separate camps, turned out to be difficult to put in place. Unlike the British, who had a well-established system for identifying Nazis, American military authorities assumed that every German soldier was a Nazi. Lacking well-trained camp commanders and guards familiar with German culture and language, they were often unable to distinguish between patriotic or nationalist convictions on the one hand and fascist convictions on the other, frequently confusing nationalism with Nazism (Buecker 1992, 34). It was not until late in the war, when the authorities tried to select democratically inclined prisoners to participate in the in the Special Projects reeducation programs (see pp. 47–50 below), that American authorities paid serious attention to this issue. Estimates of the number of Nazis in American POW camps made at the time range widely. According to several studies made in late 1944, forty percent could be considered pro–Nazi, including eight to ten percent who were classified as fanatic and about thirty percent classified as deeply sympathetic (Krammer 1991, 149).

In early 1945, reacting in part to charges that the army was "coddling" German POWs and the fact that American food reserves were declining, the previously ample food rations for POWs were cut significantly. This was particularly true for meat, sugar, canned fruit and vegetables. As Krammer pointed out, the American public believed that the rationing was the War Department's response to revelations of Germany's poor treatment of American prisoners and the horrors of Auschwitz, Dachau, Buchenwald and Bergen-Belsen which had come to light recently. The prisoners themselves were resentful of these cuts and saw them as "childish punishment" on the part of their captors. Responding in part to criticism from POWs, and the International Red Cross and complaints by American work supervisors that the POWs were too weak to work efficiently, food rationing was eased, and by fall 1945, food rations were returned to previous levels. Depending on local camp conditions and the time they were repatriated, "on the average German POWs lost about 10 to 12 pounds" (Jung 1972, 51).

While not all prisoners had universally positive experiences, and even some sympathetic POWs were not uncritical of what they observed, there is general agreement among observers, analysts and the majority of former prisoners themselves that they were well treated (Billinger 2000, Billinger 2008, Krammer, Powell 1989). In some areas the camps came to be known as "the Fritz Ritz" (Krammer, 28). Striking a more ironic note, Alfred Andersch, who was interned in several camps and became one of Germany's most respected postwar authors, referred to the camps as the "golden cage" (*Goldener Käfig*).[11]

From Maximum Security to Maximum Utilization of Labor: Creating Opportunities

Although all combatants in the Second World War made use of prisoner of war labor, and the 1929 Geneva Convention specifically permitted captor nations to use the labor of their captives, primarily concerned about escapes and sabotage, the Provost Marshal General's Office considered the German POWs strictly as a "burdensome security problem" (Smith 1945, 45), not a potential source of labor. In the first three months after the arrival of the first contingent of prisoners, only a small number of prisoners were put to work providing services within the camps or military installations—working as cooks and bakers, doing laundry, and repairing shoes, clothes and motor vehicles. For security reasons, the idea of putting large numbers of these "dangerous Nazis" to work hardly seemed like a viable option.

When the United States encountered persistent and growing manpower shortages in early 1943, the initial preoccupation with security concerns, however, gradually gave way to a new concern: the maximum use of German POW labor. A first step was taken in spring 1943 when the Provost Marshal General's Office reluctantly decided to make more systematic use of prisoner of war labor within the camps and on military bases, where POWs were increasingly employed in a variety of menial labor and clerical jobs. This decision helped free some American military personnel for more important tasks directly associated with the war effort; it did not alleviate the persistent and ever-growing labor shortages in the civilian labor market.

Despite the importation of temporary labor from Mexico, Newfoundland, the Bahamas and Jamaica and the new selective service deferment regulations for agricultural workers, such shortages were particularly pressing in agriculture (Heisler, B. 2007, Wilcox 1947). Responding to persistent urging from the War Manpower Commission that the American war effort might be endangered by manpower shortages in agriculture and related industries, and following a torturous debate, in summer 1943 the War Department agreed to make POW labor available for the private sector on the condition that all requests for prisoner of war labor were to be "channeled through military authorities by the War Manpower Commission," and all contracts issued were to "be executed and administered by the War Department."[12] In accordance with the agreement, employers seeking to use POW labor had to submit a request to the local employment office of the War Manpower Commission indicating the type of work to be done and demonstrating that no other labor was available to do the job. To placate the concern of unions, employers were required to pay the going wage rate for the type of work in the area in question. The prisoners in turn were paid eighty cents a day in script redeemable for merchandise in the camp canteen, with the difference going into the U.S. Treasury.

As was the case for their general treatment, the labor of prisoners of war was guided by the legal restrictions spelled out in the 1929 Geneva Convention on Prisoners of War. According to Article 31 of the convention, prisoners could not be employed in work "having direct connections with the operation of war, in the manufacture and transport of arms or munitions of any kind, or on the transport of material destined for combatant units" (McKnight 1944, 54). Additional restrictions applied to rank, physical ability, and types of work to be performed. Officers could not be required to work and noncommissioned officers could be required to work only in supervisory positions. Even enlisted men could not be required to perform "degrading and menial" and "unhealthy and dangerous" work or work that was beyond their physical ability. To comply with these rather vague provisions, the Prisoner of War Employment Reviewing Board was set up to determine what constituted "permissible employment" under the Geneva Convention.[13]

Given the wartime labor situation, there was no shortage of "permissible employment," and although private employers seeking to employ prisoners of war confronted a bureaucratic certification process, demand for POW labor grew rapidly and soon outstripped supply (Lewis and Mewha 1955, 126).[14] Despite some initial reservations concerning this new labor source, employers came to rely increasingly on prisoner of war labor, and employers' organizations from different parts of the country soon competed directly for prisoner of war labor allocations. By 1944 the labor of German prisoners of war had become an important and integral part of the temporary wartime labor supply.[15]

As the war was nearing its end, American employers, in particular in agriculture, in all parts of the country, became increasingly concerned that they would soon lose the POW labor they had come to depend on.[16] In spring 1945, employers' organizations pressured the War Department to bring additional prisoners from Europe.[17] Complying with these requests and to alleviate the severe overcrowding of Allied prisoners of war in Europe, the last shipment of POWs arrived in the United States a few days after V-E Day.

At the height of POW employment, almost three months after V-E Day (July 31, 1945), a total of 140,000 POWs were working in contract labor. Of these 85,000 were employed in agriculture and 55,000 in nonagricultural work (Fairchild and Grossman 1959, 195).[18] Although German POWs worked to dig ditches, to clean up after hurricanes and snowstorms, and in forestry, their work was most important and appreciated in agriculture and canning. While not all employers were equally satisfied with their work and the prisoners themselves disliked some of their work assignments— especially picking cotton — there is general agreement that German prisoners of war contributed significantly to helping ensure agricultural production during the war.[19] In summing up their assessment of German POW labor during World War II, Lewis and Mewha conclude:

> The most important lesson of all to be remembered is that the use of prisoners of war during World War II was essential to the welfare and economy of our nation. U.S. military personnel were released for combat duty, and civilians were transferred to essential work. Crops vital to the economy of our nation were harvested that otherwise would have spoiled, and war industries were able to continue operations in the face of the civilian manpower shortage. Both civil and military authorities have stated that they could not have performed their functions except for the use of prisoner of war labor [265].

The decision to make maximum use of the labor of German prisoners of war, however, necessitated significant changes in the administration of the program, the structure and location of camps and previous security policy.[20] The centralization of POW administration and decision-making in Washington made it difficult to respond to regional and local labor needs. Much of the agricultural production was not in the South and Southwest where most of the camps were located but included significant locations in the Midwest (corn, wheat, vegetables) and other parts of the country (potatoes in Idaho and Maine, grapes and fruit in California and Oregon, apples in Pennsylvania and Maryland).The traditional camp structure housing several thousand prisoners proved unwieldy and did not allow for the efficient distribution of prisoners for seasonal agricultural work.

To address these issues, the Army Service Command introduced several changes beginning in fall 1943. Disregarding earlier concerns about escapes and sabotage, the Provost Marshal General's Office built new camps and made increasing use of military facilities in locations where labor was most needed, including in the Midwest, and near both coasts.[21] Decisions concerning the location of camps, their size and layout, and the allocation of prisoners to the camps, which had been made by headquarters in Washington, were decentralized to the nine regional service commands considered to be more in tune with and responsive to local conditions and needs.[22] It also created a new type of camp, called a "side" or "branch" camp, small temporary camps "established solely for work"(McKnight 1944, 49). Housing between 150 and 1,000 captives, side camps were located in the vicinity of large agricultural production, their size determined by specific labor needs in a particular area.[23]

The new camp structure was accompanied by a more relaxed security policy. The initial policy of "lock them up inside barbed wire and keep them there" was replaced by a policy of "calculated risk," specifically aimed at facilitating and optimizing POW employment,[24] as officials came to realize that the risk of escape turned out to be minimal and there had not been a single act of sabotage.[25] A new system stationed guards only at the perimeters of fields or the exits of buildings where POWs worked. Within army posts, "roving patrols" moved periodically between POW workplaces to register their presence. In addition to deploying fewer guards, the new security policy included using POW officers and noncommissioned officers as supervisors and interpreters.[26] Fewer guards made more Americans available for work in areas where German POWs could not be employed, and POWs were found to work more efficiently and effectively in smaller groups with less supervision.

By 1945 it was not uncommon that only one guard was assigned to work groups of over 100 prisoners and that this lone guard often fell asleep while the prisoners were working, leaving them basically unsupervised. Observations made by the prisoners themselves, by the War Manpower Commission and by the Red Cross attest to lax and even absent supervision. For example, POW Rudolf Hinkelmann noted that "the guarding by the Americans became very superficial" (as quoted in Geiger 1996, 89; see similar observations in Choate, 1989, Buck 1998, O'Brien, Isern and Lumley 1984, Pabel 1955, Reiss 2005). Delegates of the International Red Cross visiting Camp Greeley, Colorado; Fort Custer, Michigan; and Camp Phillips, Kansas, observed, "We were particularly surprised at the large number of work groups that worked without any guards" (Jung 1972, 179, Reiss 2005, 109ff). And a report by the rural industries supervisor of the War Manpower Commission of his visit to Camp Remer, Minnesota, makes a point of noticing "the absence of guards with rifles" and muses that perhaps the guards were concealed at a strategic distance, or "the prisoners of war were given full privileges of the honor system" and "working much the same as any other lumber camp employing free labor" (Pluth 1975, 299).

While effective in maximizing the use and flexibility of POW labor, these changes also produced several unanticipated consequences: they provided significant opportunities for German prisoners of war to travel through the American countryside, to observe the "American way of life" and to interact with Americans, both military personnel and civilians, including women and children.

An Astonishing Introduction to America

The 378,000 men who had been drafted or volunteered for the Wehrmacht had hardly anticipated that they would spend several years as involuntary migrants on American soil. They were a diverse population that included conscripts and volunteers, professional soldiers of all military ranks (including 40 generals), and a range of political ideologies and convictions, including convinced Nazi ideologues as well as convinced opponents of National Socialism —communists and socialists—(Strafbataillon 999)[27] and many *Mitläufer*, opportunists, and apolitical men.[28]

They had fought in different military campaigns and represented different military units. They were captured at different times and places, and their war experiences and the circumstances of their capture also differed. They arrived on American soil between fall 1942 and as late as spring 1945, with some prisoners arriving several days after V-E Day. They were gradually repatriated to Europe between summer 1945 and July 1946.

The first group to arrive on American soil were men of Erwin Rommel's famed Afrika Korps, captured between fall 1942 and German capitulation in May 1943. Altogether some 140,000 so-called Afrikaner were transported to America, far exceeding the 50,000 men originally anticipated. They were joined by 50,000 men captured during the Italian campaign in summer 1943. The largest contingent were the 182,000 men captured between the Normandy invasion in June 1944 and German capitulation in May 1945 (Jung 1972, Powell 1989, 40).

The three contingents differed in terms of their military training, commitment to the German war effort and war experience. Although they ultimately had to surrender in North Africa, the soldiers of the Afrika Korps were a proud, elite fighting force (see discussion in Jung, 9, Krammer, 161). While not all were convinced Nazis, most were nationalists and they were generally committed to the German war effort. At the time they were captured (fall 1942/spring 1943) Germany was still "far removed from collapse" (Jung 1972, 9), and they could imagine a final victory despite their defeat in North Africa. As Jung points out, the men of the Afrika Korps did not have a "sense of soldierly inferiority"; and "their military order had been preserved substantially" (ibid.). Since they were first to arrive and their units and solidarity had remained intact, the Afrikaner had a large impact on life in the camps and on subsequent arrivals.

The second contingent was less cohesive as a unit and included men who had been wounded on the eastern front and reassigned to defend Italy against the allied invasion. Their experiences in the war had been more negative overall. The third contingent, the *Westfrontgefangenen* (prisoners from the western front) was a heterogeneous group that included experienced soldiers who had fought at the eastern front, and had often been wounded and reassigned, as well as many young men taken from school with only rudimentary training, and older men conscripted into the Wehrmacht in Hitler's last-ditch effort to avoid the defeat. Unlike the men of the Afrika Korps, some of these men had experienced defeat at the eastern front; all had seen and experienced the increasing devastation and relentless bombing of German cities and the increasingly dire living conditions and food shortages that plagued the Wehrmacht and the civilian population. They had also been able to observe and experience firsthand the superior equipment of the Allied forces. Many were disillusioned and believed that Germany could not prevail against the superior Allied forces. Not surprisingly, the different experiences, training and commitment of these contingents was the source of some conflict within the camps. In particular, the Afrikaner accused the *Westfrontgefangenen* of being cowards and traitors for not believing in the final victory (Jung 1972, 9).

Independent of where they had been captured, be it in North Africa, Italy, France or Germany, all German POWs were transported to the United States on returning liberty ships and passenger ships such as the *Queen Mary* (usually in large convoys because of possible German U-boat attacks). Their transatlantic crossing lasted between six and twenty-two days depending on the type of ship and the danger posed by U-boats patrolling the Atlantic. During their crossing they were mostly confined below deck, but were allowed to come up for a few hours a day. They disembarked in New York; Newport, Virginia; and Boston, where they were processed (registered, deloused, given POW uniforms) and placed on Pullman trains that took them to their final destination, the prisoner of war camps.

Their train journeys typically lasted several days. As they passed through major cities and the vast countryside of the Midwest and West, these involuntary migrants were able to get an initial glimpse of America. They were impressed by the vastness and geographic expanse of the country and above all the fact that unlike Europe, America did not show any physical damage and destruction. On the contrary, people seemed to live a peaceful and seemingly prosperous life. Indeed, what most struck the German prisoners were the bright lights that illuminated American cities and the large number of automobiles circulating and parked even in front of modest houses.

During their initial journey and after arriving at their final destination, few prisoners had contact with military personnel and such contact was limited to formal communications between captors and captives, between prisoners and guards. American camp commanders were happy to leave much of the organization of camp life to the Germans, a fact that would contribute to the initial domination of many camps by convinced Nazis who were better organized and often tyrannized their fellow prisoners.

The policy changes accompanying the decision to make maximum use of prisoner of war labor, however, significantly expanded the prisoners' opportunities to travel and see the American countryside and opened a variety of opportunities for prisoners and Americans, military and civilians, to interact on a regular basis within and outside the camps. Although previously a few prisoners had been moved from one camp to another, mostly for political reasons (to remove troublemakers, especially Nazis who were placed in special camps, and to protect prisoners who might be threatened by their fellow prisoners), the labor program required that prisoners be moved frequently from camp to camp wherever their labor might be needed, often over considerable distances (e.g., from the South and Southwest to the Midwest and East) and to different kinds of camps, main camps and side camps. Thus, they might be moved between main camps in very different parts of the country, such as New Mexico and Illinois, and once in a main camp, they might be moved to a side camp, or more typically, several side camps in succession and then back to the main camp. For example, during his one-year internment on American soil, Helmut Hörner, who arrived in April 1945 and returned to Europe in June 1946, was interned in seven camps in five states (Hörner and Powell 1971). Often hundreds of miles by train, and shorter distances by truck, these journeys allowed prisoners to see a good deal of the American countryside and many major American cities, such as New York, Chicago, and St. Louis. As the trains frequently stopped in stations, the POWs could observe the comings and goings of civilians and even interact with them.[29]

Prisoners of war working in various jobs—the motor pool, the kitchen and bakery, the warehouse and storage unit, the infirmary, the administrative office — within the camps and on military bases had regular contact with American military and civilian personnel who were supervisors or even coworkers. The contract labor program allowed prisoners to spend several hours daily outside the confines of their camps where they also had contact with American civilians. Although they were accompanied by guards, as noted above, over time, their supervision became increasingly lax. This was particularly the case in the temporary side camps set up for agricultural work. There a relatively small number (between one and 300) of prisoners were housed in temporary constructions, such as tents, or unusual locations, such as college campuses, a ballroom, and even a rodeo arena.

Daily transportation from the camp to the work site was usually by truck. Farmers (and frequently their wives and even daughters) picked up the prisoners in the morning at the camp and returned them in the evening. For example, the wife and daughter of a farmer in Minnesota who employed German POWs in fall 1945 did not recall that they had been accompanied by guards, and noted that "the entire operation was run on an honor system" (Buck 1998, 96). On the way, prisoners might pass through small towns, where they could observe the comings and goings of the civilian population. Drivers might stop at roadside stores to buy beer and soft drinks, leaving prisoners unattended in the back of trucks while local people offered cigarettes or went into the store to buy chocolates, candies, and fruit (Powell 1989, 205). In short, as Reinhold Pabel observed, "You could almost forget that you were a prisoner of war" (Pabel 1995, 139).

Enemies Become Friends

As German prisoners of war worked in the camps and on military bases, in the kitchen (cooking, baking, cleaning), in the storage unit (storing food and other equipment), in the motor pool (cleaning and repairing vehicles) and in military hospitals (as orderlies and lab technicians), as they harvested apples in Washington and Oregon, oranges in Florida and California, beans and corn, oats and onions in the Midwest, potatoes in Idaho and Maine, and cotton in Alabama and New Mexico, and as they were delegated to remove snow and clean up damage from floods and fires, these involuntary "visitors" discovered America and the American people.

At the work site, especially if they were working on family farms in the Midwest, prisoners frequently had contact with employers and their families, including wives and children. It was not unusual for farmers to provide additional food, cold drinks, candy and treats to their POW workers, and even to invite them to share a family meal (Clark 1988, 4; Cowley 2002, 25, 153; Hahn 2000; Heintz 1998, 119–20; Powell 1989, 205; Thompson 1993, 64).

On their part, Americans exhibited considerable curiosity toward the visitors from the start. When the first trainloads of prisoners arrived and they were marched to the camps, entire towns would turn out to watch them (Krammer 1991, 44; Reiss 2005, 94–96). Military personnel, including guards and even commanders of camps, frequently expressed admiration for the organization and military cohesion of their charges (Pluth, 246ff). Although fraternization with the prisoners was strictly illegal, the POW literature and my own interviews suggest that fraternization was widespread (Billinger 2000; Clark 1988; Fiedler 2003; Geiger 1996; Pabel 1955; Reiss 2002, 126ff).[30]

It was not unusual for Americans to initiate contact with prisoners working among them, a fact that raised considerable concern among military authorities. Thus, the minutes of a conference on prisoner-of-war labor between the War Department and the War Manpower Commission in January 1944 note that the "biggest problem is not to keep prisoners from making advances to people. The problem is to keep the people from fraternizing with prisoners—feelings of sympathy being manifested by attempt to give the gifts."[31] A January 1944 circular from the War Department warned that "the fraternization of Army and civilian personnel with prisoner of war is unauthorized, improper, objectionable and contrary to good order and discipline ... and will not be tolerated."[32] In July 1944, the commanding officer of Fort Benning, Georgia, expressed some consternation, remarking that "it is amazing how much curiosity there is on the part of civilians and unauthorized military personnel towards the prisoners" and "there seems to be an uncontrollable desire [among Americans] to watch them and try to communicate with them" (quoted in Reiss 2002, 121).

Curiosity about the "visitors" was not restricted to men. Particularly concerned about fraternization between American women and German prisoners, the army made special efforts to reduce their potential contact with the enemy (Reiss 2005, 494). Such efforts, however, did not prove very effective. For example, an intelligence report from Camp Fort Hays, Kansas, in October 1943 notes with some consternation that "the girl stu-

dents at Fort Hays Teachers College made every effort to get close and
fraternize with the prisoners; in many cases they have been successful"
(quoted in Reiss 2005, 495). While rumors that some POWs had married
American women were unsubstantiated (Reiss 2005, ftn. 84.124), there
are several accounts of romantic relationships between German prisoners
of war and American women (Fiedler 2003; Oberdieck 1995; Powell 1989;
Reiss 2005; Waters 2004, especially footnote 93). In two documented cases,
romantic relationships between POWs and American women led to marriages after the war (Carlson 1997; Schulz 1996). A recent article in the
Bangor Daily News (Bright 2008) reports the story of a former POW, Wolfgang Ritter, held at a camp in Princeton, Maine, who fathered a child with
a Native American woman from a nearby reservation. When Ritter visited
Princeton in 1980, he adopted the child, a son.[33]

Not all Americans were sympathetic to the "visitors" among them.
Some saw them as incorrigible Nazis and protested that the German prisoners of war were treated far too well, that they were "coddled."[34] Yet, in
the context of increased personal contact, many Americans who were initially weary of the "Nazi" soldiers in their midst came to see the Germans
not as hardened Nazi ideologues out to sabotage, kill and rape American
civilians, but rather as "ordinary guys," "victims of circumstance" (Tom
Kocher quoted in *Chicago Tribune*, June 5, 1996), as "folks like us" and
"boys next door" (Billinger 2000).

The Provost Marshal General's Office was well aware of the unintended and undesired consequences resulting from personal contacts
between prisoners and Americans. A pamphlet, *Handbook for Work Supervisors of Prisoner of War Labor*, published by the army Service Forces, notes
that "the prisoner of war labor program gives the prisoner a chance to
closely observe the average American citizen, the way he lives, the opportunities afforded to him, and his relationship with his government and
fellow citizens" and warns that work supervisors avoid talking about
American problems (especially race) to avoid "an undesirable effect on
the opinions prisoners hold with regard to American life."[35]

Toward the end of the war, recognizing the unique opportunities to
educate German prisoners of war in democratic principles, the Provost
Marshal General's Office took some formal steps aimed at reeducating a
select group of democratically inclined POWs "to create an attitude of
respect for American institutions, traditions and ways of life and thought."
The Provost Marshal General established the Special Projects Division in
June 1944.[36]

The first project of the division was the "Factory," which opened shop

at Camp Van Etten, New York on November 1, 1944, and was moved to
Fort Kearney, Rhode Island a few months later (March 1, 1945). The men
selected for this program represented an intellectual elite of German
POWs, including writers, teachers, publicists and journalists. Indeed, a
requirement for participation in this program was graduation from the
German *Gymnasium* with the *Abitur* degree (a prerequisite for university
studies). Together with their American leaders, most of whom were well
versed in German culture and language (many were exiles from Germany),
the select group of POWs at the Factory went to work. They reviewed and
produced reeducation materials (books and articles) that were to be distributed in the camps; they also made a thorough study of the books in
camp libraries, especially books that had arrived from Germany. Books
deemed to be pro–Nazi were removed and replaced by paperbound books
commissioned by the Factory. These included classic works by German
writers such as Thomas Mann, Carl Zuckmayer, and Heinrich Heine, and
American and British writers such as Joseph Conrad and Ernest Heming-
way. In addition to producing these literary works, the Factory published
its own pamphlets describing the United States and its institutions written
in both German and English.[37]

The men at the Factory also published *Der Ruf* (The Call), a very
sophisticated German-language periodical designed for the most literate
prisoners with the hope that they in turn would influence their comrades.
It was distributed in the camps and sold for five cents. The front page of
the first issue, which appeared on March 6, 1945, featured a lengthy article
entitled "The Inner Power," which discussed the human soul in the eyes
of Schiller, Goethe and Schopenhauer. Even members of the Special Projects team joked that it "would have been difficult for Thomas Mann to
understand." The educational experts at Fort Kearney also examined and
analyzed the numerous individual camp newspapers to determine the
degree to which they were Nazi, anti–Nazi, neutral or religious. Their
studies of these papers showed that over time they had become more neutral and more anti–Nazi.

After German surrender when it became known that many of the
German POWs on American soil would not return directly to Germany,
but would be transferred to Britain and France to work for an additional
one or two years as forced labor, the reeducation program shifted into
higher gear. To counteract the news that was seen as damaging to the morale
of German POWs, and to save some of the more democratically inclined
prisoners from such a fate and prepare them to assist the American occupation forces in Germany, the Special Projects Division set up three addi-

tional special camps at Fort Eustis, Virginia, Fort Getty and Fort Wetherill, Rhode Island.

The largest and best known of these was the program at Fort Eustis. Its purpose was to teach the "essence and summary of reeducation" to 23,142 specially selected men in twenty-three six-day cycles.[38] The first cycle began on January 4, 1946, and the last ended on April 5. Some 2,000 men participated in the program in each cycle. All cycles culminated in a formal ceremony with guest speakers and valedictorians. The program at Fort Getty trained some 700 men as administrators to assist the occupation forces, while Fort Wetherill trained 55 future policemen for the same purpose.

All graduates of these programs were spared additional time in forced labor and returned directly to Germany, via France. Since the number of POWs from each of the seven service commands selected to participate in these programs was limited, many men who would have qualified for the program based on their democratic inclinations and cooperative attitude could not participate. Ending up in England and France, many of these men resented their fate.

The reeducation programs have been subject to some scholarly debate. The general conclusion has been that formal efforts at reeducation had little effect on the overwhelming majority of German POWs (Jung 1972; Lowe Kunzig 1946; Robin 1995; Smith 1996) and many ordinary POWs considered these efforts as elitist and propagandist. Giving credence to Provost Marshal General Allen Gullion, who was opposed to the Special Projects Division, American historian Lewis Carlson observed, "For most ordinary German soldiers, the everyday experiences and contacts with Americans probably did more to change their hearts and minds" (quoted in *Chicago Tribune*, June 5, 1996). "The German POWs will tell you they hated the propaganda, but they loved the way Americans lived" (Lewis Carlson, quoted in *The Milwaukee Journal Magazine*, October 1, 1995).[39]

Returning to Europe

Given the increasing importance of POW labor as the war progressed, it is hardly surprising that employers expressed considerable anxiety after V-E Day when, following the Geneva Convention, prisoners were to be repatriated. Although the War Manpower Commission had sent telegrams to all agency regional directors in August 1945, informing them that the War Department intended to return all German (and Italian) prisoners of war "at the earliest practical moment," and instructing them to "discontinue the uses of prisoners of war in contract employment,"[40] repatriation was slow. Three months later, and six months after V-E Day (November 1945), only 73,178 prisoners had left the United States, and the dependence of American agriculture on their labor was an important factor (Billinger 2000, 167).[41] Responding to protests by American farmers, in January 1946, eight months after V-E Day, President Truman announced a sixty-day delay of repatriation for essential workers.

Although the war in Europe ended in May 1945, it took an additional year until all German POWs returned to Europe. Despite considerable lobbying efforts from organizations and individuals urging the government to extend their stay, or to allow some to remain in the United States permanently,[42] all German POWs had left American soil by July 22, 1946.[43] The timing of repatriation was dependent on how "useful" and "cooperative" POWs were deemed. Those deemed uncooperative, useless (older men, sick and injured men), officers, and non–German citizens, including Austrians, were returned first.

On their return to Europe, the vast majority of POWs (290,000) passed through Camp Shanks, New York. After crossing the Atlantic, most disembarked in Le Havre and were transported by truck to the nearby massive holding camp, Bolbec. (Some men who disembarked in England stayed in England or went directly to Scotland.) While they had hoped to return to Germany, for half the German POWs held on American soil (178,000) returning to Europe did not mean a direct return to Germany: they ended up spending one to two additional years as forced labor in England and France.

The decision to transfer German POWs to England and France was controversial and in violation of the Geneva Convention's Article 75, which stipulated that POWs "shall be released and repatriated without delay after the cessation of active hostilities."[44] It was based in part on President Roosevelt's insertion into the final protocol at the Yalta Conference, February 1945, mentioning that German POW labor might be used to rehabilitate Europe, and the American government's wartime agreements with Britain and France regarding the future of German POWs in American hands. The British insisted on regaining some of "their" original POWs. The French also desired POWs for agricultural labor and rebuilding. Although most were POWs under American control in Europe, their numbers were supplemented with POWs returning from camps on American soil. Thus, 123,000 men from U.S. camps went to Britain and 55,000 men ended up in France.[45] Overall, the men who spent additional time in England, compared to those who ended up in France, were still among the luckier ones. By 1946 they worked without guards and there was a good deal of fraternization between the Germans and British civilians. In France, where POWs often worked in mines and as mine sweepers, conditions were often poor and mistreatment was not infrequent.

2

An Astonishing Introduction: Thirty-five POWs Experience America

The previous chapter provided a brief general outline of the conditions and circumstances that defined the experiences of German POWs on American soil. In this chapter I turn to the particular experiences of the thirty-five men I interviewed.

Autobiographical memories are not the product of original impressions and experiences stored in people's memories like computer files that can be called upon at any time. They are constructions of the past from the perspective of the present. At the time of the interviews my respondents were in their late–70s and early to mid–80s, and most had neatly constructed life stories. This was particularly apparent for several men who had been interviewed repeatedly by local newspapers and whose responses to my questions often appeared rehearsed.

Given their age, my respondents had some difficulties remembering exact dates beyond the most important. Some respondents provided considerable detail about their experiences, while others frequently excused themselves by saying, "Sixty years is a long time to remember." While it was easier for them to talk about specific events, with few exceptions they had greater difficulties remembering and relating their feelings and sentiments. Thus, while all respondents felt that their time as POWs in the United States represented a significant event and a formative experience, they often struggled to provide more specific answers to my queries.

Except for dates relating to their captivity and release, and the dates they immigrated to the United States, recollections of other dates and events, such as transfers to camps, tended to be vague. Although I followed an interview questionnaire that covered the same topics and questions in

all interviews, as might be expected, some respondents were more artic-
ulate, more thoughtful and more talkative than others. Several men also
made statements that in the light of my research seemed questionable or
inaccurate. Rather than commenting on these inaccuracies I decided to
let the respondents speak for themselves.

At the time of the interviews, several respondents had written or were
writing memoirs. These range from works that were self-published to
unpublished material they willingly shared with me. When relevant I supplemented the interview data with information from these memoirs.

To introduce my respondents, I present their stories and experiences
in approximate chronological order of their arrival on American soil,
beginning with the first contingent, the seventeen members of the Afrika
Korps, and ending with the thirteen *Westfrontgefangenen*.

The Afrika Korps

"Aliceville will always be in my heart, because I got another chance in life.
Except for the fact that we were behind barbed wire, we had nothing to
complain about. We were treated well. We were safe" (Horst U., Camp
Aliceville, Alabama).

"We never had it so good" (Hans W., Fort Robinson, Nebraska).

"You knew that you were safe, and all the others had a chance of getting
killed. I knew that I would survive" (Alfred M., Camp Algona, Iowa).

"Wir waren zufrieden dass der Krieg für uns zu Ende war." "Das Lager-
leben war gut. Ich hatte eine schöne Zeit und habe viel gesehen." ("We were
content that the war was over for us." "Life in the camp was good and I had
a good time and saw much") (Hermann F., Camp Blanding, Florida).

"Aliceville provided stability for the first time" (Hermann B., Camp
Aliceville, Alabama).

"I felt I had to make the best out of the situation." "The summer of 1944
was a very happy time." "USA made a big mark on my mind" (Heinz R.,
Camp Grant, Illinois).

"Captivity was liberation" (Rudolf T., Camp Forrest, Tennessee).

"We had access to luxuries we had not seen." "I tried to benefit from my
camp experience" (Horst von O., Camp Concordia, Kansas).

These quotes from my interviews with members of the Afrika Korps
express their sense of relief: they were safe and life in the camps was generally good and even "happy." The men had followed a common trajectory
from capture in North Africa to brief internment in holding camps in
North Africa (Oran, Casablanca and Marrakech) and eventual transporta-

tion to the United States. Although most were transported directly from North Africa to the United States, a few were first sent to England, where they were interrogated by the British, crossing the Atlantic a few weeks later. Their transatlantic journeys took between six days and three weeks, depending on the kind of vessel — liberty ship, troop transporter, ocean liner — and the dangers posed by German U-boats in the vicinity, most traveling in large convoys.

The Afrikaner I interviewed were not among the first cohorts to be transported to the United States. All seventeen men arrived on American soil between June and September 1943. They disembarked in Boston, New York, or Newport News. After they were processed (registered, deloused, given POW uniforms), they were placed on Pullman trains which took them to their destinations, large camps or military installations in the South, Southwest, Midwest, and West (Alabama, Arkansas, Colorado, Illinois, Iowa, Kansas, Nebraska, Oklahoma, and Texas). Except for the four officers who were interned in officer camps where they remained for the duration of the war, my respondents were eventually transferred to other camps and most were moved several times.[1] The distances they traveled between camps were often substantial, covering several states and regions.

The labor program, which had begun in spring 1943, was already in place when they arrived, but not yet in full swing. Compared to the later arrivals, in particular the *Westfrontgefangenen*, the men of the Afrika Korps were less likely to work immediately after their arrival. Except for the four officers and one NCO, my respondents all ended up working in various capacities in camps or on military bases and as contract workers for private employers. While contract workers were primarily employed in agriculture and forestry, some were called upon to clear snow and debris, rebuild structures after hurricanes, and even help build new camps and dismantle existing camps. Here are their stories.

Horst U. was twenty years old when he became a POW on American soil.[2] He was born in January 1923 in Breslau (Lower Silesia, today Wroclaw, Poland) but grew up in Teuplitz (Kreis Sorau, today Zary, Poland) where his parents owned a mail order meat business. After completing the *Volksschule* he attended the *Handelsschule* (trade school), graduating with a degree in bookkeeping in 1939. Before he was drafted in April 1941, Horst worked in his parents' business.

Horst believes that he was "selected for the Afrika Korps" (Kampfgruppe Bürgermeister) "because of my good physical condition." He completed his basic training in Bad Freienwalde, near Berlin, and left for North

Africa around November 1941. On his way, he spent about three months in Naples, where his unit readied themselves for their upcoming deployment by updating their equipment. From Naples he flew to an airstrip at Cap Bon (northeast of Tunis) and was transported to Sousse and on to Pont du Fahs. In North Africa Horst was variously assigned to the 10th Panzer Division and to the 90th Light Division. He became a prisoner of war when he was captured by British forces at Cap Bon in May 1943. After a short stay in a holding camp in North Africa, Horst crossed the Atlantic on the troop transporter, USS *West Point*. His transatlantic journey lasted eleven days. He disembarked in Boston, where he was processed and placed on a Pullman train. Horst arrived at his final destination, Camp Aliceville, in the small town of Aliceville, Alabama, on June 3, 1943, "two days after the camp had opened." On his train journey to Aliceville, Horst was particularly impressed by the luxurious quality of the train "which was first class" and equated his journey with "going on vacation."

Horst spent a year in Camp Aliceville where "we had excellent food." Sick "with bouts of malaria," which he had contracted in North Africa, he did not work. Instead he spent "most of the time in the camp hospital." Summing up his time at Aliceville Horst stated: "Except for the fact that we were behind barbed wire, we had nothing to complain about. We were treated well. We were safe."

In spring 1944 when Horst's health had improved, he was transferred to Camp Gordon Johnston in western Florida, at the time a small branch camp for a contingent of 250 POWs from Aliceville. They lived in tents and most were working on the large American military post. Horst worked in a number of different jobs, including in the warehouse, the PX kitchen and the motor pool where he was "in charge of the captain's car."

Horst spoke English (and French) which he had learned at school. "I didn't have the language barrier problem." As he put it, "I was fortunate that I made contacts when I was a prisoner." His most important and memorable contact was with the captain at Camp Gordon Johnston. Although he does not remember his name, he recalls that the captain "left ice cold Coca-Cola and chocolates and offered to help me immigrate after the war." On one occasion, Horst drove the captain to Tallahassee for a meeting; and on another occasion the captain took Horst to a private picnic in nearby Carrabelle, Florida.

Horst also took advantage of the educational program offered at Camp Gordon Johnston. In addition to taking classes in history, geography, and advanced English, he particularly enjoyed a course entitled "Fundamental Questions of Right and Wrong." "This taught me to analyze the difference between right and wrong, not only for World War II, but for all the historical stories." He is particularly proud of the "Certificate of Achievement" dated March 16, 1946, that he received.

In March 1946, ten months after V-E Day, Horst was transferred to Camp Telogia, a side camp of Gordon Johnston. At Telogia he worked outside the camp, cutting timber. He did not like the camp or the work: "Thank God we stayed there only a short time." Two months later, in May 1946, Horst was moved to Fort Benning, Georgia, from where he was discharged. Passing through Camp Shanks, he crossed the Atlantic on a liberty ship, disembarking in Liverpool. Horst ended up in Normanhurst near the town of Battle in Sussex, where he spent eighteen months working in a gypsum mine.

At Normanhurst Horst worked with three POWs and one English worker drilling holes into the gypsum rock which they then filled with explosives. "We looked like snowmen after all that dust and our eyes and mouths were plugged up with dust." As the English worker was paid by the tonnage, he always pushed them to increase their production. To supplement his diet, Horst "went into the house shoe business." Taking advantage of the option of working above ground on transmission belts, Horst made slippers from old transmission belts and ropes, using the belts for soles. English women would buy the slippers in exchange for food (cocoa, cheese, bread and flour). "Every Friday we received a pound cake, but I was never able to save a piece for Sunday, so I improvised, I cut my white bread into thin slices, spread a cocoa paste on top of it, then put a thin slice of pound cake on it and kept going until I had a cake the size of a full loaf of bread, and I must say, it tasted very good when you are hungry."

Hermann B. was born in June 1921 in Stuttgart,[3] where he attended Catholic elementary school. After graduating in 1936, he completed a four-year apprenticeship as a printer with a local newspaper, passing the journeyman examination in 1940. He was drafted in January 1941 after serving in the *Arbeitsdienst*. Serving with the tank division, Hermann was first sent to eastern occupied Poland near the border to Russia. From there he participated in the attack on Russia on June 21 (he remembers being surprised since there was supposed to be a nonaggression pact). Encountering little resistance, his unit was able to advance deep into Russian territory. He was wounded by friendly fire and first sent to a hospital in Smolensk and later to the small town of Schwäbisch Gmünd to recover. While recuperating in Schwäbisch Gmünd he met his future wife Katie. Hermann and

Katie were engaged in October 1942. Discharged in late October, Hermann returned to active duty with the 10th Panzer Division in northern France. Responding to Eisenhower's invasion of North Africa, the 10th Panzer was dispatched to Tunisia. Passing through Naples by train in December, Hermann and twenty other soldiers boarded a plane which took them to Tunis.

Hermann's Afrika Korps career turned out to be short. He was captured by British troops in Tunis in March 1943, three months after his arrival. Transported first by train to Oran, where he spent a few days in an American camp, Hermann embarked on a liberty ship. Traveling in a large convoy he arrived in New York after two weeks at sea. Like Horst, he was processed and placed on a Pullman train which took him to Aliceville, where he arrived on June 2, 1943. Recalling the faces of the curious civilians who lined the road to "see the supermen of Hitler's army," he mused, "They detected no supermen, but a bunch of tired young men."

Although he was worried about the future, in particular his family and fiancée, he recalled that "Aliceville turned out to be a nice camp." Hermann did not work at Aliceville. Although they had books and musical instruments, a band and a soccer team, "there was not much work to do and soon boredom set in." To pass the time, Hermann, who did not speak English, decided to learn the language. He recalls that several prisoners who knew English were willing to teach others from memory as they "did not have books or other materials." Hermann remembers that the English class they organized was very large in the beginning. Most participants dropped out, but Hermann stuck it out. In addition to learning English, Hermann recalls taking other courses offered in the camp, but unlike Horst, he does not remember any specifics.

Hermann was among a minority of respondents who expressed some anxiety about Nazi fellow prisoners at Camp Aliceville. As he put it, "I did not talk about politics and kept my thoughts to myself." "Overall," he said, "you had to walk a fine line."

Like Horst, Hermann was transferred to Camp Gordon Johnston in spring 1944. At Gordon Johnston he worked in a variety of jobs on base, sorting clothes in the warehouse, repairing cars in the motor pool and as an orderly in the hospital (the infirmary for guards and prisoners). When the sergeant needed five men to work in the bakery, Hermann volunteered for the job. He recalls baking 400 loaves of American bread each day. While working the oven, which was "pretty automatic," Hermann had time to practice his English with Sergeant Sish, who was in charge of the bakery. The two men became friendly and frequently "joked with each other."

In the process, Hermann's English improved and when the American chaplain needed an interpreter, Hermann volunteered. "The overall atmosphere became very cordial," he recalled, and "the chaplain would bring me additional food." Hermann also commented on the lax supervision at Camp Gordon Johnston: "When we worked Sundays we did not have an escort. The guard trusted us and often went to sleep telling us to alert him in case a supervisor should show up."

In February 1946, Hermann was transferred to Camp Telogia ("a bad camp"), where he stayed for two to three months cutting wood. "We worked from dawn to dusk and had to meet quotas or we were punished." After a brief two-week stay at Fort Benning, Georgia, Hermann was transported to Camp Shanks, from where he embarked for Europe. Crossing the Atlantic on a liberty ship, Hermann volunteered as an interpreter. In this capacity he was introduced to Captain Goodies and given a private cabin, and he ate at the captain's table with the officers.

Hermann disembarked in Le Havre, and was transported to Camp Bolbec in May 1946. At Bolbec he remembers filling out a questionnaire. Among the questions was, "Would you work for American occupation forces?" to which he answered yes. He also recalls that the guards were Polish and not favorably inclined toward the prisoners.[4]

Hermann was lucky. After only two to three weeks at the camp he was discharged and returned directly to Germany. Put on a train to Germany, he arrived in Nürnberg in June 1946. He continued on to Schwäbisch Gemünd, from where he was able to get a bus to Bargau where he was reunited with his bride.

Heino E. was born in 1924 in Kiel.[5] Unlike Horst and Hermann, Heino did not complete a civilian occupation. After completing middle school, he joined the Schnellkommando (a quick response firefighting team) in 1940 at the age of 16. When he was drafted in May 1942, he volunteered for the Afrika Korps to avoid being sent to the eastern front. After completing his basic training in Denmark, Heino traveled by train through Italy, passing through Rome and Naples. After arriving in Reggio de Calabria, Heino was taken by plane to Kairouan, Tunisia, and on to the front lines. On May 9, 1964, six months after he landed, Heino's unit surrendered to British forces on the coast of North Africa.

After spending six to seven weeks in temporary camps in North Africa, including an American hospital in Oran where he was treated for dysentery, Heino crossed the Atlantic on a liberty ship. He arrived in New York at Ellis Island in August 1943. There he was processed and boarded a Pullman train which took him to his first camp, Camp Hearne, Texas.

Growing up in Kiel, Heino had often talked to sailors and dreamed of traveling abroad. An "unenthusiastic soldier," he now welcomed the unexpected opportunity to "travel." On the way from New York to Texas, the train passed through St. Louis. Heino recognized the name of Texarkana, a town he remembered to be located on the Arkansas/Texas border. He recalls being particularly impressed by the cities that were "industrious by day and fully lit at night," and the fact that the Americans clearly "didn't worry about getting bombed."

Heino's first impression of Camp Hearne was the camp's water tower: "I knew you could take a bath and get a drink." It turned out that the Camp Hearne prisoners were dominated by Nazis who intimidated the others.[6] This became particularly serious for Heino, who had befriended Hugo Krauss, a fellow POW who was in the same barracks. In the night of December 17, 1943, Hugo was severely beaten by Nazi elements in the camp, and he died six days later.[7] Fearing for his life, Heino petitioned for a transfer to another camp. After a brief stay at camp Mexia, Texas, Heino ended up at Fort Knox, Kentucky, where he arrived in May 1944.

At Fort Knox, which held only 500 German POWs, Heino worked in the kitchen, the post laundry and outside the camp on tobacco farms. Although he had learned English in school, he tried to improve his English-language skills by reading magazines. This turned out to be fortunate. By chance, Heino was able to get a job as an interpreter at the discharge center for returning American GIs located at Fort Knox. His boss was "a kindly civilian, Mr. H.G. Nall," who supervised all the Germans working in the center and who "turned out to be best boss I ever had." Mr. Nall "gave me the English name Henry,"[8] and assigned Heino to supervise "all the work details at Fort Knox." In this capacity Heino drove a jeep around the camp, where he had "complete freedom." As was the case for most of my respondents, Heino was most impressed by the ample food and amenities (such as showers) at Fort Knox.

Heino also struck up a friendship with a fellow POW, Walter B., a friendship that would turn out to be crucial for Heino's later immigration. He was discharged from Fort Knox in March 1946, and traveling east he arrived at Fort Shanks. Although Heino thought he was going home, like Horst, he did not return to Germany, but disembarked in Liverpool. From there his journey continued by train to Scotland where he spent one and a half years in eight different camps, working on farms, "milking cows and shifting manure"; still, he concluded, "it was not bad." He recalls meeting Irish workers who came to help with the harvest and offered to help him escape to Ireland, an offer he declined. As he put it: "I wanted to make the best of it."

Martin F. was born in April 1923 in Chemnitz and grew up in Bielefeld.[9] He completed the *Mittlere Reife* (middle school) and began an apprenticeship as a tool-and-die maker with a company that manufactured parts for BMW. He also attended the Beuth-Schule in Berlin (the first city technical middle school). Soon after completing his apprenticeship in 1942, Martin was drafted and assigned to the paratroopers. Following a brief period of basic training, he departed for North Africa in December 1942. On May 5, 1943, Martin became a POW when his whole unit surrendered to American forces. After spending a few days in a holding camp in Oran, he crossed the Atlantic on a liberty ship. Traveling in a convoy, he disembarked in Newport News, Virginia, in early July 1943. They had been at sea for twenty-two days.

Martin's first destination was Camp McLean, Texas, a recently constructed camp housing some 2,000 men. At McLean, Martin worked in the electrical detail. In September 1943 he was transferred to Camp Roswell, New Mexico, where he worked picking cotton. In February 1944, he was transferred again. This time he ended up at Camp White, near Medford, Oregon, where he worked in the electric shop.[10] Martin, who had learned English in school, also acted as an interpreter for the group of five Germans working there.

During the Oregon pear harvest, most POWs at Camp White, including Martin, were assigned to help farmers. During the potato harvest, 250 men, including Martin, were sent to Camp Tule Lake, California, a side camp of Camp White, to harvest potatoes and onions for three or four weeks. Returning to Camp White in spring 1946, Martin helped to close the camp and was transferred to Camp Nyssa, Oregon, where he worked harvesting sugar beets.

Martin's experiences working at the military base at Camp White and on farms in Oregon and California were very positive. Working in the electrical unit of Camp White he had opportunity to observe and admire "American know-how" and technology. He recalls that the farmers he worked for in Oregon and California were friendly. In particular, he recalls a Japanese-American farmer for whom he worked harvesting sugar beets near Camp Nyssa, Oregon, who was particularly nice. At this time another farmer, who was not Japanese, showed Martin a nearby Japanese internment camp.

Among the last POWs to leave American soil, Martin left Oregon the end of June 1946. He was transported by rail to Camp Shanks, from where he disembarked in July 1946. Crossing the Atlantic on a troop transporter, Martin disembarked in Le Havre one week later. Following a short stay at Camp Bolbec, like Hermann, Martin was among the lucky men who returned directly to Germany. He was discharged in September 1946 and made his way to Germany.

Willie S. was born in January 1924 in Brandschütz (Landkreis Neumarkt) in Lower Silesia (today Prezcyce, Poland).[11] After completing the *Volksschule* in 1938, Willie began an apprenticeship as a carpenter, graduating in 1941. He volunteered for the paratroopers in Rommel's famed Red Devils regiment. He was captured in Morocco by British troops on May 13, 1943. After spending four months in an American camp, he was taken to Oran. Placed on a ship he disembarked in Liverpool, England, where he was questioned by British forces for a week. In August 1943, he was transferred to the United States. He left on a liberty ship and arrived in New York ten days later.

Willie's three-day American train journey took him to Camp Mexia, Texas, a large camp housing 5,000 POWs (see Heino E.). At Mexia, Willie worked in the field picking cotton. He recalled that the work was hard. Willie participated in a successful strike to reduce the size of the sacks of cotton they were required to fill each day. He was among the handful of POWs I interviewed who commented on the poor treatment of the African Americans he observed working in the fields nearby.

Despite the hard work, Willie was much impressed with the many cultural resources available at Camp Mexia. He recalls that they had many theater performances and two orchestras, one consisting of sixteen men, the other of sixty. In particular he also recalls that one of his fellow POWs was "a famous German filmmaker from the Babelsberg studio in Berlin."

In March 1945 Willie was transferred to Camp Cleburne, a small side camp of Camp Mexia, which "was located in an old rodeo ring." At Cleburne Willie and his comrades were delegated to a clean-up crew after a tornado hit the area. Willie also helped build a house and pens for cows. Like most of my respondents, Willie had read Karl May books when he was a boy. He fondly recalls an incident where a man wearing a cowboy hat and carrying two Colt revolvers, "a real Texan," shot out the lights at the entry of a farm, "just for the fun of it."

After six months in Texas, Willie was transferred to the Midwest. From July to September 1945 he was interned at a side camp in Marshfield,

Wisconsin, where he harvested peas.[12] He recalls that the food was bad, but that the farmer he worked for gave them additional food. While working in Marshfield he struck up a friendship with two farmers, Lester Anderson and George Yetter. Both men offered to sponsor the young German should he want to return to the United States.

In November 1945 Willie was transferred to Fort Sheridan, Illinois, where he worked as the driver for an American officer. Willie recounts that this officer once gave him an American uniform and the two men drove to Chicago. In Chicago, they ate at a German restaurant, where the waitress was very impressed with Willie's "excellent German."

In contrast to Texas, where Willie did not have much personal contact with Americans, in Wisconsin where "the people were so good to us" he had many contacts. Willie recalls that almost everyone was "of German origin" and that the grandfather of the Yetter family "only spoke German."

Leaving Fort Sheridan in March 1946, Willie was transported to Camp Shanks, from where he embarked for Europe. Like Horst and Heino, Willie did not return to Germany until summer 1947. Willie spent a little more than a year in a camp near Sheffield, England, where he worked with a crew of German POWs laying drainage pipes. Of his time and work in England, he recalls having considerable freedom, driving to the work sites in "our own truck."

Elmar B. is one of six men I interviewed born in the first decade of the twentieth century and one of four men who was married before becoming a POW.[13] Elmar was born in 1915 in Gaggenau/Baden. After attending the local *Volksschule*, he completed an apprenticeship as a butcher in 1936 and married in 1937. An early member of the Nazi Party, Elmar considered himself a nationalist. In 1937 he volunteered for the Wehrmacht, advancing to the rank of *Stabsgefreiter* (similar to lance corporal). He participated in the invasions of Poland in 1939, France in 1940 and the Soviet Union in 1941, and joined Afrika Korps in 1942. Fighting in Libya and Tunisia, he was captured by British forces in Tunisia on May 12, 1943. Before crossing the Atlantic in a liberty ship, Elmar spent some four months in a camp in Algiers. He disembarked in Norfolk, Virginia, in August 1943. His train journey of three days took him through Chicago and on to his final destination, Fort Custer in Battle Creek, Michigan.

At Fort Custer, Elmar worked in the kitchen as a supervisor. He did not know English, but took an English course. He expressed satisfaction with the general conditions in the camp, but like several of the men I interviewed, he complained about the food rationing in spring 1945. He also recalls spending a few days in solitary confinement because he tried to suppress circulation of the liberal anti–Nazi newspaper *Der Ruf* at Fort Custer, stealing the papers and throwing them away because he felt that the paper "was anti–German."[14]

Although Elmar reports having had some contacts with Americans, "mostly military personnel," and a few civilians when shopping for the camp canteen (accompanied by a guard), he does not recall any specific relationships or events. Yet, Elmar told me that he liked what he observed outside the camp. He was especially impressed by the fact that "the class structure was more open, that there were opportunities to change your position." "I liked it so well that when I came home in 1946, I said to my wife "if we get a chance to go to the United States, we should try it.'"

Elmar was among the first men I interviewed to return to Germany. Passing through Camp Shanks, Le Havre and Bolbec, in August 1946 he returned directly to Karlsruhe and his wife and two children.

Gunther K. was born in September 1924 in Gellendorf (today Skokowa), northeast of Breslau, Silesia, and grew up in the Riesengebierge (a mountain range today located in the Czech Republic).[15] After completing the compulsory *Volksschule* he attended middle school and studied an additional year at the *Landwirtschaftsschule* (agricultural school), a prerequisite for cooking school, which he hoped to attend later. In 1941 Gunther volunteered for the paratroopers (*Sturmregiment*).[16] After completing basic training, he was first dispatched to France and from there to Sicily and to North Africa, where he was captured by British forces in April 1943 (see Heino E.). Before he was transported to Oran, from where he crossed the Atlantic on a liberty ship, Gunther was interned in several British and American camps in North Africa. He disembarked in Newport News, Virginia, in August 1943.

Gunther's first camp was Camp Opelika, Alabama, a large facility holding some 3,000 POWs. In July 1944 he was transferred to Camp Blanding, Florida. He was later transferred to Camp Trinidad, Colorado, to join his brother who was interned there.[17] In August 1945, Gunther was transferred to Camp Carson, Colorado.

Gunther worked in the fields, picking cotton in Opelika and potatoes at Camp Carson. At Trinidad he worked in the office. Gunther did not speak English when he became a POW, but took classes at Camp Opelika. An avid soccer player, he spent much time playing the sport. In particular, he recalls that members of the Afrika Korps would play soccer games against the U-boat prisoners interned at Camp Blanding. He also recalls the excellent theater at Camp Trinidad.

In addition to fleeting contacts with farmers when he worked in the fields, Gunther had some contact with military personnel. In particular, he recalls an American sergeant at Camp Trinidad who would bring him cigarettes and ice cream.

Passing through Camp Shanks, Gunther left the United States in May 1946. After arriving in Le Havre, Gunther ended up spending some time in a Belgian camp, "where conditions were very bad." Luckily, a fellow prisoner wrote a letter to his brother-in-law who was a member of the British Parliament, and Gunther and several prisoners were transferred to England. Gunther ended up spending an additional year (from June 1946 to June 1947) working on farms near London.

Robert M. was born in July 1919 in Salzburg, Austria,[18] where he completed a high school education (*matura*). An early member of the Nazi Party, he joined the *Arbeitsdienst* in 1938, and in 1939 he volunteered for the paratroopers. Before he left for North Africa, Robert was stationed in several cities in Germany and in France. In December 1942 he married Olivia in Salzburg.

Robert became a POW on April 21 or 22 near Tunis. He spent several weeks in a British camp near Bone, where the "treatment was gentleman-like." Before being transported to Oran, he spent time at a second camp, where there was not enough food and water and where "most of us lost our *Tropen* (tropics) wristwatches to the American guards." Transported by train to Casablanca, Robert crossed the Atlantic on a liberty ship, arriving in Norfolk, Virginia, on June 2 or 3. "It took us four weeks to make the crossing," he recalled, and "we were very hungry." The train journey to his first camp, Camp Aliceville, took "three or four days."

In April 1944, Robert volunteered to transfer to Camp McCain, Mississippi, where he supervised work details of 20–30 men in the laundry, "feeding the washing machines or ironing shirts and pants." When he returned to Aliceville in August 1944, he worked on building a mosquito ditch in the camp. He also took courses, studying algebra, geometry and technical drawing.

In June 1945, Robert was transferred to Palmer Field Airbase near Bennettsville, South Carolina, where he spent four months picking cotton and peanuts. Working on various farms, Robert recalled that he helped a farmer take his tobacco to the tobacco market. "That man, I wish I could remember his name, gave me a quarter and told me to buy myself an ice cream. But I didn't. I was so excited to have some real money that I just kept it until it was time for us to return to Europe." Another farmer, Mr. K.B. Hodges, served him and his men a sweet potato pie, while Mrs. Hodges provided ice-cold water and served lunch, including "very large watermelons." Grateful for the treatment, Robert and his men repaired three of Mr. Hodges' trucks.

Following a brief transfer to Camp Forrest, Tennessee, where he worked on a farm picking peas, Robert returned to Europe via Camp Shanks in early spring 1946. He disembarked in Cherbourg, France, and after a brief stay at Camp Bolbec, he returned to his hometown, Salzburg, and his wife on May 27, 1946.

Hermann F. was born in December 1919 in Freiburg, Sachsen (Saxony).[19] He attended school in Ratzeburg, Pomerania, where his family moved when Hermann was a small child. After he graduated from the *Volksschule*, Hermann completed an apprenticeship in agriculture/farming in 1938. Following his one-year service in the *Arbeitsdienst*, Hermann was drafted in January 1940. He volunteered for the heavy artillery and was sent to Jueteburg for two years of training. In 1942 he was selected for the Afrika Korps. Passing through Italy (Rome and Naples) where he stayed several months, he arrived in Tripoli. Hermann was not directly engaged in fighting; he was in charge of driving supplies to Egypt. He became a POW when his company surrendered to British forces on May 13, 1943. After spending time in several British camps, he was transferred to Casablanca, from where he embarked on his transatlantic journey. He arrived in Norfolk, Virginia, September 1943.

From Norfolk, Hermann traveled by Pullman train to Alabama, ending up in Camp Aliceville. At Aliceville, Hermann worked in the kitchen where "we had a lot of flour and baked a lot of cakes." He also took courses, including a course in farming/agriculture, and he fondly recalls the musical band at the camp. In the spring Hermann worked outside the camp, "cutting wood in teams of three men."

In September 1945 when Camp Aliceville was to be closed, Hermann was transferred to Camp Drew, Mississippi. There he worked, first clearing weeds from cotton fields and later picking cotton. He remembers the farmer as "anti–German," accusing the POWs of being poor workers, especially when compared to black people. The commander of the camp, however, proved to the farmer that the Germans actually had picked the cotton cleaner than black workers and withdrew the POWs from this farm. Hermann was assigned to a dairy farm, where he ended up "running the cow barn," because "the wife could not deal with chores." Coming from an agricultural background, Hermann enjoyed this work. Hermann's next camp was in Leesburg, Florida, where he was assigned to pick oranges. Moved again, he arrived at Camp Belle Glade, a temporary camp next to the Everglades Experiment Station. His first job was to work at a bean cannery. When their cigarettes were rationed following news stories of liberated concentration camps, Hermann and his buddies went on strike on April 4 and April 5, 1945. The strike was eventually settled and the Germans received their cigarettes.[20]

Hermann briefly worked with a group of POWs who helped to build the Lake Okeechobee Dike. He recalls that he had "good relations" with his boss, a man called Casper. Although Hermann did not speak English, he "got along well using pidgin English and hands and feet." He also recalls "some contact with girls who wanted to trade cigarettes."

After Camp Belle Glade closed in December 1945, Hermann was briefly transferred to Camp Forrest, Tennessee, from where he traveled by train to Camp Shanks, New York. He embarked for Europe on a troopship, the *Albany*, on February 13. After briefly stopping in Boston, Hermann disembarked in Le Havre on February 25, 1946, from where he was transported to Camp Bolbec.

Hermann was one of three men I interviewed who ended up in forced labor in France. Following a brief period of training he was put to work sweeping mines in Normandy, an extremely dangerous job.[21] He remembers that they were told that they would be released if they cleared 350 mines, but as it turned out, this was not the case. To escape from the dangerous work, Hermann took advantage of a program that offered free worker contracts to German POWs to work on French farms. He ended up working on a farm near Bordeaux for one year. He recalls that he was treated well and that he liked the farmer and his family. The farmer also had two daughters, and Hermann indicated that had they been a little older he would have stayed there.

At Christmas 1947 Hermann took advantage of contractually agreed upon four weeks unpaid vacations to travel to Berlin where his mother, sister and his future wife Hilde now lived. Hermann's father had died at the end of the war in Lumzow (now Lomzowa, Poland); his mother had fled from the Russians and was living in Berlin-Friedrichsfeld, located in the Russian sector. His sister and Hilde lived in the American sector in Berlin.

After briefly returning to France, Hermann received his discharge papers in September 1948 and returned to Berlin.

Heinz E., who was born in Düsseldorf in March 1915, was a professional soldier.[22] He had joined the *Reichswehr* as a medic in 1933, shortly before Hitler came to power. He was an NCO, "equivalent to master sergeant." Heinz arrived in Tunisia in summer 1942 and was taken prisoner at Cap Bon the following spring. After crossing the Atlantic on a liberty ship, he disembarked in Newport News in October 1943. Placed on a Pullman train Heinz ended up at Camp Campbell, Kentucky. He recalls that when the train stopped in Frankfort, Kentucky, "German Americans threw bread and butter into our compartments."

Like most of my respondents, Heinz has vivid recollections of the food, in particular of eating corn flakes and milk. He fondly remembers the excellent German cook from Baden-Baden, the library, the clubhouse and the movies and theater performances he attended. He also recalls that "all prisoners went to a nearby circus" one day.[23]

Having learned English in school, Heinz worked as an interpreter for the physician in the major medical corps, Dr. Harry Guy Brown. The two men became very friendly and Brown offered to sponsor Heinz should he want to immigrate to the United States after the war.

Heinz' stay at Fort Campbell turned out to be short. He returned to Europe in September 1944, when he was selected to accompany a hospital ship to Goteborg, Sweden, to exchange wounded soldiers.[24] After a brief stay in Goteborg, Heinz and his fellow medics were transported to the island of Rügen and from there to a coastal German town (he does not remember which one). For Heinz the war was not over. Following four weeks of leave, which he used to visit his parents, who had been evacuated and were now living in Thüringen, he returned to active duty as a medic, working in a field hospital in Erfurt.

In spring 1945, when he was driving an ambulance he was picked up by American forces and taken to nearby Gotha by truck. Although he protested that as a medic he was not part of the fighting army, Heinz became an American prisoner of war for a second time. He spent time in several American camps, last in Babenhausen, near Frankfurt, where he was in charge of putting up tents and taking out the wounded to reassign them. He was finally released from captivity in July or August 1945.

Four Men from the Hermann Göring Division[25]

Although **Hans W.** did not like the climate at Fort Robinson, Nebraska, where he spent his entire time as POW ("it was too hot or too cold") he concluded that "we never had it so good."[26] Hans, as an only child, was born in January 1921 in Leipzig. Hans' father died in 1928, and he was raised by his mother. After graduating from the *Oberrealschule*, where he had studied French and English, Hans enrolled at the art academy in Leipzig. Hans was a member of the "swing kids," German youth who listened to and danced to American music, a fact that got him into trouble.[27] In 1939 he was arrested by the Gestapo and spent a few weeks in a camp where he was interrogated, but he was eventually released.

After serving in the *Arbeitsdienst* in East Prussia for six months, Hans was drafted in 1940. Assigned to the Hermann Göring Regiment, an elite unit of the Luftwaffe, he was sent to Utrecht, the Netherlands, for basic training as a radio operator. From there he was transferred to Normandy, where he spent a year. Hans, who spoke French, recalls "having lots of contact with French people" and says he was known as "Monsieur Jean." During this time he was able to travel to Paris several times. Wearing civilian clothes he attended jazz clubs and met the famous jazz guitarist Django Reinhardt who invited him to play drums.

His time in France came to an end in the beginning of 1943 when Hans' regiment was sent to North Africa. Traveling there via Italy, they landed in Tunisia in February 1943, and they ended up living on a large farm 30 kilometers from near Tunis. He fondly remembers the time there, especially the food (couscous) and the wonderful oranges. Later they were moved nearer to Algeria, near Oran where Hans was in charge of the mess hall.

In May 1943 Hans was captured by British troops in Zaghouan (Tunis had already fallen into British hands). After marching for half a day, they were placed in a holding pen, from where they were transported by trucks to a collection center and on to an American camp in Algeria. He remembers the camp commander as "a beautiful person." Hans was put in charge of the officers' mess. He even made the menus, and he recalls that the prisoners baked a birthday cake for the camp commander.

Hans crossed the Atlantic on a liberty ship, disembarking in Newport News, Virginia, in October 1943. The Pullman train took him to Fort Robinson, Nebraska. He was among the first group of POWs to arrive in this relatively new camp. On his five-day journey from Virginia to Nebraska, Hans enjoyed seeing the landscapes they passed. He also observed "the poor quality of houses" and the fact that "there was always a car in front."

Hans did not work outside Fort Robinson. His first job was as a sign painter. Having learned English in school, Hans was able to use his language skills as a translator—"a gold brick job." An artistic young man,

Hans particularly enjoyed the cultural life at the camp. He was an active member of VARISTA (*Varieté im Stacheldraht*, Vaudeville behind Barbed Wire) and played drums and tenor saxophone in the band. Hans had numerous contacts with Americans at Fort Robinson, in particular Captain Silverman, whose portrait he painted, and a civilian painter, Gordon Rettew.

Hans does not remember exactly when he left Fort Robinson. He believes it was in the summer of 1945 when most of the POWs were transferred to other camps.[28] Hans briefly ended up in a camp in Colorado.[29] Before he returned to Germany, Hans was selected to participate in the Special Projects reeducation camp at Fort Eustis, Virginia, where he spent two weeks "learning about democracy." After a brief stay at Camp Shanks, Hans crossed the Atlantic, arriving in Le Havre. Although he spent a couple of weeks at Camp Bolbec, like all participants in the Special Projects Program, Hans was soon released directly to Germany. Since his hometown, Leipzig, was in the Soviet occupation zone and his mother had fled to Stuttgart where her brother lived at the end of the war, Hans was discharged in Stuttgart in November 1945.

Rudolf T. (Rudi) was born in July 1924 in Katscher, Silesia (today Kietrz, Poland), where he attended the *Realgymnasium*.[30] He left school two years before graduation because, as he put it, "I was fed up with school." He volunteered for the Hermann Göring Division in July 1942. After participating in the occupation of France, Rudolf was transferred to North Africa. Passing through Naples, he arrived in Tunis in January 1943. In May when his unit was retreating, facing certain capture, Rudolf tried to escape to the Italian island of Pantelleria. Making his way to the coast, he met up with two German soldiers who were building a raft. Before they could reach the island, he and his two comrades were captured by British soldiers on May 11, 1943. In a railroad boxcar he was transported to Oran, where he was handed over to the Americans and placed in Camp Chancy.

After a week at the camp he embarked on a liberty ship traveling in a convoy. On board they were told that they would go to America. Although Rudi had been afraid of becoming a POW (he remembered seeing Russian POWs in Germany), he was now relieved. He recalled, "My dreams for a world beyond the smoke-filled skies of Upper Silesia were in a sense coming true." He does not remember how many days they had been at sea when he finally disembarked in Norfolk, Virginia, in June. Here they were processed and placed on Pullman trains. Rudi recalls that many POWs were hesitant to board the trains as they could not believe that these luxurious cars were for them.

What struck Rudi about the American landscape he saw for the first time was the large number of churches and gas stations, the houses that were made of wood and the yards that had no fences. On the second day the train stopped at Springfield, Illinois. Standing on the platform, an American civilian was reading a newspaper, and when Rudi pointed at the newspaper, the man handed it to him after briefly talking to a guard. It was the *Chicago Tribune*. Rudi, who had had no news since he became a prisoner, read about Italy's making peace and the heavy bombing of Hamburg.

After traveling three days, Rudi arrived at his first destination, Camp Huntsville, Texas. It was July 1943. After several weeks without work, which he spent mostly playing cards, Rudi responded to a notice looking for someone who knew English to work in the camp office. He got the job, which put him in charge of food requisition for the camp. As the only POW working in the office, Rudi enjoyed the job, especially the coffee breaks, and he recalls that "a girl left things in my desk drawer."

Rudi remembers that the camp included both "hard-core Nazis" and "die-hard Communists" as well as a handful of "anti–Nazis." In addition to the "awful heat," Rudolf was afraid of "the Nazi elements at the camp" (he heard rumors of a list of thirteen men who were going to be killed by Nazis) and applied for a transfer. His application was successful and he was transferred to Camp Fabens, a small side camp near El Paso, Texas, housing some 200 POWs. The camp was "not much more than a cotton barn." Rudi did not escape the heat, but he felt safer in this camp. His job, however, was less agreeable; he picked cotton six days a week from mid-morning until late in the afternoon. Despite the heat and the backbreaking work, Rudi rather enjoyed his stay at Camp Fabens; he was able to leave the confinement of camp for the open country and was able "to see the town, seeing the town's main street from the back of the truck, once in the morning and in afternoon."

At Camp Fabens, Rudi tried to improve his English. He purchased a dictionary and, following it page by page, he set himself a daily quota of twenty English words. He also befriended a guard, Marvin, who was a German major in college and spoke some German. They helped each other to learn the other's language, and Rudi remembers that "Marvin was like a teacher."

In January 1944, Rudi was operated on for hemorrhoids at a hospital in El Paso and soon thereafter he was transferred to Camp Forrest, Tennessee, where he and his fellow prisoners repaired camouflage nets. Luckily he was able to leave this boring work for a job as an interpreter and translator in the camp administration. The sergeant who worked there offered to help Rudi escape to his sister's house so he would be able to avoid repatriation to Germany. After some serious consideration Rudi declined the offer. He did not want to cause difficulties for the sergeant.

Rudi left Camp Forrest and arrived in Camp Shanks in January 1946. A few days later he was crossing the Atlantic on a liberty ship. He recalls a stormy crossing. Although they had been told that they were heading for Bremerhaven, Rudi and his fellow prisoners disembarked in Le Havre. There they were loaded on boxcars that took them to Camp Compiègne. (He described the camp as having no barracks and no tents, only bare ground, barbed-wire fences and watchtowers). Rudi was lucky as he had learned some French in school, and when he saw an announcement for an interpreter, he was able to get the job. His situation improved when he was assigned to a barracks with several other German prisoners who worked in the kitchen and laundry. Rudi worked on improving his French by using a dictionary and writing down words he did not know, and tried to use his knowledge with the French staff.

At the end of May Rudi was released from Compiègne and traveled to Germany by boxcar. He was discharged in Marburg. Before he joined the Wehrmacht Rudi had never traveled outside Silesia; he had never been in western Germany and he did not have any relatives there, nor did he know anyone. He did not know where to go. When he overheard some soldiers talking about a nearby town called Alsfeld, Rudi decided to head there.

Alfred M. was born in March 1920 in Berlin.[31] After completing the *Volksschule*, Alfred began an apprenticeship in a clothing establishment which he did not complete. He volunteered for the Hermann Göring Division in 1938. As he put it, "You had two choices, volunteer for the German military and be able to apply for an elite unit, or wait until you are drafted and enter the infantry. In the infantry most got killed."

Alfred participated in the 1939 invasion of Czechoslovakia, France in 1940, Rumania in April to June 1941 and finally Russia from June to November 1941. As he put it, "We were all over the place." In March 1943 he was transferred to North Africa, traveling there via Italy. He was captured by British forces in Libya in May 1943. After a hospital stay for a broken leg he incurred when he jumped into a foxhole to avoid capture, he embarked on a liberty ship. Traveling for twenty-one days in "a convoy

of 100 ships," Alfred arrived in Newport News in August 1943. He remembers a great sense of relief: "You knew that you were safe, and all the others
had a chance of getting killed. I knew that I would survive."

Alfred's first camp was Indianola, Nebraska. During the POWs transatlantic journey they did not have a single hot meal, only C rations, and
he was overjoyed when "the first meal at the camp was a hot pork chop,
and the commander apologized that not every prisoner could have two."
Alfred spent two to three months at Camp Indianola, working in the fields
harvesting cucumbers and winter corn. In April 1944, he was transferred to
a new camp that had only recently been constructed, Camp Algona, Iowa.

Alfred's stay at Camp Algona turned out to be life-transforming. He
enjoyed the food, took English lessons, read books and magazines, and
participated in sports. He remembers that while not many men at Camp
Algona were strong Nazi supporters, there were some, but he quickly added
that they "were taken out to other camps."

At Algona Alfred worked in the cold storage facility, where he met a
young American civilian, George Hughes, who delivered food to the camp.
Alfred and George enjoyed each other's company and George offered to
sponsor the young German should he want to return to the United States
after the war.

In September 1945 Alfred was transferred to Fort Greeley, Colorado,
where he picked sugar beets and frozen cucumbers for seeds. Three months
later, from the end of November to the first part of December 1945, he
was moved to Camp Shanks from where he embarked for Europe. Disembarking in Le Havre in May 1946, Alfred spent several months in Camp
Attichy, France, where he worked as an interpreter. He returned to his
hometown, Berlin, in June 1946.

Heinz R. was born in February 1920 in Seitendorf, Saxony, near the Czech
border.[32] After completing the first year of his apprenticeship as a lock-
smith he was drafted into the Luftwaffe at age nineteen in 1939. As sergeant
in the signal corps (*Nachrichten Kommando*), Heinz was trained to operate
communications equipment (*Vermittlungsgeräte*). In fall 1942 he was sent
via Sicily to North Africa, first near Tunis, then near Algeria. He mentioned a town called "Fax" (spelling uncertain), probably Pont du Fahs.
He was stationed behind the front, transferring messages from the headquarters of Kesselring and Rommel to the front.

Heinz was taken prisoner in the spring or early summer of 1943
"somewhere between Algeria and Gibraltar." He was first transported to
Scotland, where he was interrogated by the British. Heinz crossed the

Atlantic on the *Queen Mary* two or three weeks later. He disembarked in New York in September 1943.

On his arrival in America, Heinz remembered mixed feelings: "I was struck by both confidence and fear. America — who would have thought that I would see the country of which so much was told." "It is hard to describe the impression which the gigantic skyscrapers made on me. I was young, and I came from a small town." He felt uncertain about the future, thinking about his wife (he had married Hildegard in 1942), and he felt "overpowered by the new and beautiful things, but I was also afraid."

After four days on the train, traveling "great distances for a German," Heinz arrived in Chicago at night and continued north to Camp Grant in Rockford, Illinois, where he arrived on "a sunny morning" in September 1943. Feeling that he "had to make the best out of the situation," Heinz decided to "try to get to know the country," and although as a sergeant he was not required to work, he "immediately volunteered to work."

Heinz "had to wait six weeks," to be assigned his first job. Meanwhile Heinz, who did not know English, befriended a fellow prisoner, Hans, who was older and "who always carried a dictionary" and used "the opportunity to speak with guards or civilians whenever he could." The two men would practice English together.

Finally, in November Heinz was assigned his first job, to keep the stove going in his barracks. While working he had the opportunity to converse, using a dictionary, with a guard who would come inside. "He was very patient with me," Heinz recalls, and "sometimes he fell asleep, but I wouldn't let him sleep too long because I wanted to learn English."

In January 1944 Heinz was assigned a job moving trees, driving trucks to a nearby forest. "It was bitter cold, much colder than it got in Germany." He also worked in the laundry, where they did the laundry for the entire camp. He expressed surprise that the U.S. army washed the soldiers' clothes. In the Wehrmacht soldiers had to wash their own clothes. During the winter of 1943-44 Heinz and his comrades were driven to various places to shovel show. By spring 1944 they worked without guards.

In spring 1944 Heinz and his friend Hans volunteered to help build a new camp in Battle Creek, Michigan, because they "wanted to see more of the United Sates." (This may have been Fort Custer or Percy Hospital.) On the way there, they admired the skyscrapers of Chicago: "We just looked out the windows in awed silence." He returned to Camp Grant a few months later. Heinz was one of five POWs who worked in the camp's auto shop with seven GIs. Heinz was eager to talk, but POWs and GIs were kept separate.

For Heinz the summer of 1944 was "a very happy time." He had a job driving "a huge lawn tractor to cut down thistles at an exercise field." During his work he was accompanied by a dog with long ears that he called "Schlupp-Schlupp."[33] His boss was an "elderly man" named Bill "who was like a father to me," and showed "me how to fish [for] catfish."

At Camp Grant, Heinz took courses in algebra, geometry, and English, and with a friend who had studied astronomy he formed a study group. "We were outside every night an hour or two to look at the stars." A POW named Schürmann who had been a teacher in civilian life was "in charge of the educational program and was able to get educational material with the help of the camp administration." As Heinz put it, "Anybody who wanted to continue his education could do so," and Heinz was determined to take advantage of his situation (*"wir müssen das ausnützen"*—"we have to take advantage of this").

Reading American newspapers every day, Heinz was informed about the worsening situation in Germany and he worried about his wife and relatives. "We read terrible things in the newspapers about what the Russians were doing in the East. I knew that my dear wife and my small boy, whom I had not yet seen, were in the area occupied by the Russians."

Heinz left Camp Grant in January 1946. He gave his dog to Bill, who promised to take good care of him. It is unclear whether Heinz participated in one of the reeducation camps. In the interview he mentioned that he left the United States in March 1946 after "studying democracy for about two and a half months," but he does not remember the name of the camp.[34] Before leaving the United States he "knew they [his wife and child] were refugees but I did not know where they were."

Heinz embarked on a liberty ship in March 1946. "I said good-bye to America thinking I would surely see it again." He disembarked in Le Havre, and after a brief stay at Bolbec, Heinz returned to Germany on March 23, 1946. Since the Americans did not discharge former POWs into the Soviet occupation zone, Heinz was discharged in Bad Aibling, Bavaria, and discovered that his wife and child were now living in Dresden. "After three years as a POW I was free again."

Three Officers: Wolf-Dieter Z., Horst von O. and Gerhard H.

Wolf-Dieter Z. was born in December 1915 in Kottbus.[35] After he graduated from the *Gymnasium*, he studied banking at the Université de

Neuchâtel in Switzerland from 1935 to 1936. In 1936 he moved to Berlin where he worked in a bank. There Wolf-Dieter married an American woman whom he had met at a social event in 1940. That same year he was drafted into the infantry reconnaissance division. Sent to Russia, he was wounded twice. After attending officer school in Berlin, Wolf-Dieter was promoted to lieutenant.

In January 1943, Wolf-Dieter was transferred to North Africa, where he served in the 10th Panzerdivision. He was captured in May 1943 when, "out of food and petrol," they were waiting to be picked up by British forces. Transported to the United States, he arrived in New York in June 1943. His destination was Camp Concordia, Kansas, the first and largest POW camp in Kansas, which housed 1,700 officers and 600 enlisted men. On his train journey from New York to Kansas, Wolf-Dieter observed "a community in peace, a population that was well dressed, and cars everywhere."

A few months after arriving at Camp Concordia, Hans-Dieter, who spoke English, began to organize high school and college courses for his fellow POWs. As an officer, Wolf-Dieter did not work and did not have much contact with Americans at Camp Concordia. This would change when he was selected to spend sixty days at Fort Getty, where some 455 German POWs were trained for possible positions in the U.S. military occupation government. Wolf-Dieter enjoyed his stay at Fort Getty, where he spent several months as a teaching assistant. Passing through Camp Shanks, he embarked for Europe in April 1946, disembarking in LeHavre. After a one-week stay at Camp Bolbec, Wolf-Dieter was released, arriving in Darmstadt, Germany, in May 1946. Knowing that his wife had left Berlin and had sought refuge with friends in Salzburg, he immediately traveled to Austria, where he was reunited with his wife.

Horst von O. was born in July 1913 in Berlin.[36] He left home at age eleven to attend a private preparatory school graduating with the *Abitur* in 1932. Horst planned to pursue a career in agricultural estate management. Toward this goal he served as an apprentice, doing all kinds of work on a large estate in the western part of Pomerania near Mecklenburg/Vorpommern, and studied two semesters in a technical agricultural college. He started out working with different people, and he eventually managed a farm of his own.

Horst was drafted in 1939. Serving in an armored reconnaissance battalion he participated in the invasion of France, breaking through the Maginot Line and on to Calais and Cognac. After the armistice with France, his unit moved back across France and on toward Moscow. He returned to Germany after his unit suffered massive losses in Russia in the winter of 1941. Horst's next posting was to North Africa. From France they went to Tunis via Naples. In mid–February 1942, Horst became the aide of the 10th Panzer Division's first general staff officer, Lieutenant Colonel Claus von Stauffenberg. After Stauffenberg was severely wounded in a battle with the British, he was sent to Germany and Horst never saw him again.[37]

Horst was captured by British forces in Tunis on May 11, 1943, when his entire unit surrendered. He was first transferred to Algeria and placed in French custody. From there he was transported by boxcar train (*Güterwagen*) to Casablanca, a journey that took eight days. From Casablanca they crossed the Atlantic to arrive in Staten Island, New York, from where they were transported by train to Camp Concordia, Kansas.

As an officer Horst did not work, but after the armistice he volunteered to put together and delegate German work crews assigned to farmers. This allowed him to get outside the camp, where he had contacts with American civilians, but he did not develop any particular relationship.

Horst's "whole attitude toward America was governed by curiosity." Given his educational background, he was particularly interested in learning about food production and the American agriculture system and tried to find books about these subjects. Like Wolf-Dieter, Horst helped organize a school in the camp where German prisoners could finish the *Abitur*. He also took a course through the camp's extension program at Kansas State University (then Kansas State College) for which he received credit in Germany.

Like his friend Wolf-Dieter, Horst was selected to participate in the two-week reeducation course at Fort Getty in July 1945, and like Wolf-Dieter he stayed on as a teaching assistant. Leaving the United States in January 1946, he crossed the Atlantic and disembarked in Le Havre. Horst was discharged to Germany and arrived in Frankfurt by train on January 31. His first destination was Wiesbaden, where he had a girlfriend.

Gerhard H. was born in 1922 in Wiedenest, a small town sixty kilometers east of Cologne.[38] After attending the *Volksschule* for five years, he transferred to the *Realgymnasium*. In 1935 his family moved to Koblenz, where he continued his schooling. He would graduate with the *Abitur* in 1939. Beginning in 1936, Gerhard participated in a student exchange program with English students on the Isle of Wight, and an English student came to live with his family for a couple of weeks in 1937. During the following two years Gerhard also spent some time with his family in Canterbury, England.

After graduating from the *Realgymnasium*, Gerhard volunteered to join the Wehrmacht, in the hope of finishing his military service before entering the university, so he would not have to disrupt his studies later. Before joining the Wehrmacht, he was drafted into the *Arbeitsdienst*. After working on the *Westwall* (also *Siegfried Line*[39]) for seven months, in October 1939, he finally joined the Signal Corps and in December he was sent to Posen (Poznan) for basic training.

In July 1940, Gerhard was dispatched to Camargue, in France, from where they were supposed to go to England. Instead, in mid–October, he ended up in northern France (Pas-de-Calais), Floringhem. A dedicated soldier, Gerhard was soon promoted to corporal, and in April 1941 he was selected as an officer candidate and sent to Leipzig to attend officer school. He graduated four months later as a newly minted lieutenant.

In late September 1941, Gerhard was transferred to the *Panzerarmee-nachrichtenregiment* 10 in Baumholder, a unit destined for North Africa. Finally, in spring 1942 they left for Naples, where Gerhard briefly became "a soldier tourist." Gerhard arrived in Tripoli in April 1942. Traveling by train toward the East, he arrived in Tobruk in time for the German retaking of the city on June 20, 1942. In July he fought in the battle at El Alamein, where he was wounded and spent some time in a field hospital. After he returned to Tunisia, Gerhard was taken prisoner when Rommel surrendered to the British on May 12, 1943. This was the beginning of his time as a POW that would encompass "sixteen camps in six countries," from North Africa to England and Scotland and to the United States. He was interrogated in North Africa, England, and Scotland, because one person in his unit had cracked the British code. He did not know anything about this.

In October 1943, Gerhard embarked for the United States on the *Queen Mary*, leaving from Glasgow. He disembarked in New York six days later. It was October 12, 1943, Columbus Day. After six days below deck, Gerhard "had no idea where they were," and he and his fellow POWs "gazed with amazement at the New York City skyline."

Gerhard's final destination was Camp Crossville, Tennessee (800 officers and 500 enlisted men) where, except for a brief stay at a hospital in Nashville, he stayed until his release in 1945. As an officer he did not work. He recalls the excellent food of breaded pork chops, string beans, corn muffins and Jell-O. "There was so much food, we couldn't eat it all."

Around Christmas 1944, Gerhard received an unexpected postcard from his father, Major Friedrich H. A World War I veteran and reserve officer, Major H. had commanded an armored battalion, first on the Russian front and later in Normandy, where he was captured. The postcard informed Gerhard that his father was now interned at Camp Trinidad, Colorado. After petitioning to be transferred, Friedrich H. was allowed to join his son at Camp Crossville.

Gerhard did not have contact with Americans at Camp Crossville. He passed his time playing soccer and tennis and taking courses offered at the camp. He also enrolled in a correspondence course offered through the University of Wisconsin which enabled him to receive credit in Germany for three semesters of university work in modern languages. When officers were offered the opportunity to work after the German surrender, Gerhard declined. (He recalls that about forty percent accepted the offer.) He felt that he wanted to be true to his fatherland (*Vaterlandstreue*).

Gerhard recalls some conflicts between Nazis and other prisoners at Camp Crossville. However, he does not recall any violence ("no holy ghost, no *Scharfmacher*"—"agitator"). At the same time he observed that "two outspoken anti–Nazi prisoners in the camp were shunned and isolated."

Accompanied by his father, Gerhard returned to Germany at the end of January 1946. He recalls a stormy voyage on a liberty ship, when "everyone except my father and I were seasick." After arriving in Le Havre, they were transported by truck to Camp Attichy (near Compiègne in northern France, a large camp of some 100,000 prisoners run by Americans). After four weeks at Attichy, Gerhard and his father were discharged. Traveling by train via Strasbourg, they were released in Darmstadt, where they arrived on January 30, 1946.

The Five Men Captured in Italy

As a group, the five men who became prisoners of war during the Italian campaign were somewhat younger than the Afrikaner; they were born between 1921 and 1926. Some had served in Russia and had been reassigned, and others were on their way to North Africa, but due to German surrender in North Africa, they never made it there.

"I was excited about the change in my life and did not have trepidations about my future." "The war was over for me and I was looking forward to seeing America" (Rupert M., Camp Blanding, Florida).

"When I set foot on American soil I was home." "The day I became a POW was the day that changed my life" (Harry H., several camps in Wisconsin).

"We were happy to be out of the war, a roof over our head and all the beer we could drink" (Kurt P., several camps in Wisconsin)

Rupert M. was born in September 1926 in Trechtinghausen/Rhein.[40] At the age of 17 (in 1943) he was drafted out of school. After serving as *Luft-waffenhelfer* (air defense helper) for one year, he volunteered for the airborne troops (paratroopers) "to avoid being drafted into the SS." Rupert received his basic training as a radio technician in France and was dispatched to Italy in February 1944, where he participated in the end phases of the Anzio battles. Hiding in a farmhouse at Passo Futa, he was captured by the Americans on his 18th birthday.

Rupert was first taken to a camp near Livorno. In November the POWs were told they would go to the United States. Transported first to Naples and then to Oran, Rupert crossed the Atlantic on a liberty ship traveling in a convoy of seventy ships. The journey took three weeks.

Rupert had learned English in school and was able to act as a translator for the guards and crew on board the ship. "For me the war was over; I just could not bring myself to think of the men on the back of the ship as enemies." In particular he struck up a friendship with Sergeant Thomas Bunch, who gave him his address and told him to write.

When they disembarked at Hampton Roads, Virginia, Rupert marveled at the brightly lit harbor. Placed on a Pullman train, he traveled south to Florida. "The train rolled through the night. Well-lighted places amazed us. It seemed there was no war going on." He ended up at Camp Blanding, where he was the youngest prisoner among the 1,000 German POWs interned there.[41] He recalls that the inmates had made everything ready for the new arrivals and were waiting for them. "We were seen as heroes," he recalls.

Like Hans W., Rupert did not work outside the camp. Soon after arriving, he tried to contact his friend Thomas, only to be told that POWs were not permitted to correspond with American military personnel. Making good use of his English skills, Rupert served as an interpreter in the shoe repair and tailor shop. As the job was not particularly demanding, Rupert had opportunities to talk with Jim, a U.S. Army veteran who supervised the shoe repair shop at night. He described the atmosphere as "very congenial." "When Jim was in a good mood, he gave me a nickel for a Coke." Rupert also recalls the many cultural activities at the camp, in particular the theater, and the band that frequently played for the Americans.

After almost two years at Camp Blanding, Rupert left in February 1946. He was transferred to Camp Shanks and crossed the Atlantic after a week's stay. Believing that he was returning to Germany, he was greatly surprised when they disembarked in Liverpool, England. In Liverpool he was loaded on a train that took him to Ayrshire (in southwest Scotland).

After working in agriculture picking potatoes in Aberdeen, Rupert was transported by truck to Cheltenham, Gloucestershire. His new job was to stack mattresses. Allergic to the dust, he was reassigned to work in the fields. The camp was in a small village, and they were given bicycles to get to work and were able to move around freely during the day. In fall 1946 Rupert was transferred to Tonbridge (Kent), where he worked threshing grain.

Although the work was unpleasant, Rupert had considerable contact with British people and recalls that "the British were very friendly." At Cheltenham he dated a young woman, Doris; at Tonbridge he had supper with the farmer's family, and on Christmas he was invited to a dinner at another family's home. Before returning to Germany in March 1948, Rupert spent a few months in Dover, where he worked laying curbstones for a new housing development.

Josef G. Josef was born in 1923 in Saarbrücken.[42] He was drafted in 1942 after graduating from the *Gymnasium*, and he volunteered for the Afrika Korps in which he served between June and December 1942. While stationed in Italy, he became ill. After hospitalization in a German military hospital in Italy, he was transferred to Garmisch, where he spent two months recuperating. Although he was reassigned to Tunisia, he landed in Sardinia and spent several months defending the island for the Germans.

After they encountered fierce fighting, Josef's company retreated and moved on to Florence and later Venice. Josef was taken prisoner by British forces after two weeks of fighting near Pescara. He was briefly interned in a temporary camp and then transferred to a camp near Algeria, where he spent three months. In March 1944 he embarked on a liberty ship, arriving in Norfolk, Virginia, three weeks later. Josef's train journey across much of the United States took him past Chicago to his final destination, Camp Atlanta, Nebraska.

Josef had learned English in school and used the opportunity to read books to improve his language skills. When he learned that the Americans were looking for someone who could identify malaria parasites in the hospital laboratory, he applied and got the job. Although he had no formal medical training, as he put it, "I had been hospitalized with malaria when I was stationed in Sardinia and the doctor had shown me my parasites under a microscope." Working in the laboratory he had many contacts with American officers and enlisted men. In particular he struck up a friendship with Lieutenant Corenti. He recalls that Americans often discussed politics in front of him (clearly a violation of anti-fraternization rules) and he was particularly interested in listening to their discussions.

With the exception of several short trips to side camps with Lieutenant Corenti, Josef spent his entire time in Camp Atlanta. He recalls that the conditions at the camp were good until V-E Day, when they deteriorated, but they improved again by fall 1945. He also remembers that Nazis were separated into special compounds.

Josef was discharged from Camp Atlanta in February or March 1946. Traveling by train to San Francisco, he was placed on a ship that passed through the Panama Canal and eventually took him to Liverpool. He spent almost a year in England at Camp Selby. Although he worked "mostly digging ditches," he had "a good experience there." Major Kemp treated the prisoners well and he had "much contact with the civilian population." They were allowed outside camp during day. He also established a long-term family relationship with an Anglican rector whom he taught German. Josef was discharged in 1947 and returned to his native Saarbrücken.

Harry H. was born in 1924 in Metzdorf, near Kulmbach, Oberbayern (Upper Bavaria).[43] After attending *Volksschule* in Ziegelhütten, he transferred to the *Realschule für Jungen* in Kulmbach (which became an *Oberrealschule* in 1939). He completed six grades in the *Oberrealschule* (three grades short of the nine grades required for the final degree, the *Abitur*), when he volunteered for the *Sanitätsoffizierslaufbahn* (medical officer career) in the Luftwaffe (air force) on August 1, 1942.

Like Hans W., Harry was a jazz enthusiast (he learned to play jazz piano and had many jazz records) and a free spirit. He did not take well to regimental life. In 1943 he was fired from the program for *"Charakterliche Uneignung"* (roughly translated as "lack of character") and given orders to join a unit at the eastern front. As fate would have it (or rather luck), the night before his departure, Harry ran into an acquaintance who illegally changed his orders to place him in a paratrooper unit destined for Italy.

Harry's paratrooper career turned out to be short.[44] After heavy fighting, he was captured by the Americans on September 16, 1943, near Florence (Highway 65, Borgo San Lorenzo). Only twenty-two men in his company survived. Harry, who had some training as a medic and spoke English, was able to help wounded American soldiers (the Americans did not have a medic). Grateful, the American officer in charge offered to exchange Harry for Americans, but Harry chose not to be exchanged. He was taken to a camp between Livorno and Pisa. After two weeks, he was taken to Oran by ship, from where he crossed the Atlantic. "We left Oran, went through the Straits of Gibraltar [and then] into New York Harbor." Harry "had read a lot of books about America" and vividly recalls his arrival in New York as "probably the most impressive day of my life. It was a beautiful October day, 29th of October, 1944. The captain of the troop transport ship that I was on, with hundreds of others, allowed us to go up on the upper deck. I'd seen pictures of the southern tip of Manhattan. I'd never been there, but here I am. It's just like in the movies, my mother would say. That's when life began for me. It sounds strange but it's true."

Placed on a Pullman train, Harry arrived at Camp Chaffee, Arkansas. He recalls that the prisoners hesitated to board the train when they saw the upholstered seats, believing that there must be something wrong. On the way, he expressed surprise at the luxurious appointment of the Pullman train and the sumptuous breakfast of scrambled eggs and orange juice.

At Camp Chaffee, Harry admired the clean barracks and the fact that the beds had sheets. As an NCO Harry did not work initially. Bored and "tired of playing cards" by Christmas, Harry signed up to work. He was placed in a separate camp for NCOs who volunteered to work to prevent retaliation from Nazis who saw this as collaboration with the enemy. Since it was winter he was put in charge of stoking the furnace for six of the barracks, a job he did until the end of February or beginning of March, when he was reassigned to work in the kitchen, peeling potatoes and making pancakes. At the end of May/beginning of June, Harry was transferred to Fort Sheridan, Illinois. His train journey took him past Chicago, the city that would become his home after the war.

While normally at Fort Sheridan, Harry was frequently transferred to several side camps, working in agriculture. At Waupun, Wisconsin, he worked in the pea harvest; at Thornton, Illinois, he picked cocktail onions; at Galesville, Wisconsin, he worked in a canning factory; at Billy Mitchell Field, Wisconsin he worked on farms and in a sauerkraut factory. At the end the year he was transferred again. This time his destination was Vaughn General U.S. Army Hospital in Chicago, where he worked as an orderly for three months until March or April 1946.

As was the case for Willie S., Harry's memories of his time in Wisconsin are very positive: "It was just like home. People were so kind, and so decent." At Billy Mitchell Field, Harry remembers, one of the farmers he worked for would invite four prisoners for a family meal on Sundays, picking them up in the morning and returning them to the camp in the evening. Harry recalls the following episode from his time in the sauerkraut factory: "I don't know exactly where that was, there were a bunch of POWs sitting on one side of the conveyor belt, and a bunch of little old ladies from Wisconsin on the other side. And I remember clearly, one of the ladies, after we'd been there a couple of days, you know, she looked at me. Well, it turned out that she had had two boys who were in the infantry in Europe, and both survived. And she looked at me, and she said 'Jeez,' she said, 'You know, I'm looking at you, and you remind me so of my two boys. I just can't believe that you were over there trying to kill one another.'"

After a brief stay at Fort Custer, Michigan (where he played jazz in March and April), Harry left for Fort Shanks, from where he was repatriated to Europe. He disembarked at Le Havre on May 10 and spent two and a half months at Camp Bolbec. He was never in the French part of the camp. Harry assembled a small jazz band and he managed to get a job with the Americans playing jazz in the officers' club. In November 1946 Harry was discharged directly to Germany, arriving in Kulmbach by train.

Heinrich T. was born in 1921 in Daetsdorf (near Jauer, today Jawor, Poland), Silesia.[45] In 1925, he moved with his parents to Berlin/Schöneberg. In Berlin he attended the *Volksschule* and completed an apprenticeship as a baker that ended with the journeyman certificate in 1939. In 1940, Heinrich was drafted into the infantry. He participated in the occupation of Poland, and after a brief stint in France he was sent to Russia, near Leningrad, in December 1941. Fortunately, Heinrich was part of the support forces. He worked in a bakery and was not at the front. When he contracted yellow fever he was sent to a field hospital near Riga, Latvia, where he recuperated for four weeks.

Heinrich is not sure about the exact sequence of events following his recuperation. He remembers being sent to Vienna and Czechoslovakia, but does not remember where he went first. He does remember ending up in Stuttgart, where he received orders to be sent to North Africa. In April 1943 he arrived in Sicily, spending time near Gela and Licata. Given the German capitulation in North Africa in the following month, Heinrich never made it to North Africa. In heavy fighting in Italy, most of his company had been killed. Heinrich was sitting in an orange grove with no ammunition when he was taken prisoner by the Americans in summer 1943. He was transported to Tunis and on to Oran from where he crossed the Atlantic on a liberty ship, arriving in Newport or Norfolk (he is not sure) in September 1943.

The Pullman train took him to Camp Tonkawa, Oklahoma. Heinrich stayed at Tonkawa for six months. He did not work. In spring 1944 he was transferred to Camp Gruber, Oklahoma. At Camp Gruber he first worked in the motor pool and then in the bakery. At the bakery he and his fellow POWs went on strike when they were asked to work longer hours. The strike proved unsuccessful, and Heinrich and a fellow POW were punished by being placed in detention with only bread and water. Heinrich remembers, "It was not that bad because comrades were able to smuggle us food."[46] Thereafter he worked in the kitchen, cooking and cleaning. He does not recall having had contact with Americans at Camp Gruber.

Heinz was discharged in fall 1946. He traveled to Camp Shanks and then crossed the Atlantic. He disembarked in Southampton, England. He ended up in a camp in Stratford on Avon, an old English air force camp, where he worked in the kitchen and on several farms. He recalls that the barracks were very comfortable and the British people were very friendly. In particular he remembers that he was frequently given a ride by local people and was once invited into Shakespeare's house. After a year in England, Heinrich returned to Germany in 1947.

Kurt P. was born in 1922, in Kuhnern (near Neumarkt, today Środa Slaşka) Silesia.[47] After graduating from the *Volksschule*, he completed an apprenticeship as a stonemason in 1941 (the certificate —*Zeugnis*— is prominently displayed on his office wall). He moved to Berlin where he worked as a stonemason in construction. After several deferments he was drafted in 1943.

Kurt ended up in southern Italy, where he was captured by British forces near Naples on November 6, 1943. After a few days in a temporary camp (the basement of an Italian home) he was transported by boat to Le Havre, France, from where he crossed the Atlantic on a liberty ship, disembarking in Norfolk, Virginia. Deloused, given clean clothes, a blanket, and cigarettes, Kurt was put on a Pullman train which took him to Camp Ellis, Illinois, via Chicago.

After spending five months at Camp Ellis, cleaning machinery and doing chores around the camp, Kurt was transferred to several side camps in Illinois and Wisconsin. At Camp Barron, Wisconsin, he picked asparagus; at Camp Lodi, Wisconsin, he picked peas; at Camp Columbus, Wisconsin, he worked in canning and on a sheep farm; at Camp Hoopston, Illinois, he helped make rope from hemp. Finally Kurt spent a few weeks at Camp Hartford (near Milwaukee), where he worked in cheese making and canning. Most of these side camps were makeshift, set up specifically for temporary agricultural work. Prisoners often slept in tents, and worked with little supervision (see Harry H.). Camp Hartford was particularly memorable, as it was located in a beautiful ballroom. Kurt remembers the luxurious quality of the parquet floor. "It was the best prisoner of war camp in America."

The POWs moved from camp to camp "just like migrant workers," Kurt recalls. He had contacts with several farmers, many of whom were of German origin. He recalls that the manager at the cheese factory at Juneau (Camp Barron) "took us out for dinner in town, in an American restaurant in Juneau, can you imagine? A bunch of prisoners of war — people coming in there with 'POW's on their back, going in a civilian restaurant?"

Kurt also recalls being involved in a brief successful strike at Camp Barron. When they arrived at Camp Barron in August 1944, they had not been paid for work done at their previous work site. Unable to buy cigarettes and other treats, they went on strike. When they were paid the following day, they resumed work. Summing up his experience in an interview with Wisconsin Public Radio, Kurt concludes, "Everybody was happy. ... We were happy to be out of the war, a roof over our head and all the beer we could drink. There were no problems."

Kurt left the United States in May 1946. Traveling from Fort Shanks to Le Havre and Bolbec, he ended up as a farm laborer in France. Kurt worked for two farmers. The first treated him very badly. When Kurt wrote a letter of complaint to the supervising officer, he was transferred to another farm, where conditions were much better. In late 1948, when Kurt received permission to attend the wedding of his girlfriend's sister in Germany, he simply did not return to France as promised. Instead in Kurt traveled to Königstein, the small town in the Taunus Mountains north of Frankfurt where he had met Emilie, his girlfriend. Kurt and Emilie were married later that year.

Thirteen Westfrontgefangenen

"My life was saved and changed forever when I was taken prisoner by the Americans" (Peter E., Camp Aliceville, Alabama).

"I was not bitter regarding all circumstances, I was really lucky" (Henry K., Fort Chaffee, Arkansas).

"I felt like an angel in seventh heaven" (Ernst F., Camps in the Midwest and New Mexico).

"I always wanted to see the world"; "I learned a lot about America."

"When we were working outside the camps we saw the way people lived."
(Ludwig N., camps in Washington and Montana).

"This huge, wonderful country impressed me no end. Put this together
with the friendship I had developed with Mr. Lykins, and it is no wonder
that within me the thought firmed that I simply have to come back to the
United States." (Henry R., several camps in California).

"I was relieved and overjoyed when I was captured by the Americans"
(Erich K., Camp Ogden, Utah).

As a group, the men captured during and after the Normandy invasion were the youngest. Most were born between 1925 and 1927. Variously
known as the *Franzosen* or *Westfrontgefangenen*, they represented a broad
range of war experiences. They included seasoned soldiers who had previously fought on the eastern front, but most were young men who had
been drafted out of school in Hitler's last desperate effort to defend Germany.

Henry K. was born in 1923 in Teltge/Münster as one of eleven children.[48]
After completing the *Volksschule* in 1937, Henry started, but did not finish,
an apprenticeship as a mechanic. When he was drafted in fall 1941 he
joined the paratroopers to avoid being drafted into the SS. (See similar
sentiments expressed by Rupert M.) After three months of basic training
near Breslau, Henry was dispatched to the Russian front. He was seriously
wounded in 1943. To recover, he spent time in hospitals in Breslau and
later Koblenz and the Oberpfalz (Upper Palatinate).

Having recovered, Henry was promoted to sergeant and dispatched
to Normandy in 1944. He was captured near Remagen when his unit was
retreating from advancing American forces. He recalls that he and the
twelve men he was leading were hiding in a cellar in a small town, when
the mayor of the town told him that it was pointless to resist and they
capitulated in March 1945. Taken to Le Havre, Henry crossed the Atlantic
on a liberty ship, arriving in New York in April 1945. He remembers that
Roosevelt had died when they were about to embark and they had to stay
below deck for most of the trip. He believes that the Americans were afraid
that there might be a revolt among the prisoners.

His American train journey took him to Fort Chaffee, Arkansas, outside Fort Smith, a large POW camp housing some 3,000 prisoners. Unlike
my other respondents, Henry has negative memories of his train trip to
Arkansas. He recalls that the train was a cattle train and that the journey
was rough so that several men died.

Henry remained at Fort Chaffee for a year working in the kitchen. He noted that the food was good, but he recalled that he kept his "distance from the Americans." He did not make any attempts to learn English. He remembers that the camp commander, whom he considered "anti–German," was eventually replaced when the Lutheran and Catholic ministers launched a complaint. Yet, summing up his experience, he concluded: "I was not bitter regarding all circumstances, I was really lucky."

While at Fort Chaffee, Henry was able to get in touch with an American relative, an uncle (his mother's brother) who had emigrated in the 1920s and lived in Sylvan, Oregon. The uncle would later sponsor his immigration.

Passing through Camp Shanks, Henry returned to Europe in April 1946. He ended up spending two additional years in England doing forced labor, working on farms near London. Like most of my respondents, Henry had considerable contact with British people and his memories were very positive. "I met a wonderful English family," he says, including a woman who lived with her mother and owned a beauty salon. He volunteered to help in their garden and home. When Henry returned to his hometown of Teltge in 1948, he found his family alive and well.

Oskar S. is the youngest man I interviewed.[49] He was born in December 1927 in Rastenburg, East Prussia (today Ketrzyn, Poland). After completing the *Volksschule*, he started an apprenticeship as an electrician in 1942. He was drafted into the *Arbeitsdienst* early in 1944. Drafted into the Wehrmacht six months later, he was sent to Unterwangen, near Königsberg (today Kaliningrad, Russia) for basic training. Following a brief stay in Linz, Austria, Oskar ended up at the front in Normandy, where he became a prisoner of war near Cherbourg on June 23, 1944, shortly after the invasion on June 6. He was transported to England, from where he crossed the Atlantic, arriving in Boston in July 1944. Oskar was barely seventeen years old.

Oskar's train journey took him first to Fort Custer, Michigan, but he was soon transferred to Fort Sheridan, Illinois, and on to Hartford, Wisconsin, where the POWs lived in an old ballroom (see Kurt P.). Like Kurt P. and Harry H., Oskar worked in agriculture, picking potatoes and tomatoes, in a milk factory where they made concentrated milk, and in a sauerkraut factory (see Harry H.). Commenting on the "lax supervision," he remembers that "one guy even left to visit with a girl."

Except for his brief stays at Fort Custer and Fort Sheridan, Oskar spent most of his POW time in small side camps, where formal opportunities to learn English were limited or nonexistent. Unlike Kurt P. and Harry H. who were in similar camps, Oskar did not have much contact with Americans and he did not learn English during his captivity.[50]

Passing through Camp Shanks, Oskar left for Europe in May 1946. Arriving in Le Havre, he had the misfortune of ending up as forced labor in a French coal mine near Pas de Calais, where he was "working eight hours a day and eating cabbage soup," and where the overall "conditions were very bad." Released for "health reasons" in spring 1948, Oskar was unable to return to his home, which was now under Polish administration. Nor could he join his parents, who now lived in the Russian Occupation Zone, so he joined his brother who had moved to Göttingen after the war.

Ernst F. was born in 1925 in Stettin.[51] He attended the local *Gymnasium* through the eleventh grade when he was drafted in August 1943. He volunteered for the army because he had been told that he would be drafted soon into the SS, "the very last thing I wanted to happen to me." (See similar comments made by Rupert M. and Hermann K.). He was accepted into the Signal Corps. Following brief training in Danzig (Gdansk) and Thorn (Torun), Ernst's unit was dispatched to Baumholder in the Palatinate. At the end of April 1944 they were dispatched to St.-Nazaire, France, and ten days later to Normandy, where they arrived on May 16, 1944.

Ernst was working laying telephone cables and the workers were told that the Allied invasion would happen soon. He became a prisoner of war on June 18, 1944, at 7:30 in the evening, twelve days after the invasion. He was eighteen years old.

Ernst did not like being a soldier and when he was sent to sergeant school he made deliberate mistakes to avoid being promoted. From the start, he recalls, "I aimed at becoming a prisoner of the British or Americans." When his goal became reality, his first thought was, "Thank God, no more rifle drills." He says, "After eight months in the German army, I was happy that this episode of my life was over."

Ernst was first transported to England. Disembarking in Southampton, he was transported to London by train. After spending four days being interrogated, he was again placed on a train. This one took him to Liverpool, from where he embarked for the United States on July 1, 1944, on the *Argentina*, an ocean liner of the South American Line that was traveling in a convoy because of the danger presented by German U-boats.

Ernst's transatlantic journey lasted twelve days. He recalls that they were allowed forty-five minutes on deck each day. He disembarked at Ellis Island, New York. After being processed he was placed on a ferry to Hoboken, New Jersey, where the POWs boarded a Pullman train. Passing Manhattan, he marveled at the skyscrapers, which were all lit up. "It was like Utopia coming from the dark of Europe."

The train took them up the Hudson River, then passed near Niagara Falls, through Ontario and past Detroit. He arrived at his final destination, Fort Custer, Michigan, on July 13, 1944. Ernst recalls that one of the POWs arriving with him at Fort Custer found his brother who was an American GI stationed at Fort Custer.

After only five days at Fort Custer, Ernst was transferred to Camp Ellis, near Peoria, Illinois. On the way there, they were passing through Chicago. At Camp Ellis, they were greeted by their "comrades" from the Afrika Korps with, "You traitors, you communists." Ernst's stay at Camp Ellis turned out to be short. On July 29 he was transferred again, this time to Eureka, Illinois, a small side camp where prisoners were housed in the Eureka College gymnasium. Ernst recalls that there was only a single wire and two guards assigned to the camp.

At Eureka, Ernst worked in the corn cannery in the nearby town of Washington. On the bus between the camp and the cannery, they sang German songs. During their break they had a chance to talk to the civilian workers, "who were very friendly." On Sundays, a German-speaking pastor provided church services at the camp. Although the work was rather monotonous, Ernst enjoyed his time at Eureka: "the weather was perfect, food excellent, and the treatment terrific."

On September 6, Ernst was transferred to Camp Grant, Illinois. "It was a good place to be, we had a piano, a library, pool hall, bands and theater." Ernst also recalls receiving books that his father had sent him and took advantage of courses offered in the camp, in particular a course in geometry and English. At night they roasted corn. Ernst was assigned to the potato harvest nearby and he recalls that at lunch break, an American couple would drive up in a Cadillac and give each prisoner a Baby Ruth candy bar.

Ernst was spared "a cold winter in the northern states" when he was transferred again on October 10. This time he was heading south. On the way he passed through St. Louis, then Little Rock and into Texas near the Mexican border. He arrived at his destination, Fort Bliss, Texas, on October 13. From there they were transported by truck to their new "home," nearby Camp Hatch. Three days later they started picking cotton, a job they universally disliked. He recalls that they were punished for "poor cotton picking" by getting only bread and water to eat. Supervision was extremely lax and the guard would often tell them he wanted to sleep and they should wake him if a superior should come. Otherwise the camp provided diversions, including a movie every week. When the cotton harvest ended in February, there was not much to do, so they were put to work cutting trees and cleaning the camp.

In May 1945, Ernst broke his glasses, and he was taken to Fort Bliss to be fitted with new glasses by a local optometrist. "In the waiting room I sat among GIs and almost felt like one of them." In May it was time for more field work, this time to hoe weeds. Ernst worked for several farmers, in particular Mr. Mundy, Mr. Hitchcocks and Mr. Alvarez. "We had a good time on Mr. Mundy's farm," he recalls. "The guard left us in peace and sometimes we could swim in the irrigation ditches." Mrs. Hitchcocks would serve them a bowl of Jell-O and Mr. Alvarez presented "each of us with huge watermelons." Ernst particularly liked picking tomatoes, a job that allowed him to eat as many as he wanted. In September Ernst was back picking cotton. Picking cotton "was rough." "We had to fulfill a quota and the food was insufficient, especially there was not enough salt." "The farmers sometimes gave us salt and additional food."

A committed anti–Nazi, Ernst remembers that there were Nazis at Camp Hatch, but that there were no fights. Ernst was the only POW I interviewed who told me that he subscribed to *Der Ruf.*

In January 1946, after fifteen months in Camp Hatch, Ernst was transferred to another side camp in Ysleta, where he worked in the kitchen. Selected to participate in the Special Projects reeducation camp at Fort Eustis, Hans left Camp Hatch on March 2, and arrived in Virginia after "a very nice trip in a very comfortable train" on March 5. After completing the two-week course, he left Fort Eustis on March 18. Ernst traveled north to Camp Shanks. On the way, the train passed through Washington, D.C., where "we all had a glimpse of the lighted capitol." On March 24, 1946, Ernst embarked for Europe. After disembarking in Le Havre, he spent a couple of weeks at Camp Bolbec ("an awful camp") before he was finally discharged to Germany.

Johannes (John) S. was born in 1924 in Bremen.[52] After attending the *Volksschule* he completed an apprenticeship in shipbuilding. Before he was drafted in 1942 at the age of eighteen, John worked in a shipyard as a draftsman for submarines. He also went out on submarines to test them. Given his civilian background, John ended up in the navy.

After some basic training on a small island in Holland, John was dispatched to Cherbourg, where he was assigned to a kind of coast guard during late 1943 and early 1944. His unit also was in charge of placing mines in the harbor. When the invasion started in June 1944, he was assigned to protect the arsenal. When Americans came they jumped into the river. The colonel in charge of his unit told them to surrender. The Americans told him to throw his personal belongings away because "everything is better in America." They were then marched to the beach. On the way, he recalls, there was an incident in a small French village where people were celebrating liberation. John had always liked jazz and had belonged to a Jazz club in Bremen were they listened to forbidden records (see also Harry H. and Hans W.). He had also learned to play the accordion and he asked his captors if they had an instrument. They did and he played some American songs for them.

After marching to the beach they were placed on ships that took them to Southampton and on to a POW camp on a racetrack near London. There he was interrogated by the British since he had worked on submarines and they wanted to know secrets. However, John said he did not divulge any. From London he was transported to Edinburgh by train. On the way he saw British people in train stations giving "V for victory" signs.

After a week's stay in a camp in Edinburgh, John was transported to Glasgow from where he disembarked on the *Queen Mary*. He arrived in New York in July 1944. After the usual procedures he was put on the train to Alabama. On the train, the guards told them that since they had a long ride ahead, they should change seats in such a way that they could put up their feet and sleep.

John's first camp was Camp Opelika, Alabama. At Opelika, John worked cutting trees. He remembers the oppressive heat in July and August, and although they were provided with salt and ice water, the job "was tough." Fortunately, after three months, John was briefly transferred to Camp Rucker and then to Camp Montgomery, Alabama, where some 300 POWs worked in a large army supply depot. John worked in the warehouse unloading and loading supplies. This was hard work, especially given the heat and sun.

One day when he was sweeping the floor he advised the woman in charge of keeping records how to improve her recordkeeping. She followed his advice and he was permanently assigned to her and her black assistant. Mrs. Richardson was the wife of the first sergeant in the camp and "she was very friendly." The three of them got along quite well; the black man even gave John a wallet for his birthday. Sometimes when they were loading and unloading supplies, the Americans told them to drop crates of beer, which would allow them to drink the unbroken bottles. John recalls the excellent food but also recalls that the food deteriorated after German surrender and that Americans became less friendly. He also took the opportunity to learn English and tried to improve his skills by reading books.

Towards the end of his stay, John broke his hand while working on a forklift. He was taken to the hospital and could not work after the incident. In October 1945 he was transported to Camp Shanks, and after a brief hospital stay of three days, he returned to Europe on a U.S. Army hospital ship, the *Wisteria*. Disembarking in Cherbourg, he was worried about the mines they had laid, but found that they had been cleared up. John returned to his hometown, Bremen, in October 1945.

Heinz F. was born in 1926 in Berlin/Neukölln.[53] After completing the *Volksschule*, Heinz started an apprenticeship as tool and die maker when he was drafted in the *Arbeitsdienst* in late 1942 and after a two day visit at home, he was immediately drafted into the Wehrmacht.

After brief training as a fuselier in the Mark Brandenburg, Heinz was sent to France (outside Paris) where he stayed for six months. He was then transported to Italy and on to North Africa (Tunis). Before he arrived there, the Germans had surrendered and Heinz was sent to Poland and on to Russia, but the Germans soon had to retreat from both. This episode took less than six months, and Heinz found himself back in Brest, France.

He was captured on his birthday in 1944. At the time of his capture his unit of 300 had been reduced to only fifty men. They had horses with a cannon. When they were bombarded, an impact directly behind him hit the horses and they fell on him, saving his life. He and two comrades tried to get back to another unit. On their way they came across American soldiers, and one of his comrades was hit in the stomach. Heinz patched up the wounded comrade and was able to escape by hiding in the fields, eating green apples and milking cows. They were also able to steal some C rations. After three days of hiding, they decided to walk on and saw many dead bodies. Heinz was shot in the head, but not seriously wounded. When he was cold he took a jacket from a dead American soldier. Exhausted, they fell asleep, and they were woken up by American soldiers pointing guns at them. They were taken to a provisional camp, where they were disinfected. In the process Heinz took off his dog tag. He had also lost his *Soldbuch* in the bombardment. This meant that he did not have any identification.

They were placed on a ship to New York, but the Americans kept Heinz apart because they thought he might be an American. Heinz did not speak. The American physician who tried to interview him talked to him in German and Heinz answered so that it was clear he was not an American. He was immediately taken from the group of American wounded and placed with the other Germany POWs on the ship.

After arriving in New York (he thinks it was Harlem), they were placed on a train to Houlton, Maine in late 1944. Camp Houlton was not their final destination; four or five days later they were transported by trucks to a side camp. (He does not remember the name of the camp. It could be Lake Spencer, or Seboomook). Before departing they were given cigarettes and toiletries for which he eventually paid with the money they made.

At the camp he first worked as a lumberjack. He recalls that they were taken to the woods on trucks, each with twenty-five men, and worked in teams of two cutting timber. There was only one guard and he was usually drunk. After a few months Heinz was put to work digging up potatoes for about two weeks. He also befriended another German POW, Karl-Heinz B., who was older and took the young Heinz under protection. (Karl-Heinz went straight home to Germany after the war and later visited Heinz in Berlin. He was a chauffeur for the American occupation forces and came to Berlin with an American officer, and he took the time to visit Heinz briefly). Karl-Heinz, who was the spokesman for the POWs, got Heinz a job in the kitchen, peeling potatoes, making pancakes. Heinz recalls that the kitchen staff included a German butcher "who made great salami." They were allowed to have pigs which they slaughtered to make the salami. The food was good and plentiful.

Heinz remembers having some contact with Americans. One was a doctor whose name he does not remember. He was "a very nice man," and one of the prisoners drew a portrait of him. One of the guards with whom he traded was a middleman between the Germans and the guard. He sometimes let Heinz listen to the radio.

Heinz does not remember the exact date he left Maine. He believes "it must have been sometime in 1946." He recalls returning to Europe via the St. Lawrence Seaway to New York, and crossing the Atlantic. He disembarked in England but does not remember the port. Heinz spent a year in a camp near Coventry working for a chicken farmer nearby. Heinz could have returned to Germany in 1948. When he received a letter from his mother telling him that things were bad in Germany, he took advantage of the British offer to remain as a civilian contract worker. When he finally returned to Germany at Christmas in 1950, he found out that his mother was sick.

Ludwig N. was born 1926 in Rottenburg/Neckar.[54] After completing the *Volksschule* he attended the *Technikum* (technical school) in Stuttgart. When he was drafted in 1944 he volunteered for the air force (*Flugnach-richtendienst*). Following a brief training in Augsburg he ended up in France, near Nancy, where he was wounded on August 29, 1944. In an ambulance, Ludwig was transported to a nearby field hospital where he was operated on under chaotic conditions. After three weeks in the field hospital he was well enough to be transported to Trier, Germany. He remembers the constant attacks and air raids, and he hid in a basement for two weeks. Ordered to rejoin his unit in early November 1944, Ludwig was captured in France on March 20, 1945.

After internment in several transition camps, where he was interrogated, Ludwig was transported to Cherbourg, where he was among the 2,500 German POWs placed on the last ship to the United States. He arrived in New York Harbor on May 8, 1945, the day the war in Europe ended. His train journey across the United States took him to Camp Florence, Arizona (outside Phoenix). On the train they passed through Santa Fe. Like most of my respondents Ludwig had read Karl May and was now able to see the "wild west" landscapes described in May's many books. He was "overwhelmed by a sense of adventure." "I liked geography outside Europe, and learned a lot about America," he recalled. Unfortunately Ludwig was never in a camp where he could take formal courses.

At Camp Florence Ludwig did not work. "All we did is walk around the fence and exchange experiences." Ludwig, who was determined to make the best of the situation, used the time to talk with his fellow POWs from whom, he remembers, he learned a lot. In particular, he befriended an older man, Dr. Meier, who had been a judge in civilian life. (Meier later went to Fort Eustis and afterward returned to being a judge in Germany). "We talked about the future, and he reinforced many thoughts I already had. He had a young daughter, and he wanted her to come to the United States. I felt the same way. My dad had gone through World War I and had lost everything after the war. I wanted to get away from all that" (quoted in Carlson, 217–18).

After four weeks at Camp Florence, Ludwig was transferred to a side camp in Glasgow, Montana, where he worked in sugar beet fields. Sometime in the summer Ludwig was transferred to Fort Lewis, Washington, where most POWs worked as lumberjacks. Ludwig worked in the kitchen, cleaning up and serving food. In late fall 1945 Ludwig returned to Montana and then to Florence. This time he worked picking cotton until March 1946.

2. An Astonishing Introduction

Ludwig's stay in each camp was short. He did have some contact with Americans working in sugar beets in Montana, and as a lumberjack at Fort Lewis, but he did not develop any lasting relationships. He does recall that a farmer gave him additional food and cigarettes and would even buy him things on request. He also recalls a farmer in Montana who "spoke my dialect" (Schwäbisch — Swabian) and "who turned out to be a German Russian." "When we were working outside the camps we saw the way people lived. What interested me was the vastness of the country and the openness of the society."

Ludwig left Camp Florence in March 1946. Like Johann G., Ludwig returned to Europe via San Francisco and the Panama Canal, stopping for three days in Guantánamo Bay, Cuba. He finally disembarked in Glasgow, Scotland, in April 1946. He spent two years in several camps in Scotland and England, including near Stratford (see Hermann F.). In England he worked in road construction (see Rupert M.) and housing tracts in the London suburbs. Although Ludwig had learned English in school, he had not had much opportunity to improve his knowledge in American camps. So he practiced English in England, mostly by reading. He also remembers attending a concert at the Royal Albert Hall. Most important, perhaps, was that he made many friends in England, including one person who arranged for and paid for his transportation to immigrate to America.

He remembers a particular event that he found deeply moving. He and twenty other POWs were invited to attend a picnic hosted by German Jews who had fled to England who treated them "as if nothing had happened." After two years in England, Ludwig returned to Germany on May 23, 1948.

Erwin H. was born in Lemberg, Silesia (today Lwów), in 1927.[55] His father, a Lutheran minister, died mysteriously during a trip to Berlin and his mother had died earlier, leaving Erwin and his two sisters orphans. Erwin attended a boarding school from which he graduated in 1944. During vacations he spent time on his uncle's large farm. After graduating, Erwin joined the Luftwaffe and was assigned to the paratroopers. Following a brief period of basic training near Berlin, his unit was sent to Belgium and Holland at the end of 1944. There he was captured by Canadian forces near Venlo in early 1945.

After spending two to three weeks in a large camp in Le Havre, Erwin was among some 1,000 men who were put on a ship. Only after they passed England did they realize that they were going to the United States. It took the liberty ship twenty-three days to cross the Atlantic. He arrived in New

York, tired but also excited. After the men were deloused and given POW uniforms, Erwin's Pullman train passed through Philadelphia and went on to Richmond, Virginia. Erwin ended up in Camp Butner, North Carolina, in early summer 1945. At Camp Butner Erwin worked for a farmer who came to pick up three or four POWs in the morning and brought them back in the evening. Later in the summer some 200 POWs, including Erwin, were transported by truck to Scotland Neck, where they picked peanuts. After a few weeks he was transferred to New Bern and a temporary tent camp where he picked peanuts and cotton for two months.

While working at Scotland Neck, Erwin was friendly with a farmer, Manford Lawrence. He recalls that Lawrence would serve his POWs breakfast before work every day, "which was against the rules." As Erwin observed wryly, "He got more work out of us this way, by being nice."

Erwin was among the last German POWs to be returned to Germany in summer 1946. He believes he left through Camp Shanks and spent a few days at Camp Bolbec until he was put on a train to Germany. Unable to return to his home in Silesia, Erwin ended up in Babenhausen, a large American base in the state of Hessen.

Johann G. was born in 1925 in Gelsenkirchen.[56] After completing the *Volksschule* and gaining his journeyman's certificate (*Gesellenprüfung*) as an electrician, he was drafted in 1943. Stationed in Königsberg, he became a dispatcher driving a motorcycle between units. Pushing into Russia, he was wounded in November 1944 and, after spending time in a field hospital (*Feldlazarett*), sent to Berchtesgaden to recuperate. He was released in March 1945 and given seventeen days of leave to spend with his parents. Johann had papers to join a tank division (*Panzerdivision*) in Berlin. While in town, he was picked up by Americans who had just arrived. He was taken across the Rhine and loaded on a railroad car. He traveled for three days all over France. Johann arrived in Cherbourg, and there he spent two weeks in a camp administered by the Americans with French guards. He was one of 1,000 men selected to be transported to the United States, and embarked on a liberty ship traveling in a convoy of ninety ships heading for New York. There they disembarked after nine days at sea. His cross-country train journey took him to Camp Florence, near Phoenix, Arizona, where he arrived one day before V-E Day, May 7, 1945. At Camp Florence he spent four weeks "with nothing to do," so he tried to learn English. Since there were no organized classes, he recalls, "I learned what I could."

Johann was soon transferred to a camp near Preston, Idaho, where he arrived the end of May 1945. His stay at Camp Preston turned out to be life-transforming. After briefly working in the camp's kitchen, Johann was put in charge of supply. "From that day on, I had the best job in the camp." In this capacity he drove a jeep (accompanied by a guard) through the Idaho countryside and "met all kinds of people and my English improved every day." Coming from the industrial Ruhr Valley of Germany, Johann was enchanted with the pristine nature of the Idaho countryside and the mountains.

While procuring food for the camp, Johann befriended two Americans, a farmer and a gas station owner. Both men took a liking to the young German and offered to sponsor him should he want to return after the war. Mr. Hansen, the gas station owner, told him, "Hans, I like you. You are a fine boy. If you would like to come back to the USA, let me know and I will try to get you over here."

In June 1945 Johann was briefly assigned to work in sugar beets. The following December he helped dismantle the camp. Passing briefly through Ogden, Utah, where he stayed one week, he continued to Stockton, California, where he arrived around Christmas 1946. Two months later, in February 1946, Johann was transported to San Francisco from where he embarked for Europe. The return trip took twenty-one days. He traveled through the Panama Canal, to Cuba and France, and eventually disembarked in Liverpool, England. Johann spent two years in English camps near the town of Kettering where he worked on several jobs, in a cleanup crew, in a smelter and on a farm owned by George Thompson. Johann and his fellow German POWs were allowed to go out during the day, but had to be back in the camp at night. When he finally returned to Germany in May 1948, Johann had only one dream, "to go back to the USA, with all the wonderful people."

Otto L. was born in 1925 in Halle and grew up in Osnabrück.[57] After graduating from the *Mittelschule* (middle school), he attended a *Fachschule* (trade school), the Staatliche Versuchsanstalt für Kleintierzucht (for small animal husbandry) in Hamm. In December 1942, he was drafted into the *Arbeitsdienst*. Six months later he was drafted into the Wehrmacht. His basic training took place in Ameland, a west Friesian island in the Netherlands. In November or December 1943, Otto was moved to Marquise, a town in the Pas-de-Calais, France, where he received further boot camp training on an abandoned former German air force field. From there he was transferred to Cap Gris-Nez (near Calais). His unit was scheduled to go to the Somme, but they were rerouted and Otto became a prisoner of war when he was captured by American forces with a British liaison officer in a small village in France near the Belgium border on September 7, 1944. Two of his German POW comrades who had been POWs in World War I told him that the war was now over for them.

Transported by Jeep and surrounded by GIs, Otto was taken to a temporary camp near Compiègne. On the way there he was given food and conversed with GIs who asked him what it was like to fight for Hitler. After a few days in the camp, Otto was transported by jeep to Cherbourg. On the way he marveled at American army equipment and organization, the abundance and the waste of gasoline.

In Cherbourg they were given uniforms, shoes, and wool blankets; they were deloused and were given a warm meal. From Cherbourg, Otto crossed the English Channel to Southampton and went on to Liverpool, from where he embarked on a troopship to cross the Atlantic, arriving in New York early in October 1944. He recalls that he was treated well on ship, that the ship was clean and the food was great. They were also allowed to be on deck during the day.

After being processed, Otto was taken to Camp Fort Benning, Georgia. He recalls the luxurious Pullman trains with upholstered compartments with a guard at each end. Passing through Washington, D.C., and Atlanta, Otto and the other POWs arrived at Fort Benning, where they were unloaded, divided into companies and marched to their barracks. "Overall the treatment was friendly," Otto recalls.

At the camp there were already POWs, mostly from the Afrika Korps. He remembers that they were generally helpful about "the ropes of life in the camp," but he also remembers some conflicts between the Afrikaner and the newcomers. However, he hastened to add that these conflicts did not involve violence.

Otto spent most of his captivity at Fort Benning, where the "treatment was good." He recalls that the "housing was standard U.S. army barracks" and that he particularly enjoyed having sheets "for the first time." He also recalls that the POWs had constant information about the war in Europe, that the camp command listened to shortwave radio and typed up news they made available to prisoners daily before breakfast.

Otto believes that their good treatment can be partially explained by the fact that "the camp was in [the] South and they were white." Given his background and training in small animal husbandry, Otto worked at a pigeon loft in the communication division, where he had daily contact with American military and "made many friends." In particular, he struck up a friendship with a young American paratrooper from Utah named Earl Jackson, and Cornel Adams, who was in charge of the pigeon loft.

When Otto expressed an interest in immigrating after the war, both men offered to sponsor him. Earl Jackson warned Otto that Adams was from Texas and that the climate there was very hot. In contrast, Earl told Otto that Utah had a great climate. The two young men cooked up the idea of raising chickens and turkeys in Utah after the war.

Otto also used his time to improve his English by reading and talking daily at work with U.S. Army personnel. He recalls that at the camp there was a POW who worked on a farm who was given a car by the farmer to drive himself back and forth to work.

In fall 1945 Otto was moved to a temporary camp in Idaho where he harvested potatoes. In November o December 1945 Otto was transferred to Camp Forrest, Tennessee. In January 1946 he was transferred to Camp Shanks, and he embarked for Europe in late January 1946. He disembarked in Le Havre and was transferred to a camp run by the U.S. Army where returning German POWs were sorted according to their physical fitness to work on farms and mines in France. Otto was lucky in that his physical condition was deemed inadequate and he was put on a train to Germany. After spending a few weeks in various camps in Germany, Otto arrived in Osnabrück at the end of April 1946, almost one year after the war had ended.

Henry R. was born in 1926 in Braunschweig.[58] After attending the local *Volksschule* until the fifth grade, Henry transferred to a middle school. He then attended vocational school, while simultaneously working at the *Niedersächsiche Motorenwerke*. He graduated in 1942 with a degree in mechanical engineering.

Soon after graduating, in January 1943, Henry received his letter of induction. After six weeks of boot camp he was deployed to Russia. Fighting partisans near the town of Tarnopol, 40 kilometers west of the old Soviet-Polish border, they were moved closer to the Russian front, where he and his company were briefly captured by Russian forces. They were eventually rescued by arriving German troops. Although he hoped to be able to return to Germany, Henry was transferred to Belgium near Herentals, where he was trained in explosives.

He was captured near Caen, France, September 1944. From Caen the prisoners were marched to Cherbourg, and from there they crossed the channel, disembarking near Hampton, England. In a British camp near Hampton he was questioned "in perfect German by British officers who seemed to know everything about me." After two weeks he was transported to Glasgow from where they embarked on the *Normandy*, an ocean liner that had been converted into a troop transporter. Five days later Henry disembarked in Hoboken, New Jersey. "I had now become a POW on American soil," he remembered. Traveling for five days on a Pullman train, passing "through the most fascinating areas," Henry arrived at Fort Hall, near Pocatello, Idaho. Henry admired the beautiful countryside and expressed amazement at the ample food and the quality of the camp itself.

Henry was assigned to a group of fifteen POWs to harvest sugar beets. He remembers his first Christmas Eve, when a delegation from the YMCA "brought all kinds of goodies, such as fountain pens, cookies, razors, books, writing paper." He also recalls working for a farmer who "made us welcome" and "whose children tried to communicate with us."

Several months later Henry was transferred to Camp Cooke, California, traveling by truck "through an unbelievable countryside, mountains and gorges, rivers and deserts." At Camp Cooke, Henry was assigned to build and repair roads inside the camp. His job entailed driving a truck to the beach to get sand. Having studied mechanical engineering, Henry enjoyed hanging around the motor vehicles in the camp. In his spare time he played soccer.

Soon Henry was transferred again. His new base was a temporary camp of tents housing some 600 POWs called Camp Corcoran, northwest of Bakersfield. At Camp Corcoran, Henry had a significant and consequential encounter with an American civilian, Mr. Lykins, whom he met by chance. "Here I experienced some of the best times," he recalled, "For here is where I met Mr. Lykins while we worked in an orange plantation."

Henry tells the following story: He had been picking oranges on a quota system. Having finished his quota, he roamed around the orange grove (owned and operated by the Boswell Company), when he encountered a man in front of a house who was busy sawing and hammering. When the man noticed him he waved to him to come over. Although Henry's English was very limited and the man did not speak any German, they were able to communicate "with hands and feet." The man invited Henry to help him with his work and the young German obliged. The following day when Henry came back the man handed him a dictionary. With the help of the dictionary, Henry was able to communicate better and better. The relationship between the older American and the young German POW lasted several months. "Mr. Lykins was unquestionably the most profound, yet subtle, influence in my life. Because of him I gained perspective, and a burning desire to go back to the United States."

Henry was the only POW I interviewed who told me that he tried to escape. He escaped with a friend, but was captured after a few days and returned to the camp, where he was briefly incarcerated. In late June 1945 Henry returned to Camp Cooke and from there he traveled by truck to a camp near Stockton, California. In Stockton they boarded a train, this time going east with a final destination of Camp Shanks.

Henry's transatlantic journey took him to Ostend, Belgium, where he arrived in September 1945. He would spent several months working in mines in Belgium. After an escape and capture he was transferred to England, where he spent two years working on farms. He returned to Germany in November 1947.

Erich K. was born in 1926 in Czernowitz, Romania.[59] Ethnic Germans (*Volksdeutsche*), the family moved to Salzgitter, Germany, in 1939 when Erich was thirteen years old (*Umsiedler*).[60] He became a German citizen in 1941. After completing the *Volksschule* he began an apprenticeship as a mechanic, but was drafted, first into the *Arbeitsdienst*, and then into the Wehrmacht in January 1942. He joined the paratroopers. Like Henry R., he was first sent to Russia, and after the German retreat he was delegated to Normandy, where he was captured a short time after the invasion near Cherbourg.

"I was relieved and overjoyed when I was captured by the Americans" (*Standard Examiner*, June 16, 1952). Again like Henry, he was first transported to England where he spent two months before crossing the Atlantic, arriving in New York. Erich's first camp was near Billings, Montana. After picking sugar beets for a few months he was transferred to the army Service Forces Depot in Ogden, Utah, where he spent twenty-one months.[61]

In Ogden, Erich received training as a medic and worked in the hospital dispensary. A certificate from the Station Hospital, Utah Army Service Forces Depot, dated 23 April 1946 states that Erich K. "has rendered very satisfactory service in the Dispensary at this Hospital for the past twenty months. He has been a cooperative and resourceful worker."[62] Given his job, Erich had many contacts with Americans; in particular, he remembers being friendly with a nurse, Dorothy, who later sent care packages to Germany.

Erich did not know English when he became a POW. Like others, he also took advantage of the educational opportunities provided at Ogden, where he took courses in English and geography. In his spare time, he played soccer and learned how to box "to defend myself from bullies in the camp." Erich was among the lucky POWs who returned directly to Germany, where he was discharged in August 1946.

Peter E. was born in 1917 in Kiel.[63] After completing the *Volksschule*, he completed an apprenticeship as *kaufmännischer Angestellter* (commercial clerk) in Munich. In 1940 he married Johanna.

Peter was drafted in 1939, and after a brief deployment in France in 1940, he was sent to Poland in 1941, advancing to the Russian border. He participated in the attack on Moscow where his company suffered heavy losses. "I knew then for sure that the war was lost for Germany," he says. Wounded, he ended up in a hospital in Poland.

Having recuperated, he joined a troop put together in Munich, and again ended up in France, first in Besançon and Mâcon and then Normandy. It was there that he was taken prisoner of war by the Americans in June 1944. An NCO (*Feldwebel*, highest rank of noncommissioned officer in the Wehrmacht) Peter was first transported to England and left from Liverpool, disembarking in New York in July 1944. Peter's first POW camp was Camp Aliceville. As an NCO he did not work. He used his time to learn English, to act and direct plays and to perform in the camp orchestra.

After a brief stay in a camp in South Carolina, Peter was selected to participate in the special projects school at Fort Getty, Rhode Island, where he spent two months being trained for administrative posts in Germany. For Peter, the experience at Fort Getty was life transforming and he was keen to return to the United States at the earliest possible time. Passing through Camp Shanks, Peter returned to Munich, Germany, in October 1945.

Siegfried (Sig) K. is the only officer among the *Westfrontgefangenen* I interviewed. Sig was born in 1924 in Stettin and grew up in Berlin.[64] He attended the *Gymnasium* to the *Obersekunda* (third to last grade) and was drafted in 1942. In October of that year, Sig was sent to Stettin and Elbing (East Prussia) where he received his basic training (*Reserveoffiziersausbildung*—RoB). After completing his training in June 1943, he was dispatched to the Russian front, where he was wounded in September 1943. To recuperate he was sent a military hospital (*Lazarett*) in Upper Silesia (Oberschlesien), and later in several locations in Germany, including Schwerin until the beginning of June 1944. Later that month, Sig attended the *Kriegsschule* (war college) in Metz (required for all officer candidates, *Offiziersanwärter*) and was promoted to the rank of lieutenant. He returned to the front near Metz and later near Aachen, in September. He was wounded again on October 15, 1944, near Aachen.

Sig became a prisoner of war on November 18, 1944, in Appweiler, north of Aachen. His first days as a POW were spent in the U.S. Army field hospital in Lüttich. He was transferred to Cherbourg and crossed the channel to Southampton. From there he was transferred to a field hospital camp in Reading. After he recuperated he was transferred to Camp Moreton (near Stratford on Avon). In January 1945 Sig left England via Bristol and embarked for the United States, arriving in New York after thirteen days at sea, January 21, 1945.

His train journey lasted four or five days and took him around New York City to Camp Dermott, Arkansas (an officer camp that used to be a Japanese relocation camp). On his train trip to Arkansas, Sig commented on the slums around New York and the poverty in Appalachia. He was particularly amused by the fact that on the way they passed through "Stuttgart, which was north of Hamburg."

Sig spent one year at Camp Dermott. As an officer he did not work. He used his time to take courses through Ohio University in organic chemistry and physiology. (He gave me a copy of his certificate.) Although he had learned English in school, he also studied English to improve his skills.

Sig recalls that the performances of "the excellent symphony orchestra" at Camp Dermott were attended regularly by American officers. He also recalls some conflicts between Nazis and anti–Nazis, "but no overt violence or murders." When the Americans asked officers to volunteer to work after German capitulation, conflicts erupted between those willing to volunteer and the rest of the POWs in the camp. Recalling the "severe rationing of food," Sig felt that the Americans were using food as a way of "persuading" the officers to "volunteer" for work. Sig did not volunteer.

Sig also recalls that one of his POW comrades received a visit from his aunt who had traveled from Boston to see her nephew. For his part, Sig had no contact with civilians and very little with American military personnel.

In January 1946, Sig was transferred to Camp Shanks, and after a brief stay of four to five days he embarked on the USS *Elgin* on January 25, 1946. After eight days, he disembarked in Le Havre and ended up at Camp Bolbec. He remembers that the "conditions in the camp there were poor," that the guards were "Polish *Freiheitskämpfer*" (Polish freedom fighters) and that they "ate corn mash." After an inspection visit from the Red Cross, Sig was transferred to Camp Wings, 30 kilometers from Bolbec. Camp Wings, which was basically a farm, represented "a one hundred percent improvement."

Returning briefly to Bolbec on March 26, Sig was placed on a train in the direction of home. Passing through Saarbrücken, he arrived in a discharge camp in Regensburg, where he was discharged on April 10, 1946. Sig made his way to his parents' house and his fiancée Beate who had found refuge in Marktredwitz (Oberfranken, near Bayreuth).

Summary and Analysis

The above interviews reveal a broad spectrum of backgrounds and experiences. They include members of the Afrika Korps who arrived in the United States in 1943 as well as men who became POWs during and after the Normandy invasion who arrived in 1944 and 1945, including one man who was captured in his hometown and arrived in the United States after V-E Day. They include men who served at different fronts as well as men who had less extensive war experiences.

The men I interviewed were interned in a variety of camps located throughout the United States, in the Midwest and South, Southwest, Northeast and Northwest. They spent time in standard POW camps, on military bases, and in side camps. While a few were confined to only one camp during their entire captivity, most were frequently moved from camp to camp; and these were often located in different geographical areas.

My respondents' POW experiences reflect many of the general themes reported in the literature. During their initial train trip to the camps and later during their transfers to other camps, they had opportunities to see the American countryside. They often remarked on the vastness of the country, the wide and open spaces, and the brightly illuminated cities they passed through. They were impressed by the luxurious Pullman trains that took them to their camps, the material conditions of their camps, in particular the quantity and quality of the food (especially when compared to the food they had in the Wehrmacht), the comfortable barracks (sheets for the first time, hot showers), and the camp amenities (books, magazines, theaters, bands and orchestras, sports facilities, canteens and medical services).

Although all commented on their overall good and "fair" treatment by their captors, a few men complained about the rationing of food at the end of the war. Two men (Hermann F. and Henry K.) also remarked on what they considered unfair or unreasonable treatment. Thus, Hermann F. complained about an "anti–German" farmer and Henry K. reported that a camp commander who was "anti–German" was eventually replaced. Four respondents were involved in strikes, one for pay owed (Kurt P.);

one about the hours they were required to work (Heinrich T.); one to reduce the size of the cotton sacks they were required to fill (Willie S.); and one (Hermann F.) for cigarettes. Several men interned in the South and Southwest commented on the poverty and racial inequality and segregation they observed, but only two men (John S. and Heino E.) had any direct contact working with African American men in camps located on military bases.

Three respondents, all members of the Afrika Korps (Heino E., Rudolf T., and Hermann B.), expressed concerns and fears about "Nazi" fellow prisoners, and two of these men (Rudolf T. and Heino E.) were transferred to other camps. Three additional men (Hermann B., Hans W., Gerhard H.) reported political tensions in their camps, but they were quick to point out that there was no violence. Even when queried specifically, the vast majority of my respondents did not recall such concerns. This is particularly true for the men who arrived after 1944, when the American authorities had recognized the dangers posed by Nazi elements in some of the camps and had begun to move the most convinced Nazis and anti–Nazis into separate camps. This supports Ron Robin's conclusion that reports on Nazi terrorism in the camps had been exaggerated (1995). Indeed, in a poll of departing prisoners conducted by the Provost Marshal General's Office (PMGO) at Fort Shanks, only sixteen percent indicated that they had been afraid to express anti–Nazi opinions in their camps.[65]

Except for the four officers and one NCO, my respondents worked in a variety of jobs in the camps and military bases and as contract workers in agriculture, canning, pulpwood, snow removal, and construction. The *Westfrontgefangenen* spent most of their captivity in side camps working primarily in agriculture and canning, in the timber industry and in clean-up crews. This is hardly surprising given the fact that they arrived when the labor program was in full swing and POWs were transported to the United States in part to fulfill the ever growing demand for additional labor.[66]

My respondents left American soil between 1945 and 1946. The timing of their return generally reflects official PMGO policy. According to this policy, the first group to be repatriated were men considered too old, too young, officers and noncommissioned officers, the sick or mentally ill, those considered "untrustworthy" and "uncooperative" (which included most "Nazis"), and men deemed important for German reconstruction such as miners, construction workers, policemen and civilian administrators as well as Austrian citizens (Billinger 2008, 172).[67] All were returned directly to Germany. Thus, Johannes S., who was injured, returned in

1945; Elmar B., who had been punished for destroying copies of *Der Ruf*, returned in 1946; and Robert M., the Austrian citizen also returned in 1946. The "super-democrats," as the men selected for the Special Projects reeducation camps were called, also returned directly to Germany after completing their courses. Peter E. returned in 1945, Hans W. and Heinz R. in 1946. All four officers, Horst von O., Wolf-Dieter Z., Gerhard H. and Sig K., also returned in 1946.

Unfortunately, many men who were deemed "cooperative," especially if they were working in agriculture, were often repatriated last. Ludwig N., and Martin F., are good examples. While slightly more than half of my respondents returned directly to Germany (such as Hermann B., Martin F.), fourteen men ended up spending additional time doing forced labor in England and France. These men returned to Germany in 1947 and 1948. There seems to be no relationship between the time they left American soil and whether they were repatriated directly to Germany or spent additional time in forced labor in England or France, and it is also impossible to determine why some of my respondents ended up in England or France, whereas others returned directly to Germany. For example, although Horst U.'s and Hermann B.'s POW experiences were very similar, Horst ended up in England, whereas Hermann returned directly to Germany.

For the men I interviewed, captivity on American soil was a form of *Bildungsreise*.[68] During their unexpected sojourn on American soil, they had opportunities to travel in the American countryside, to observe how Americans lived, to learn English and to interact with Americans, both military and civilian.

OPPORTUNITIES TO TRAVEL AND OBSERVE AMERICA

While a few men, including all four officers, spent their entire captivity confined to one camp, most were frequently moved from camp to camp. While most respondents were moved in a relatively geographically restricted area, such as the Midwest, the South, the Southwest or the Northwest, by German standards, the distances they traveled were enormous. Several men were transferred to camps in different parts of the country, often traveling long distances between camps. A good example is Ernst F. who spent time in several camps in the Midwest and in New Mexico, where he experienced very different landscapes, cultures and climates.

Although the side camps, set up specifically for temporary work, lacked many of the amenities found in larger base camps (e.g., theaters, libraries, music, organized sports, classes), the men who spent most of their time in side camps had more opportunities to observe the world outside the confines of their camps. Several respondents remarked on the fact that although the work might have been unpleasant, they enjoyed the fact that they worked outside the camps and were able to observe "how Americans lived."

LEARNING ENGLISH

Formal opportunities to learn English varied from camp to camp. As the side camps were temporary and makeshift, men who spent most of their captivity in side camps had fewer formal opportunities to learn English or to take other courses that were frequently offered in the large base camps. Yet, with the exception of three men, all respondents learned some English and those who had known English when they were captured were able to improve their skills. Where available, several men took advantage of English courses offered in their camps; others tried to learn from fellow prisoners, or by reading dictionaries and books and practicing their skills with guards or civilian employees. Several respondents took advantage of opportunities offered to further their general education, taking courses in a variety of subjects, such as geography, history, psychology and science, and one man was able to enroll in courses offered by the extension services of an American university. Four men were selected to participate in the Special Projects reeducation camps, where they further perfected their English and "learned about democracy."

Since there are no systematic data on the general POW population in America, it is difficult to know to what extent my respondents might have differed from the vast majority interned on American soil. A survey titled "Poll of German Prisoner of War Opinion" conducted by the Provost Marshal General's Office sheds some light on this issue. The aim of the survey was to gather information "concerning the attitudes and opinions of the prisoners." A questionnaire was administered to 22,153 German prisoners of war from all nine service commands at Camp Shanks "immediately before their repatriation."[69] The answers to the questionnaire of these "run-of-the-mill" prisoners were deemed "a basis for the measurement of attitude of the average German prisoner of war at the time of his repatriation." Although the questions focused primarily on the prisoners' attitudes toward democracy and the wrongs committed by the Nazi regime, one question addresses their knowledge of English.

Question 11 asked respondents about their knowledge of English before coming to America and at the time of departure. Eighty-four percent indicated that they did not know any English when they became POWs. At the time of their return to Europe, only seventeen percent reported not knowing some English. At the same time the percentage of men claiming to have known "a little English" increased from ten percent at the time of arrival to fifty-four percent at the time of departure, and the percentage of those with a fair knowledge increased from four percent to twenty percent. Only two percent claimed that they had known English well when they became POWs, a percentage that increased to eight percent. Compared to the men responding to the Fort Shanks survey, my respondents were more likely to know English when they arrived and more likely to have learned English during their captivity. Only one percent reported not having learned any English. Although it is impossible to judge their English knowledge and skills when they became prisoners, a larger number of my respondents (eight men, or twenty-four percent, compared to twelve percent in the survey) reported that they knew some English when they arrived in the United States, a fact that allowed them to communicate with their captors (see comment by Horst U.) and frequently work as interpreters in the camps, where they were more likely to have sustained contact with Americans and further improve their linguistic skills.

CONTACT WITH AMERICANS

Unfortunately the Fort Shanks survey did not ask any questions concerning contacts between prisoners and Americans. Although the literature on POWs in the United States indicates that personal contacts between Americans and POWs were not uncommon, the evidence is anecdotal: we do not know exactly how pervasive such contacts were, and neither do we know anything about their degree of intimacy. Given the lack of information, it is impossible to determine systematically whether the contacts reported by my respondents differed significantly from those of the "run-of-the-mill" German POWs.

Nonetheless, the numbers and the nature of the contacts reported by my respondents are impressive. The majority had contacts with Americans, both with military personnel and civilians. While the nature of these contacts varied from fleeting and superficial to more sustained and in depth, for at least half of my respondents contacts with Americans represented an important and memorable part of their American experience.

Three men, Otto L., Heinz E. and Alfred M., who spent most of their time in only one camp, were able to develop significant long-term relationships with Americans in the camps. For Otto L. and Heinz E., who spent their captivity on military bases, these relationships were with military personnel. Alfred M., who was held in a large standard POW camp, developed a relationship was with a civilian who delivered food to the camp. Except for Heinz E. who was repatriated after only one year, Otto L. and Alfred M. spent two and three years respectively in captivity, a significant time span allowing for the development of more in-depth relationships. All three men returned to Germany with a promise from their American friends to help them return to the United States as immigrants.

Four men developed relationships with farmers they worked for (Johann G., Willie S., Kurt P. and Heinz R.) and four (Johann G., Willie S. and Kurt P.) returned to Europe with promises of sponsorships. While Heinz R. developed a close relationship with the farmer he worked for, this relationship did not result in a similar promise. In this case, the farmer, whom Heinz described as "elderly," probably could not or did not want to take on the responsibility of sponsorship. As we will see in the following chapter, Heinz, who was eager to return, was unable to find a sponsor and ended up immigrating first to Canada.

Henry R. had a significant chance encounter and important relationship with a civilian he met outside the camp. Although Mr. Lykins gave Henry his card and encouraged him to contact him, Henry was unable to locate Mr. Lykins after his return to Germany.[70] Hans W. developed a friendship with Gordon Rettew, the civilian painter at Fort Robinson, and was friendly with Captain Silverman. Similarly, Horst U. became friendly with a captain he worked for at Camp Gordon Johnston and Heino E. developed a cordial relationship with Mr. Nall while working at Fort Knox. Erich K. developed a friendship with a nurse he worked with at Ogden Supply Depot who would later send him care packages to Germany.

Although Hermann B., John S. and Josef G. worked with Americans in the camps, these relationships were more fleeting and did not continue after the war. Others, like Harry H., Martin F., and Ludwig N., who worked in agriculture, also had casual and fleeting contacts with farmers they worked for. Ernst F. had passing contacts with famers in New Mexico.

Only two enlisted men (Henry K. and Oskar S.) and two officers (Siegfried K. and Gerhard H.) reported that they had little or no personal contacts with Americans. This is not unusual for the officers, Siegfried K. and Gerhard H., who were not required to work and had the privilege of having German POW enlisted men as servants in the camps. Although Horst von O. and Wolf-Dieter Z. did not have contact with Americans at Camp Concordia, they worked closely with Americans at Fort Getty.

The men who had learned English in school were generally able to use this knowledge to work as interpreters in the camps, and in this capacity they had easy contact with American military and civilians. Others who did not know English used their time to learn the language and were able to translate their new skills into interpreter jobs. While opportunities to learn English clearly varied, depending on the time of arrival and the types of camps, we cannot discount the role played by individual personality characteristics, such as curiosity, open-mindedness and flexibility. Several men (Ludwig N., Ernst F., Heinz R., Hans W. and Harry H.) reported that they were curious about America and about the American people and that they wanted "to make the best" of their unanticipated sojourn.

In addition to Horst and Wolf-Dieter three or possibly four respondents participated in the Special Projects reeducation programs at Fort Eustis and Fort Getty: Ernst F. and Hans W. spent time at Fort Eustis; Peter E. spent time at Fort Getty; Heinz R. reported that he was sent to a camp "to learn democracy," but he does not recall the name of the camp. This means that five, or most likely six respondents, eighteen percent of the men I interviewed, participated in these formal reeducation programs. As the total number of men who participated in these programs was 23,000, the men I interviewed were twice as likely to have participated (eighteen percent as compared to seven percent).

There are no systematic data on the distribution of age, occupation and other socioeconomic characteristics of the 380,000 German prisoners of war held on American soil. My respondents were overwhelmingly young men when they became prisoners. Given their age, they were perhaps more flexible and open to new experiences than their older colleagues. As a group the men in my sample appear to stand out on two dimensions for which we do have some comparable data: their knowledge of English and their participation in the Special Projects reeducation efforts. This suggests that on the whole, and compared to the majority of their fellow POWs, my respondents had already developed a more open, more pro–American stance before they returned to Germany.

3

Repatriation to Germany
and Return to America

In the aftermath of total war, devastation and destruction, life in Germany was a daily struggle and constant challenge. Cities lay in ruins, transportation was in shambles. Until the currency reform in 1948, inflation was rampant and money was worthless. Food and housing shortages were pervasive and unemployment was high (Ermath 1993; Hardach 1984; Klessmann 1991; Kramer 1991).

The resident population in the four occupation zones (American, British, French and Soviet) was highly mobile and uprooted. In the words of Richard Bessel, "Germany had become a land of the homeless, the dispossessed and the displaced" (2009, 247). Evacuees were returning from the countryside where they had fled from the constant bombardment; ethnic Germans who fled or had been forced out from the eastern provinces of Silesia, Pomerania (which had become Polish), the Sudetenland (Czechoslovakia), and northern East Prussia (Soviet Union) added thousands to the population in the remaining occupied Germany. In 1950, eight million of the fifty million residents in the Federal Republic (founded in 1948 from the western occupation zones) were refugees and expellees (*Vertriebene*) from the lost German territories and 1.4 million were refugees from the Soviet occupation zone/German Democratic Republic. An additional 5.2 million were returning former POWs. As German historian Klaus Bade put it, the resident population was characterized by "multiple border experiences"—*vielfältige Grenzerfahrungen* (Bade 1994).

Although food supplies began to improve in the late 1940s, unemployment remained high until the mid–1950s. In March 1950, almost five years after the war had ended, unemployment in the Federal Republic still stood at 12.2 percent and housing shortages remained troubling. Allied bombing had destroyed a quarter of the housing stock. The destruction was particularly significant in the large industrial cities of the Ruhr, south and middle Germany and the port cities in the North, and they were particularly devastating for working-class households whose housing was traditionally located in inner cities, near train stations, industrial production and harbors.

Millions of city dwellers had to share apartments, often with strangers, and many lived in basements and temporary shelters, such as gymnasiums and barns. The lack of privacy and the cultural differences between people who were forced to live in close quarters with strangers frequently created tensions and resentments. Young people who wanted to get married confronted significant housing problems, and frequently ended up living with parents or in-laws (see respondent Heino E.).The housing problems were particularly severe for the masses of refugees and expellees from the East. In the fall 1950, seventy percent of natives but only thirty percent refugees lived in their own apartments in the Federal Republic of Germany. Although housing conditions improved in the mid–1950s, in 1957 some 400,000 people still lived in former army barracks and camps, and housing scarcity eased only in the late 1950s and early 1960s.

The beginning of the Cold War was accompanied by considerable fear and anxiety among the German population, many of whom believed that the potential outbreak of hostilities between the Soviet Union and the United States and its allies would be carried out on German soil. In 1955, when the so-called *Wirtschaftswunder* (economic miracle)[1] was in full swing and the Federal Republic of Germany had signed a labor recruitment with Italy to recruit temporary workers, seventy-two percent (seventy-nine percent in big cities) of Germans surveyed said that they "felt not safe from a nuclear attack."[2]

It is hardly surprising that the desire to leave Germany and to begin a new life abroad was widespread among the population throughout the late 1940s and early to mid–1950s and officials and the press spoke of *Auswanderungsdrang* ("emigration pressure"). Surveys conducted by the public opinion research organization EMNID in 1951 and 1954, found that respectively twenty-nine and thirty-one percent of respondents would emigrate immediately, perhaps, or under certain circumstances. This figure declined somewhat in the second half of the 1950s when economic and social conditions improved significantly.[3]

Data collected by the Bundesamt für Auswanderung (Federal Agency for Emigration — an agency set up by the West German government)[4] on the major reasons why people sought to emigrate show that the top two reasons in 1951 were economic and occupational ("unemployment," "economic insecurity," "poor occupational prospects"), followed by "friends and relatives abroad." While the percentage of respondents indicating unemployment as a reason for emigration declined after 1953, the percentages of those indicating poor occupational prospects and economic insecurity actually increased between 1951 and 1956 (Grothe 1959). Yet, despite a widespread desire to emigrate, emigration remained an unfulfilled hope for millions.

The desire to emigrate, however great, is only a first step in a complex process that may or may not result in successful immigration. Beyond the simple "push and pull" paradigm, emigration involves more than objective socioeconomic and political conditions and prospects in the home country (push factors) and perceptions of conditions and opportunities in the country of destination and expectations about a better life (pull factors). Both include subjective, personal and experiential dimensions that are difficult to document. Thus, the way individuals and families perceive the conditions in the home country vary based on their prior experience and their sense of relative deprivation. Similarly, perceptions of the country of destination vary depending on the type and sources of information available and past experiences with that country. These may be based on relatively abstract and general information from media and books, on more personal, secondhand information from visitors or relatives, or firsthand observations and personal experience derived from prior visits.[5]

While personal knowledge and experiences of the possibility of a better life add weight to more objective socioeconomic and political factors, migration does not take place in a social and political vacuum. As numerous studies have shown, it involves social connections and networks in the home and the receiving country, and above all it is ultimately dependent on the immigration policies of potential countries of destination.

The prewar social networks of much of the German population were seriously disrupted by the economic, geographic and social dislocation of the war and its aftermath. Such disruptions were particularly pronounced for the refugees and displaced persons from the eastern provinces and the Soviet occupation zone/German Democratic Republic. At the same time, previous German immigration to the United States in the period between the two world wars meant that the personal networks of thousands of Germans extended to the United States, where they had relatives. Thus, a survey in March 1958 reported that thirty-five percent of respondents indicated that "someone" in their family had "once immigrated to America"(Noelle and Neumann 1965, 550), and as indicated by the data collected by the

Bundesamt für Auswanderung, "relatives and friends abroad" was the fourth most frequently mentioned reason why people were seeking to emigrate.

Whatever their reasons for wanting to leave Germany behind, Germans seeking to immigrate confronted significant hurdles in the form of exit permits, the limited availability and financing of overseas transportation and, perhaps most important, the immigration policies of the potential countries of destination. Until 1949, it was exceedingly difficult for ordinary Germans to leave the occupied territory. With the unconditional German surrender on May 7 and 8, 1945, German state power ceased to exist and Allied military governments controlled all legislative and executive power, including migration. According to the Allied Control Council Law No. 161 of March 7, 1945, and the Proclamation No. 2, which came into effect on September 20, 1945, all potential emigrants were required to have an exit permit issued by the Allied powers.[6] The official purpose of these permits was to prevent Nazi war criminals from leaving, to make their prosecution easier, and to forestall a dispersal of National Socialist ideology (Steinert 1995, 22).

Individuals whose travels were in the interest of the occupying powers, such as several hundred German scientists, were able to leave and immigrate to the United States under the auspices of Projects Paperclip and Overcast (Freund 2005; Lasby 1971; Laney 2008). The Truman Directive on Displaced Persons of December 1945 allowed 40,000 displaced persons (mostly forced workers from Eastern Europe who were in Germany at the end of the war) to leave and immigrate between 1946 and 1948. Between 1946 and 1949 the military authorities gradually relaxed the criteria on issuing travel document, to include opponents and victims of the Nazi regime; close family members of citizens of Allied countries such as spouses, parents and children under the age of 21; and so-called compassionate cases (persons who needed medical treatment abroad, children and old people with relatives abroad, and displaced persons traveling outside of organized migrations). Germans who applied for exit permits under these categories had to pass a background check by the Berlin Document Center to determine possible involvement in the NSDAP and associated Nazi organizations.

The Allied Combined Travel Security Board, responsible for processing travel requests, gave permission to travel only to individuals who had an entry visa to a country of destination and a person or organization outside Germany that would pay for their transportation. War brides, individuals with close relatives abroad, and scientists and technicians had the best chances of getting exit permits, while even Germans persecuted by the Nazi regime often had difficulty proving their opposition activities and rarely qualified for exit permits. Until 1948 all former members of the Wehrmacht were automatically excluded.

In February 1949, the western military governments dropped all exit visa restrictions for women who passed the security check. Given German government concerns about the emigration of men needed for reconstruction and in recognition of the serious gender imbalance caused by the war, men still had to obtain an official declaration that they were dispensable for the labor market. Two months later, however, the Manpower Advisors of the three western zones concluded that a further liberalization of the emigration regulations would have no negative repercussions for the German economy and allowed the emigration of men under the same conditions as those for women. Although they retained the right to exclude specific professions, the Allied military governments lifted the last remaining travel restrictions for western Germany in July 1949. This meant that ordinary Germans, including members of the former Wehrmacht, were free to leave.

While freedom to leave a territory is a prerequisite for migration, it is meaningless if it is not accompanied by permission to enter another country. By the time exit restrictions were lifted, several traditional immigration countries reopened immigration to German citizens— the United States, Canada, Argentina, Brazil, South Africa and Australia. Among these, the United States (*Traumland Amerika*, or "dream land America")[7] had long been the preferred destination for German emigrants and it remained so after the war.[8]

In the post–World War II period, immigration to the United States continued to be governed by the 1924 Immigration and Naturalization Act. Aimed at restricting immigration from eastern and southern Europe by establishing a national origins quota system, the act provided a relatively generous annual quota of 25.957 for Germans.[9] Although American consulates began to accept visa applications, as early as March 1946, when the annual quota was officially reopened, visas were restricted to special groups, including victims of National Socialism, close relatives of citizens of the United States, in particular children of American citizens, and husbands of American women who had been married before July 1932 (Reimers 1981; Steinert 1995; Freund 2004).

Between 1945 and 1949 several hundred German scientists and technicians were able to immigrate under the auspices of Projects Overcast and Paperclip (Freund 2004). The War Brides Act of 1948 allowed some

14,000 German women to join their new American husbands. The Truman Directive on Displaced Persons of December 1945, which had allowed 40,000 displaced persons to immigrate between 1946 and 1948, was replaced by the 1948 Displaced Persons Act, which allowed some additional 205,000 displaced persons to immigrate between 1948 and 1950. Originally aimed at helping individuals from Eastern Europe who had been forced by the Nazis to migrate to Germany as slave labor or prisoners of war, and who could not return to their countries of origin, in 1950 the Displaced Persons Act included so-called *Volksdeutsche Vertriebene* (ethnic Germans, but not German citizens) who had been expelled from their homes in Eastern Europe. All were counted against the German quota (Freund 2004, 217).

In June 1948, United States Foreign Secretary George C. Marshall declared that the emigration of German nationals and ethnic Germans would be permissible as long as security preventing the emigration of war criminals was maintained and the emigration of displaced persons would not be affected. Three months later, in September 1948, President Truman lifted the ban on immigration of ordinary Germans, including members of the former Wehrmacht, and large masses of people rushed to the American consulates. By June 1949, they had received half a million applicants (Reimers 1981; Freund 2004, 166–168).[10]

Yet, as the available quota continued to be filled by people belonging to the preferred categories, including displaced persons and close relatives of American citizens (especially husband, parents and children), the chances for ordinary Germans who did not fall into these categories of obtaining a visa continued to be poor.[11] An article in the German weekly newsmagazine *Der Spiegel*, entitled "Hunters for Quota," outlining the difficulties confronting would-be German immigrants quoted the U.S. Consul General for Germany, Marshall Vance: "No one gets out without relatives or friends in America and without dollars" (September 25, 1948, 3). It was not until 1952 and the McCarran-Walter Act that restrictions were eased somewhat, a fact that is reflected in the surging number of German immigrants in the mid–1950s.

While the oversubscribed quota system presented a formidable hurdle, American law also required that would-be immigrants have an American sponsor, a person who would guarantee that the newcomer would not become a burden on the welfare system. Sponsors could be relatives or voluntary organizations, such as churches and welfare organizations. Active military personnel were automatically excluded from sponsorship. Until 1952 when it was repealed with the McCarran-Walter Act, the Alien Contract Labor Act of 1885 (a response by Congress to the importation of foreign laborers, especially from China, to work in the United States) did not formally allow American employers to sponsor an immigrant.[12]

An affidavit from the sponsor pledging his support for the newcomer until his naturalization (usually at least five years) had to accompany the application for immigration. Sponsors had to provide information concerning their financial well-being. Yet, there were no fixed rules concerning the amount of income or other financial assets. If the sponsor was a relative, officials were more likely to accept a lower income, and consular officials evaluating immigrant applications often gave preference to "an affiant that can show that he (the sponsor) has some convincing legal or moral obligation to support the prospective immigrant" (Auberbach 1952, 5).

The process of getting a visa was complex and often took more than a year. The would-be immigrant had to apply by letter accompanied by a self-addressed, stamped envelope. In addition to the requisite application form and supporting papers, including the crucial letter of sponsorship, all would-be immigrants were subject to a medical examination and interviews with members of the consulate and the Immigration and Naturalization Service.

Finally, would-be-immigrants needed to obtain and finance their overseas transportation. Until the early 1950s such transportation was difficult to find as the number of transatlantic ships was limited, air transportation was still in its infancy, and the fare for both was beyond the means of most would-be immigrants. There were no German ships; only a few freight ships offered cabin spaces. Transportation on foreign ships had to be paid in dollars, and the German Central Bank did not permit Germans to purchase foreign currency until 1952. Since they had to find someone abroad to pay for their transatlantic passage, the vast majority of immigrants were dependent on relatives, friends or organizations abroad willing to sponsor them and to pay for their transportation.

Returning to Germany and Immigrating to America[13]

Given the multiple hurdles they confronted, it is hardly surprising that despite strong objective push factors, immigration to the United States remained an unfulfilled hope for thousands of Germans, including an unknown number of former POWs.[14] My respondents were among the lucky ones who succeeded. Although their return journeys "to the place where we had the good life" (Otto Fernholz, Camp Ruston[15]) reflect many of the difficulties encountered by all German emigrants, they also reveal the multifarious connections between their first American experience as captive enemy soldiers and their return as immigrants and future citizens.

Horst U. returned to Germany in September 1947. His mother had fled from their home in Lower Silesia, first to Berlin and later to Dresden where she had survived the war; his stepfather, who had been fighting on the Russian front, had been reported missing in action and was later declared dead. Horst could not return to his prewar home, and British and American forces did not release prisoners into the Soviet zone where his mother lived. Horst "found refuge" with friends of his parents' who lived in Eystrup/Weser (Lower Saxony-Niedersachsen).

Before he became a prisoner of war Horst had some indirect, second-hand experience with America. His biological father had worked for Interpol and moved to the United States in 1922, the year Horst was born. As a child Horst had dreamed of seeing his father and immigrating to America. Horst's experiences as a prisoner of war strongly reinforced his desire to immigrate and he "wanted to get back as soon as possible."

Although he had considerable contact with Americans and an especially friendly relationship with a captain at Camp Gordon Johnston, Horst had lost the addresses of his contacts during his time in England. "So, I had no more addresses. I had no way of contacting anybody." Horst's plans to return "as soon as possible" were stifled by the lack of a sponsor. Except for his biological father, who had disappeared into thin air, and unlike some of my respondents, Horst did not have relatives in the United States.

His dream of returning to the United States on hold, Horst supported himself by working in "several small office jobs." In November 1948 he married Else, a young woman from Nürnberg, and the couple had three children. In 1951, taking advantage of his English skills, Horst was able to find more steady employment as "an accountant for petrol and oil" with the British occupation forces in the city of Celle. Although he was working, he was concerned about "the lack of opportunities in Germany due to high unemployment," and continued to pursue his quest to immigrate, searching for a sponsor. He was finally successful in 1954 when the World Church Services in Switzerland agreed to sponsor Horst and his family. It took an additional two years until they finally received a visa in 1956. Horst, Else and their three children embarked on the *General Langfitt*, leaving from Bremerhaven, and finally arrived in New York in December 1956. As Horst put it, "It took me nine years until I found a sponsor."

The family was first settled in Rose Hill, Michigan, where their local sponsor, the Afternoon Guild of St. James Church, had set up an apartment for them. They also found a job for Horst at the McLouth Steel Corporation in Trenton, Michigan. Having good English skills and experience in accounting, Horst worked first in the superintendent's office; later he moved to a supervisory position where he was in charge of recording operations. The company, which used German steel technology, received equipment from Germany and Horst acted as an interpreter for the German engineers. In 1985 Horst retired, and seven years later Horst and Else moved to Florida.

In 1963 Horst was able to sponsor his only surviving relative in Germany, his mother, who joined them in Michigan. Horst and Else became American citizens in 1974.[16] In Grosse Isle, Horst was "very active" in the German American community, especially the German American Club, where he served on the board. He was interested in preserving German heritage and raising German Americans to be proud of that heritage. Yet, the family did not continue to speak German at home and the three children born in Germany lost their German-language skills.

Although Horst does not have relatives in Germany, he and Else have returned to visit several times, "but not regularly." In the interview Horst expressed some criticism of his adopted country. While he "enjoyed the freedom," he was particularly critical of the lack of universal health care and "the violence and crime." Like most of my respondents, Horst has fond memories of his POW time and has visited his former POW camps, including Aliceville in 2004.[17]

Although Horst U. and **Hermann B.** arrived at Camp Aliceville at the same time and their stay on American soil included similar camps and experiences, their paths to immigration turned out to be different. Like Horst, Hermann was transferred to Camp Gordon Johnston, Camp Telogia and briefly to Fort Benning, leaving for Europe from Camp Shanks, New York. Like Horst, Hermann had contacts with military personnel at Camp Gordon Johnston. Unlike Horst, Hermann did not know English when he arrived on American soil. Yet, he was interested and eager to learn the language, and eventually was able to act as an informal interpreter.

When Hermann returned to Germany in June 1946, he immediately made his way to Schwäbisch Gmünd and on to nearby Bargau, the small town where his fiancée Katie lived. Hermann and Katie were married three months later and Hermann, who had completed his apprenticeship before the war, was able to get work as a printer in Stuttgart. Although Hermann was never unemployed, he felt that "things were bad in Germany." Not seeing much of a future in his homeland, he convinced his young bride, who had a large family and was not eager to leave, that they should immigrate to the United States, "the first chance we get."

In 1948, listening to American Forces Radio, Hermann heard that President Truman had "lifted the ban on immigration." He immediately went to the American Consulate in Stuttgart, where "the girl was very helpful." As with Horst, Hermann's friendly relationships with Americans did not produce a possible sponsor. Unlike Horst, whose immigration was delayed by the lack of a sponsor, the B. family was among the thousands of Germans who were able to activate their network of American relatives. It was Katie's uncle in Niles, Michigan, who offered to sponsor the young couple, and Hermann and his family were among the lucky few who received a visa shortly after their application. Yet they had considerable difficulty finding transatlantic transportation from Germany. In October 1949, with their transportation paid by Katie's uncle, they (including a daughter born in 1948) finally managed to find a space on the SS *Mauritania*, leaving from Cherbourg, France.

After disembarking in New York, the young family traveled to Niles by train, where the local newspaper reported on their arrival.[18]As a skilled printer with good English skills acquired during his captivity, Hermann had no trouble getting a job with the *South Bend Tribune*. He worked there for thirty-one years until his retirement in 1986. In 1992 Hermann and Katie moved to Florida, where they live near one of their three daughters.

Hermann and Katie became American citizens in 1954. Like Horst, Hermann has been active in German American organizations. In Niles, he was president of DANK (Deutsch-Amerikanischer National Kongress— German American National Congress) from 1980 to 1983, and the family regularly attended the local Oktoberfest. The B. family frequently visited Germany; their last trip was in 1999. Unlike Horst, Hermann does not recall any anti–German sentiments toward him or his family. Hermann also kept in touch with and corresponded with Charles Campbell, the American soldier with whom he worked at the bakery at Camp Gordon Johnston. Like Horst, Hermann has visited Camp Aliceville, attending two reunions for former POWs held at the camp organized by the Aliceville Museum in 1989 and 2002.

What he likes most about the United States is "the ability to have more freedom." He particularly enjoys the more relaxed lifestyle in Florida, where at the time of the interview, the B.'s were active members of the Polish Club (mostly for the festivities and the dancing). The couple likes to dance and Hermann often plays the accordion while Katie sings old German folk songs.

Still in captivity in the United States, **Heino E.** had heard from POWs captured at the western front and from letters from his parents that his hometown, Kiel, had been totally destroyed. He was prepared for the worst. When he returned from England in September 1947, he found the city in rubble, but his parents and sister had survived. Although the apartment where they lived had been damaged by bombing raids, it was still standing. Despite his own family's survival, Heino was shocked to discover that all his classmates from school had been killed and Germany was "in worse shape than I imagined."

Although he did not feel ready to work, Heino's mother urged him to register at the labor office, so he could get the necessary ration cards. Assigned to a group of men in charge of clearing rubble, Heino heard from another former POW that the British labor office was looking for an English speaker. Heino, who had been able to perfect his English while at Fort Knox and later in Scotland, applied and was hired as a translator for the British Control Commission for Germany. Heino liked his job and the man he worked for, Mr. Thompson. In 1949 he married Ruth, who had a small apartment, and Heino, who had been living with his parents was eager to move in.

Unlike Horst U. and Hermann B., who had completed their education and worked before the war, Heino was drafted before he finished school and did not have an occupation or trade he could return to. He felt that the long-term prospects in Germany were poor. His sense of insecurity was heightened by the outbreak of the Korean War. Like many Germans, he was afraid that the war would turn into World War III, giving significant urgency to his desire to immigrate.

Although Heino's first application for a visa in 1950 was rejected, his quest was successful in 1952.[19] As was the case for Horst and Hermann, Heino's relationships with Americans did not produce a sponsor and unlike Hermann, Heino did not have American relatives. Heino's sponsor was a fellow German POW, Walter B., whom he had befriended at Fort Knox. Walter, who had many American relatives, had been able to immigrate two years earlier and had kept his promise to sponsor his friend as soon as possible.

Heino had saved enough money to pay for his family's (wife and son Jörg) transatlantic passage on the Holland-America Line, and the young family departed from Rotterdam in fall 1953. When they disembarked in New York, Walter picked them up and drove them to their new home in Minneapolis, Minnesota.

In Minneapolis, Walter, who owned a duplex, was able to provide housing for the young family and Heino worked in several successive unskilled jobs. After working as a molder in a rubber company, he found work as a sales representative for a coffee company, delivering coffee to suburban Minneapolis households. His next job, as a stock clerk in the Midland Cooperatives, proved more rewarding. Heine was able to work himself up to stock auditor, doing accounting work. Using his newly acquired experience in accounting, Heino was able to get a job as an accountant in a large international car rental company. While working there he took night courses to get a BA in accounting. With his new accounting degree in hand, he was offered a job at St. Mary's Hospital as a full-fledged accountant.

When Heino's marriage to Ruth ended in divorce in 1961, he was awarded custody of their son. Now a single father, Heino joined a group of single parents. There he met his second wife Jean, a social worker. Heino and Jean were married in December 1962.

Weary of the war and with two sons (his son and Jean's son) of draft age, during the Vietnam War Heino became a Quaker and moved to Earlham, Iowa, to study for the ministry. After completing his studies, the Quakers sent him to Belize "where conditions were very bad." Heino resigned from the ministry after six months and, returning to Minnesota, he "became a Lutheran again."

Back in Minneapolis, Heino took a job as an accountant with the Salvation Army. At the same time Heino and Jean enrolled in a master's degree program in human development at St. Mary's College in Winona, Minnesota. They graduated in 1981, and with their degrees in hand they were granted a Minnesota child care license. In June of that year, the couple opened a child-placing adoption agency in Minneapolis, Los Niños International Aid and Adoption Agency.

Tired of the Minnesota winters, they moved to Austin, Texas, in February 1982. In Austin, Heino worked as comptroller at Seton Hospital while Jean was granted a child-placing license. Eventually Heino left the hospital job. Joining his wife, they opened Los Niños International Adoption Center. The adoption center proved successful and grew rapidly. (He thinks they placed 100 children in the first year). When their Minnesota license expired, they incorporated in Texas, founding the international adoption agency Los Niños Internationales. In addition to the two children from their first marriages, Heino and Jean adopted four children.

Like Horst and Hermann, Heino has been active in German American organizations, in particular the German Heritage Society in Texas. Heino and Jean have visited Germany on many occasions, the first time a year after they were married. Heino is well traveled and has taken frequent trips to Latin America and more recently to Russia and Vietnam as the executive director of Los Niños.[20] Heino sees his work in international adoption for children from third world countries as a kind of *Wiedergutmachung* (reparation). At the time of the interview, Heino was still working for the agency and traveling abroad frequently. In 2008 he stepped down as executive director of Los Niños and he and Jean continued to work part time for the agency until it finally closed its doors 2009.

Like Horst and Hermann, Heino has visited his former POW camps: Fort Knox and Camp Hearne. In fall 2001 he was invited to be a guest speaker at Fort Knox and he returned to Fort Knox in 2007, 2009 and, most recently in 2010. Like Horst, Heino is not uncritical of the United States. He believes that he had "an exaggerated idea of America," a country which turned out "not to be quite a paradise." In particular, he did not like lawsuits, and after his divorce, he even briefly considered returning to Germany.

When **Martin F.** returned to Germany in September 1946, he discovered that his father had died in 1945 and that his mother lived in Chemnitz in the Soviet occupation zone. As the Americans did not discharge POWs into the Soviet occupation zone, Martin joined an uncle who lived in Dinslaken/Niederrhein, a small town at the lower Rhine.

Like Horst and Heino, Martin was able to use his English-language skills to get a job with the occupation forces. He worked with the police department, translating documents for the British occupation forces. When police authority was turned over to German authorities in 1947, Martin decided "to return to industry." He was able to find a job as a technician in plant maintenance working for Bayer Pharmaceuticals in Leverkusen. His living quarters were supplied by the company. After this job was terminated in 1952, Martin briefly worked for the Ottinger Waggonfabrik near Donaueschingen.

Martin had been much impressed by American technological know-how and the relaxed attitude of the people he met while he was a POW in Oregon. He had thought about immigrating to the United States and had kept in touch with military personnel he had met at Camp White. As military personnel could not sponsor immigrants, he had to postpone his return to the United States.

While working in Leverkusen, he met his future wife Editha, a native of Pomerania. Like Hermann B.'s wife Katie, Editha had relatives in the United States and when Martin and Editha met she had a standing invitation from an uncle in Detroit to come to the United States. Not knowing much about the United States, Editha had been undecided. Telling her that this "was the best offer you ever had," Martin was enthusiastic about the idea. When Martin and Editha were engaged, Editha's uncle was willing to sponsor Martin and his fiancée. Editha left Germany in 1952. After briefly joining her uncle in Detroit, she moved to Chicago, where she found a job working for a newspaper, the *Prairie Farmer*. Martin joined her in Chicago in April 1953, and there the young couple was married.

Within two days of his arrival, Martin was able to get a job at Chicago Forging and Manufacturing Company. The company made auto parts, in particular hood ledges and hinges, and Martin's boss was originally from Germany. A trained and skilled engineer, Martin was soon able to move into research and development. While working there, he developed a hinge for Chevrolet that was used by Cadillac and for which he received a patent. He became an American citizen in 1959.

When the company was sold in 1962, Martin decided to look for another job. He took a job with a small company that experimented with electric discharge machinery for making hypodermic needles. In 1964, he again changed jobs. This time he was working for a company that designed air dryers for industry and he ended up designing several models which turned out to be successful. Meanwhile he started a degree program at Illinois Technical. Despite the fact that he did not finish the degree he was promoted to chief engineer. Martin retired in 1992 but continued to work as a consultant for four more years. In 1996 Martin and Editha moved to Mountain Home, North Carolina.

Martin and Editha have visited Germany frequently, but have not been back since Martin retired and they moved to North Carolina. Martin also visited his mother, who lived outside Berlin in the former GDR and said he never had any problems. Editha has also returned to visit her childhood home in Pomerania. Like Hermann, Martin has been active in DANK (Deutsch Amerkikanischer National Kongress). He also subscribes to the American German-language newspaper *New Yorker Staats-Zeitung*.

Based on his observations of civilians "from industry" at Camp White, Martin had been impressed by American business practices. Given his technical qualifications and English skills, he found it easy to find a job in Chicago. As he put it, "What counts in America is that you can show that you can do it, documents are less important." He does not recall encountering anti–German feelings or activities, a fact that he attributes to being in Chicago, "where there are many immigrants."

Leaving from Southampton in July 1947, **Willie S.** arrived at Münster Camp, the largest camp for returning British POWs in the British occupation zone. Unable to return to his home in Silesia, Willie made his way to East Berlin, where his grandfather lived. Unable to find a job in East Berlin, he decided to return to the British zone. On his way there, near the border of the Soviet zone, he accidentally encountered a former fellow prisoner from Camp Mexia. The man invited Willie to his village (Mechau, Anhalt Sachsen, former German Democratic Republic). In Mechau he met his future wife, Charlotte, a war widow with a young son who was a refugee from the East. After they married, the young couple moved to Dessau, where Willie was able to get a job as a carpenter.

In Dessau, Willie was involved in the June 17, 1953, uprising against the communist regime. Accused of destroying company property, he spent three months in jail. Although Willie was able to return to work after his release, afraid of future repressions and arrests, the couple managed to flee to West Berlin. After spending a few months in a refugee camp, they were moved to camps in West Germany, first in Ulm and then in Balingen (Württemberg). They stayed in Balingen for three years.

Working on farms in Wisconsin, Willie had developed friendships with two farmers he worked for, Mr. Anderson and Mr. Yetter. After his return to Germany, both families sent numerous care packages and kept in touch over the years. They also offered to sponsor Willie and his family (including their two children).

Having left East Germany behind, they were now eager to immigrate and, sponsored by the Yetter family, they applied for a visa. Although they were finally offered a house which would have allowed them to move from the refugee camp, Willie was committed to returning to the United States. On February 24, 1956, the family embarked from Bremen on the ocean liner *United States*. They arrived in New York on March 1 and took the train to Babcock, Wisconsin, where Mr. Yetter picked them up in his truck. When Mr. Yetter died six weeks after their arrival, his cousin Mr. Oelschlaegel took on the sponsorship. The Oelschlaegels who, Willie recalls, "took us in like their own children," bought a house for the S. family in Port Edwards and Willie found work in a nursery in nearby Nekosa. Later Willie worked in the cranberry marshes and a paper factory and tutored math for the owners' children ("who were not very bright").

Given the dearth of secure employment opportunities in rural Wisconsin, Willie and his family moved to Chicago three years after their arrival. In Chicago Willie was able to get a job washing milk cans with the help of a carpenter he had befriended at Fort Sheridan (a man who had emigrated from Germany in the 1920s). The family lived in an apartment above the Schwaben Athletic Club and Willie also worked as part-time caretaker of that facility. Four years later, the family moved to Niles, Illinois, where Willie was able to get a job as a tool maker in a company owned by a German American. He continued to work there until his retirement in 1978.

The S. family became American citizens in 1964. Like Horst, Hermann, Heino and Martin, they have been active in German American organizations, including the Chicago Football Club. They speak German with one another, and although the terrorist attacks of 9/11 made them "feel American," they confessed that they are German in their heart and "feel German."

Willie is proud of his service as a paratrooper: "They were very strict and honor was important." Having lived mostly in Wisconsin and Chicago, Willie and his wife do not recall anti–German sentiments or expressions. Both expressed concern about the direction of their adopted country: "When we came, America was still America. It is not now." They are particularly concerned about schools and education and young people more generally. Like almost all my respondents, they expressed strong opposition to the war in Iraq.

Passing through Camp Shanks and Bolbec, **Elmar B.** returned directly to Germany, arriving in Karlsruhe in August 1946. He found the city destroyed, but his wife (they were married in 1937) was living. Using his skills as a butcher, he was able to find work. At a time when most Germans did not have sufficient food, Elmar remembers eating very well and bringing food home to give to friends and neighbors.

Elmar never wanted to be a butcher, a trade his father had chosen for him. Between 1949 and 1950 he worked for the American forces as a truck driver, a job he considered far from ideal. Despite these misgivings, compared to most Germans at the time, Elmar and his family were doing quite well. He was able to buy a BMW motorcycle with a sidecar, and when the family immigrated to Canada, he was able to pay for their transportation.

Although Elmar told me that he would not have immigrated to the United States had he not been a POW, it seems unclear what really attracted him. Elmar did not have relatives and although he had had some contacts with Americans when he was a POW, his contacts had been fleeting. Unable to get a visa for the United States, the B. family applied to immigrate to Canada. They received a visa in 1951 and settled in Windsor, Ontario. After a brief period of unemployment, Elmar was able to get a job working for General Motors, a job he lost during the 1957 recession.

For Elmar and his family, Canada was only a way station, and he revealed that "we were not much liked in Canada." His final destination was always the United States. He finally received the coveted visa in 1958. They moved to Detroit and on to St. Clair, Michigan, where Elmar found a job with a German butcher, whose customers were predominantly Germans and German Americans. After seven years in this job, Elmar took a job as butcher in a supermarket from which he retired in 1980.

In St. Clair the B. family lived in a predominantly German milieu, and most of their friends were German. As a consequence, Elmar's command of English was not very good. The B. family belonged to several German American organizations, including the *Schwabenverein*. Elmar is particularly proud of a certificate from the German Consulate in Detroit on behalf of his engagement for German American relations which he proudly displays in his home. Elmar and his wife (who had died before the interview) also made frequent trips to Germany, every two years, and after they retired they traveled throughout the United States in a camper for two months.

Gunther K. returned to Germany on June 24, 1947. Arriving in Dachau, he continued to a village in Lower Bavaria where his parents had fled at the end of the war and where they now lived on a farm in one room. He moved in with them. In September 1947 he married Ursula, a young woman he had met during the war in Silesia. Ursula, who lived in East Germany after the war, had managed to escape in April 1948 by swimming across the river Elbe.

Given the crowded living conditions and the lack of a decent job, Gunther soon moved to Munich, where he was able to get a job with the industrial police (*Industriepolizei*). He worked for the Americans guarding industrial plants in the suburbs. Unhappy with the job and the living conditions, Gunther joined his brother who lived in the Rheinland and worked as a coal miner. There Gunther was able to get a job with the postal service sorting mail. Although the postal service offered to send him to school so he could be promoted to a better position, Gunther declined the offer. He felt that the money he would earn was not sufficient to support his wife and child.

Like that of many refugees from the East, Gunther's life was unsettled. "We had lost our home," he says, and he did not see much of a future in Germany. Immigration seemed like an attractive alternative and Gunther's POW experiences had been positive. In particular he had "liked the people, who were open and friendly." Yet, like Horst, Gunther did not have a sponsor. He did not have relatives in the United States, nor had he developed any significant relations with Americans during his time in captivity. As he put it, "we wanted to come to America, but there was a low quota for immigrants that year and we didn't have a sponsor." Like Elmar, Gunther decided to seek his luck in Canada, "because it was easier to go there." In 1952, the K. family was able to get a visa for Canada. Settling in Saskatchewan, Gunther was able to get a job with the Canadian postal service. Although he became a Canadian citizen in 1956, he continued to pursue his goal to move to the United States.

In 1962 Gunther traveled to California to check out possible job prospects. When he was able to get a job as an insurance underwriter in Alameda, the family, which included one child, moved to Alameda. Two years later, Gunther changed jobs to become a supervisor of ground crews for Pan American Airlines at San Francisco International Airport. Eight years later, the family moved to Paradise, California, where Gunther started his own business selling imported German manufactured awnings. When he retired in 2001, Gunther and Ursula moved to a retirement community in Roseville, California.

Like the previous respondents, Gunther and Ursula have been involved in German American organizations and frequently travel to Germany. In Paradise they founded a German American club and organized several Oktoberfests in town. Gunther did not encounter anti–German sentiments and felt that "Germans were respected because of their work ethic."

In 1963 Gunther and Ursula traveled to Trinidad, Colorado, to visit his old POW camp.[21] Inspired by their visit, the city of Trinidad organized a formal reunion for former German POWs in 1964, inviting some twenty former POWs from Germany.[22] Gunther is particularly proud of a certificate of appreciation he received at an American reunion of Veterans of Foreign Wars (by mistake, it seems).[23]

Released from Camp Bolbec in May 1946, **Robert M.** made his way back to his native Salzburg and his wife Olivia (they were married in 1942). In Salzburg, Robert was unable to find a steady job, which kindled his desire to return to the United States. He applied in the early 1950s but did not get a visa as he did not have a sponsor. (He believes this is because he was a member of the Hitlerjugend and the Nazi Party). Like Elmar and Gunther, Robert decided to immigrate to Canada instead. When Robert received a visa in 1954, he left without his wife and two children, settling in Vancouver, British Columbia. Olivia and the children joined him two years later.

In Vancouver, Robert found work in an aluminum smelter. In 1962, the family traveled to California on vacation. They liked what they saw and applied for a visa to the United States. In March 1963, the M. family finally received the coveted visa and the family moved to Anaheim, California. Until his retirement in 1980, Robert worked in various jobs, mostly in the construction industry, and in machine jobs as a tool and die maker. He also briefly attended Los Angeles Technical College. Robert and his family became American citizens in 1975.

The M. family kept connected to their German/Austrian roots, subscribing to two German-language newspapers, the *Kalifornische Staats-Zeitung* and *Das Neue Blatt*. In Anaheim they also belonged to a German club. Robert learned about the reunion of German POWs in 1989 while reading the *Kalifornische Staats-Zeitung* after it had taken place. In 1994 Robert and Olivia visited Camp Bennetsville, a trip that Robert had talked about for years.[24]

Robert liked his adopted country for being less status- and credential-conscious than Germany. As he put it, "In the United States "education is less important than 'can you do it,'" and Robert saw himself as someone who could.

Hermann F. was discharged from forced labor in France into the French occupation zone in 1948. Since he had not lived there before the war he was not allowed to stay, and since he could not return to his home in Pomerania, Hermann made his way to Berlin, where he had relatives. As he put it, "Keiner wollte mich haben" (No one wanted to have me).

In Berlin, Hermann was granted a permit only for the Russian sector, where his mother had found refuge. His fiancée, Hilde, however, lived in Berlin-Schöneberg, in the American sector. In East Berlin he first worked to clear up rubble (*Aufräumungsarbeiten*). Later he was able to get a job with the newly organized Soviet-controlled East German police unit, a job he quit when he discovered that the Russians were going to turn the police unit into a new East German army unit. After his marriage to Hilde in 1950, Hermann gained permission to move out of the Russian sector into West Berlin. Hermann could not find work for eleven months, and the young couple lived of the meager wages Hilde made selling milk in a little store. Eventually Hermann found work mixing sand and cement for a construction company.

Hermann did not see much of a future in Germany. Telling his wife that "we have lost Pomerania, we have lost eastern Germany, we have lost our home," he had made immigration a precondition for their marriage. Although Hermann had not made any significant contacts with Americans and did not have relatives in the United States, like Hermann B. and Martin F., Hermann was able to tap into his wife's network of American relatives who had immigrated in the 1920s. An aunt who lived in New York agreed to sponsor the young couple. They applied for a visa in 1950 but had to wait until 1952 to finally receive it. At the end of November they finally embarked on the SS *America* from Bremerhaven, arriving in New York on December 2.

With the help of Hilde's aunt's connections, Hermann was able to get a job at a Wonder Bread factory soon after they arrived. He worked as a machine setter for bread cutting machines. Although he had no experience with factory work, the foreman liked the hard-working and affable young immigrant, and he soon became "head machine setter" and joined the Baker and Confections Workers Union, Local 50. Hermann, who earned the nickname "Herman the German," worked at Wonder Bread until his retirement. Hilde also worked there, and, with overtime, they were able to save a thousand dollars in six months. With the help of friends who lent them $6,000, the F.'s bought a house in Averne. When they moved there sixteen German families lived in the neighborhood. Although the neighborhood is mostly Jamaican today, they have remained in the modest duplex which they share with their son, Harold. They are known as "the German family," not the "white family."[25]

Unlike previous respondents, the F.'s are not members of German American organizations. They have visited Germany several times and have hosted visitors from Germany. Hermann also visited his childhood town, now in Poland, twice, in 1982 and 1987, and they have traveled frequently in the United States. On one of their many visits to Florida, Hermann drove by the old Belle Glade camp location but found nothing that would remind him of his original stay there.

When **Heinz E.** was released from his second captivity, he was unable to join his parents, who lived in the Soviet zone. Instead he made his way to Schwarzenbach/Saale, the home of a German doctor who had invited him to spend some time to recuperate. About half a year later, in 1946, he returned to his native Rhineland. He was able to find work with the American forces in Wiesbaden, doing a variety of odd jobs. While visiting his sister in Wiesbaden he also met his future wife, Trudi, and they were married in 1949.

For Heinz the decision to emigrate "was easy." He recalls, "There was no work in Germany and I did not have many relatives." As he put it, "Nichts hat mich gehalten." ("Nothing could hold me back"). Since Heinz had a standing invitation from Dr. Brown, who had offered to sponsor him, his quest to return to the United States was relatively easy. After some delays, he received a visa in 1953, and he and Trudi left in January 1954. Arriving in New York, they were met by Dr. Brown and driven to Cincinnati, where Brown had arranged a studio apartment for them.

In Cincinnati Heinz, was able to get a job as a masseur in a men's club, where he worked for a year. Lacking an American license, he could only work as an assistant. One of his clients, Mr. Schneider, owned a wholesale drug company and offered Heinz a position in charge of the narcotics department where pharmacists would come and pick up medication.

Heinz worked in this position for five years when he found a new job with the William Merrell Chemical Company, a job he was able to get because he was a member of the same church as the owner. He worked at Merrell for nine years. He became an American citizen in 1959.

In 1962, the E.'s, who did not have children, sponsored Heinz' brother and sister-in-law. His brother was a trained colonial farmer (*Colonialwirt*) and Germany did not have colonies.[26] Moving to Florida, the two brothers and their wives started a greenhouse business in Alachua in 1969. In 1973 Heinz and his wife sold their share (the women did not get along) and took jobs at a greenhouse in Bradenton, where Heinz was in charge of taking visiting foreigners around. At the same time the E.'s started a successful flower business exporting gladiolas to Germany.

When Heinz retired in 1985, the E.'s moved to North Carolina, where they had built a log cabin in the Smoky Mountains. In 1997 they sold the house and moved back to Florida into a small retirement house in a large retirement community.[27]

Heinz and Trudi have visited Germany frequently, and a great-niece comes to visit them regularly. Heinz was active in several German American organizations, including the Bayern Verein, Schlaraffia.[28] He was very active, traveling to conventions around the world, his wife accompanying him on all trips. He was also an honorary member of the Viking Club in Cincinnati. Like the vast majority of my respondents, Heinz does not recall any anti–German sentiments.

Hans W. was lucky. His excellent English skills, perfected at Fort Robinson, enabled him to find employment as an interpreter with the newly constituted Länderrat in Stuttgart.[29] Hans, who had led a rather carefree life at Fort Robinson, recalls that life in Germany was difficult. To purchase anything, including clothes and shoes, one needed *Bezugsscheine* (requisition papers) from the Economics Office. Hans was able to get the necessary papers by selling cigarettes that he had brought back from the United States.

At the Länderrat Hans, was soon promoted to head the translation department, a job he believes he "could not have done, had I not been in America." He also met his future wife Lore, who worked there as a secretary. Until his marriage to Lore in 1946, Hans lived with his uncle. After the marriage the young couple moved in with Lore's parents.

Hans had contemplated immigrating to the United States when he was still a POW. He had remained in contact with several men he befriended at Camp Robinson, the painter Gordon Rettew, Coronel Daniels, the commander of the camp, and another GI whose name he has forgotten. Thus, when he saw an announcement in the newspaper that the German quota became available again for ordinary Germans, he immediately applied at the consulate in Stuttgart, where he was "the third person to do so." His acquaintances from Fort Robinson did not work out as sponsors, but luckily Hans had a relative, a woman called Else who lived in Maine, near Portland. Else was willing to sponsor the young couple and Hans received a visa in 1949. Embarking from Hamburg on the S.S. *Marine Shark*, he arrived in New York on June 18, 1949 (Father's Day) and immediately took a train to Portland, where his sponsor lived. His wife, who was pregnant at the time, remained in Germany and did not join him until 1950.

To pay off the money for his transatlantic journey and to support himself, Hans worked a variety of odd jobs in Portland, including dishwasher and soda jerk at Howard Johnson. Around Christmas, Hans created a couple of traditional German puppets and started a puppet show. He was fired from Howard Johnson. Unfortunately the puppet show did not support him financially and after a brief stint as a maintenance man, Hans found a job in a photography store. While working there he continued with his puppet show, which met with increasing success. The job in the photography store turned out to be consequential for Hans. While working there he met a customer who was a physician and told him he had gone to medical school when he was in his thirties, "a thing unheard of in Germany." Hans had always wanted to go to medical school but thought he was too old. Inspired by the man's story, Hans sold the house they had built in Cape Elizabeth. Lore and their two children returned to Germany, while Hans spent the summer touring with the puppet show to make additional money. In the fall of 1957, he enrolled at Northeast Missouri University (today Truman State University) in Kirksville, Missouri. He received a BS and BA degree in 1959 and was accepted at the American

School of Osteopathy in Kirksville, Missouri. He graduated in 1962 with a DO degree.

Hans and his family returned to Portland (Lore and children had returned from Germany in 1957), where he interned in a family practice. In 1963, he opened his own practice. Lore died in 1966. In 1975 Hans moved to Chicago, where he took a teaching position at the Chicago School of Osteopathy (incorporated into Midwestern University in 1993).

Returning to Portland in 1982, Hans opened a practice for sexual counseling and osteopathy. When no one came for the sexual counseling, he dropped that part. In 1985 he remarried Martha, an artist. In 1990, Hans briefly returned to Germany to recuperate from a staph infection in the spine, and after a single by-pass surgery he retired in 1991. Hans and Martha moved to Cliff Island, Maine, where Hans, a self-proclaimed "boat-aholic," went into a business building small boats. In 2000, they moved again, to their current home in Georgetown.

Hans and Martha are both active with a variety of art projects in the local community, and Hans frequently lectures on his POW experience in high schools and community organizations. A jazz aficionado, he plays drums and performs with his puppets. In 1955, when traveling with his puppets, Hans visited Captain Silverman in Boston and Colonel Daniels in San Antonio. He also visited Camp Robinson in 1961 and returned for a reunion of former prisoners organized at the camp in August 1987.[30] Hans never regretted immigrating to the United States and he is convinced that he would not have been able to do the things he did, in particular studying medicine "at an advanced age," had he stayed in Germany.

When **Rudolf T.** was discharged, he was given a note from his mother which had been originally sent to him at Camp Huntsville but had never reached him. The note informed him that she was in a refugee camp in Austria but that she did not know what happened to his father and sister. The note also gave him the address of his cousin Gerda, who lived in Zwickau, a town located in the Soviet zone.

Finding himself in Alsfeld, an unfamiliar town, and without a civilian occupation, Rudi was at a loss as to what to do, when he met former POW who had been in Russia and who was making a living in the black market selling German cameras to Americans. Since Friedrich did not know English, Rudi agreed to help him and the two men went into business together. Meanwhile Rudi had written to his cousin in Zwickau. When she informed him that his mother was now living in Tittmoning, a village in Bavaria, he immediately set out to see her. On his way there, he saw the devastated cities, including Frankfurt and Munich, which he described as "a modern Pompeii."

Finally reunited with his mother in Tittmoning, Rudi had to confront the large number of bureaucratic requirements—registering with the police, getting a residence permit, registering with the labor office and finally getting a monthly food-rationing card. For a while he worked as a farmhand, but when the farmer mistreated him, Rudi left for Munich where he was able to find a job with a circus company, moving props. The circus job was short-lived and Rudi managed to get an apprenticeship as a bricklayer with a large building company. He passed the journeyman's examination (*Gesellenprüfung*) in May or June 1948.

Rudi had stayed in touch with his friend Heinz from Camp Forrest. Heinz had been living in Braunfels, Hessen, where he was working for the Americans. When Heinz informed Rudi about possible jobs working as an interpreter for the Americans in nearby Wetzlar, Rudi traveled to Braunfels to apply for the job. With the help of clothes given to him by his friend and the English skills he had been able to perfect while at Camp Forrest, Rudi got the job.

In 1949, after the founding of the Federal Republic, Rudi moved to Giessen, where he continued to work for the Americans as an interpreter for the civil affairs officer, Mr. Ralph Cramer. All along Rudi had been thinking about returning to the United States, and when Mr. Cramer offered to sponsor him, Rudi was enthusiastic.

With Mr. Cramer's help, Rudi was able to get a visa in 1954. In September that year, he flew to New York on Scandinavian Airlines. From there he traveled by bus to Fort Madison, Iowa, the hometown of his sponsor. Before the war, Mr. Cramer had worked at the Sheaffer Pen Company in Fort Madison and Rudi hoped that he could find work there. Unfortunately the company had recently had some bad experiences with several German technicians they had hired and refused to consider Rudi because he was German. Rudi decided to try his luck in Des Moines. Having little money, he needed a job immediately, and when he was offered a job as a porter in the Savery hotel, he accepted. He said, "I was the only white person in such a job in Des Moines."

Although later he was offered a job at a news agency, he remained at the hotel, where he was promoted to assistant catering manager. In this capacity Rudi met a man who was in charge of arranging dinners at the hotel for the Drake University Athletic Club. This acquaintance suggested that Rudi should go back to school. At the time, he was thirty-one years old and people did not go to school at that age in Germany. When the man brought him application forms, he applied to Drake University, and after taking the entrance examination he was admitted.

Rudi received a BA in 1960 and two years later an MA in history, writing his thesis on Franz von Papen. While working on his MA, Rudi had taught part time at Grand View College in Des Moines (now Grand View University). He was now able to get a full-time faculty position teaching modern European and German history. In 1964, he also married Jacqueline, an American woman, but they divorced five years later. In 1977, he married Sigrid B., and he retired ten years later. Like Heino E. and Rupert M., Rudi has written an autobiography.[31]

Rudi likes to speak German and belongs to a German chat club which regularly met at a Borders bookstore in Des Moines. He does not recall any anti–German sentiments. He still has many relatives in Germany, including his sister, and has visited Germany frequently, the last time in 2001. In 1993 he also visited his former POW camp, Camp Huntsville.

When **Alfred M.** returned to his hometown, Berlin, in June 1946, he discovered that his mother had been killed in an air raid in April 1945 and that the whole neighborhood had been completely destroyed. (His father had died in 1942.) He was able to move in with his sister, who had an efficiency apartment in Berlin-Spandau, located in the British sector. He also got in touch with a young woman, Edith, whom he had met during a leave in 1942. Alfred and Edith were married on November 9, 1946. "All our clothes were borrowed; the only thing that belonged to us was our underwear."

Alfred was able to get a job as a truck dispatcher with the British occupation forces and later worked as a lifeguard at a British swimming pool. (He was an excellent swimmer and had gained the *Lebensrettungsabzeichen* [life-savings certificate] before the war.) However, when still a POW in Iowa, Alfred had decided that he wanted to return to the United States as soon as possible and his friend Hughes had offered to sponsor him. After returning to Germany, he had corresponded with Hughes, who had sent care packages. When Alfred found out that it was possible to immigrate in 1948, he applied immediately. Although it turned out that Hughes did not qualify as a sponsor, his father-in-law, Shorty Greiman, offered to sponsor his friend and his new wife.[32] The M.'s were lucky; they received their visas in November 1949 and were given three months to leave.

Unable to secure a space on a transatlantic ocean liner, the M.'s flew from Berlin to Frankfurt and Frankfurt to New York on airline tickets Mr. Greiman had sent them, costing $1,000 for the two. They were supposed to continue by air to Mason City, Iowa, but when their flight was canceled they took the train to Indianapolis and continued from there to Garner, Iowa, where they arrived in December 1949. Their trip had taken four days. On December 28, 1949, the Garner, Iowa local paper, the *Leader and Signal*, published an article with the headline "German Couple Will Settle in the Land of the Enemy."

Moving from bombed-out Berlin to peaceful rural Iowa "was quite a culture shock." As promised, Alfred got a job digging ditches with Shorty Greiman, and Edith worked as a waitress. When Alfred, whose legs were different lengths, could not continue in his job, Shorty encouraged him to find another job. For a few years he worked repairing cylinder heads at the International Harvester dealership in Garner. In 1952 he joined the Masonic Lodge and Eastern Star and later the Toastmasters. When a fellow member at the lodge who worked at General Mills in Belmont, Iowa, told Alfred that the company was looking for a laboratory assistant, Alfred applied and got the job which involved analyzing soybeans and later Vitamin E. Edith worked as a secretary for the plant manager.

When Alfred and Edith became American citizens on April 14, 1955, in Dodge City, the local paper reported on the event: "Mr. and Mrs. Alfred Mueller Sworn in Last Thursday at Fort Dodge as Citizens of United States, Culminating Five Years of Waiting."[33] In 1957 Alfred was transferred to Minneapolis, and he was later promoted to head of the laboratory. Although he formally retired in 1982, Alfred continued to work for General Mills as a consultant until his final retirement in 1985. In 1990 Alfred and Edith, who did not have children, moved to Faribault, a small town forty miles south of Minneapolis where they live in a comfortable house. Both Alfred and Edith have died since the interview.

Leaving Germany behind, they "came with a bag full of hope and the whole thing was a learning experience." When they arrived in 1949, they agreed that they would speak only English with each other. Yet they also kept contact with their German culture and heritage. Alfred traveled to Germany on several occasions. Alfred and Edith briefly belonged to DANK (Deutsch Amerikanischer Nationaler Kongress) and they continue to subscribe to the *New Yorker Staats-Zeitung*. Alfred is proud of his membership in the Hermann Göring Division and he displays many photographs and medals, including an Iron Cross, in his study. In 1993 Alfred and Edith visited Camp Algona to view a nativity scene which had been built by German POWs once held at the camp.[34]

Arriving so soon after the war, and living in a rural area, the M.'s encountered some anti–German sentiments. Edith, in particular, remembers that "people complained that I got the job as head secretary." This bothered her: "We tried so hard to fit in." Alfred and Edith remained close to the Hughes and the Greiman families who adopted them "as their own children." As they have no children their heirs are the Greimans' grand-children.[35]

Heinz R. returned to Germany on March 23, 1946. His wife and son had found refuge near Dresden in the Soviet occupation zone. Since the Americans did not discharge former POWs into the Soviet occupation zone, Heinz was discharged in Bad Aibling, Bavaria.

Heinz was able to get a job as superintendent of maintenance for American schools in Munich. An American captain helped him get his wife, son, and mother to join him in Munich later that year. Heinz "had a good time in Munich" and "liked his job." "I spoke English every day," he recalls.

Heinz' POW experiences had been very positive. When he heard rumors of another war in the early 1950s (see Heino E.) he decided it was time to leave Germany behind. Although Heinz had a potential sponsor, a teacher in Michigan City "who wanted to help Germans come to the United States," when he applied for a visa he was told that the quota was full. Like Gunther, Robert, and Elmar, Heinz and his family opted for Canada instead. They arrived in Kitchener, Ontario, in 1954 and Heinz worked as a welder. Yet Canada was never intended to be their final destination. Heinz wanted to go to the United States, "the land [where] I always had in mind to return." Four years later, in 1958, they were able to realize his dream. After a short stay in Kansas, Heinz and his family settled in Des Plaines, Illinois, not far from where he had spent time as a POW.

Heinz had no trouble finding employment at a large company producing stainless steel equipment for hospitals, and he was soon promoted to head foreman. He retired from the company in 1983. Heinz and his family became American citizens in 1963. At the time of the interview the family lived in Milwaukee, Wisconsin.

Heinz and Hildegard have visited Germany many times and they still have relatives there. In turn, their German relatives visit them frequently. They are not members of any German American organizations. They speak English and German at home, but, as they point out, "increasingly English because of the grandchildren." Their son Tony became a professor of German literature. They have also traveled extensively in the United States, "driving everywhere."

Heinz is convinced that his time as POW was crucial for his later immigration. His recollections of his POW time were very positive and he took advantage of his unexpected circumstances: "Wir müssen das ausnützen." As he put it, "You have to know the country. I would not have known the country."

Released from Camp Bolbec after one week, **Wolf-Dieter Z.** arrived in Darmstadt, Germany, in May 1946. Knowing that his American wife had left Berlin and had sought refuge with friends in Salzburg, he immediately traveled to Austria. In Salzburg he was able to get a job working for the American Occupation Forces in Restoration of Allied and Other Properties. His wife returned to the United States in 1946, and as the husband of an American citizen Wolf-Dieter was able to join her in 1947. The couple settled in Montclair, New Jersey, the home of his wife's family, and Wolf-Dieter became a citizen in 1950. In Montclair, Wolf-Dieter opened a small pharmaceutical company importing pharmaceuticals from Germany. Ten years later he sold the company.

At Camp Concordia, Wolf-Dieter had struck up a friendship with Arnhold Bleichroeder, an American sergeant in the Intelligence Corps whose family had left Germany in 1937. Twenty-two years later he went to work at the Bleichroeder family bank in New York, where he continued to work at the time of the interview.

Wolf-Dieter travels frequently to Germany both as a private citizen and for business. He has several relatives in Germany, including two brothers. He lives an international life and is active in several international and German American organizations: the American Council for Germany, the Foreign Policy Association, the Policy Institute at the New School and Deutsch Amerikanische Handelskammer (German American Chamber of Commerce).

Horst von O. was discharged to Germany and arrived in Frankfurt by train on January 31. He recalls traveling with a group of nine former POWs. Given the destruction, they could not find a place to stay. Even the underpasses in the train stations were filled with refugees, so Horst and his companions spent the night on the cold station platform. Horst's final destination was Wiesbaden, where he had a girlfriend. In Wiesbaden he was able to find a job in the *Landesministerium* (State Ministry) for food and agriculture. In August he moved to Berlin, where he found employment with the United States military government, as a liaison in food distribution.

In Berlin he met his future wife, Judith, an American citizen, at a social function. Horst and Judith were married in September 1948. As the husband of an American citizen he was able to immigrate, and the couple moved to Rochester, New York, his wife's family hometown. When Horst was accepted to study agricultural economic and international finance at Cornell University, the couple moved to Ithaca where Judith worked in the Department of Rural Sociology, putting him through school. After receiving a Ph.D., Horst took a teaching position at Michigan State University. Two years later, the couple left for the Philippines on a Rockefeller-financed post at a small university outside Manila, where they stayed until 1963. At that time his wife returned to the United States, while he made several short-term missions to Papua New Guinea for the World Bank. After briefly returning to Michigan State, Horst joined the World Bank full time in 1964.

Living outside Washington, D.C., Horst has many friends at the World Bank and frequently attends lectures at the German Historical Society and the Friedrich Ebert Foundation. He even continues to attend professional conferences in the field of agricultural development.

Transported by train to Strasbourg, **Gerhard H.** was released in Darmstadt on January 30, 1946. He traveled to his hometown, Koblenz, which had suffered major damage during the war. Gerhard immediately applied and was accepted to the University of Marburg to study modern languages, a course of study he had pursued through the extension service at Camp Crossville and for which he had received credit. Yet after three semesters in Marburg, and after getting married (to Heidi, a woman from East Prussia) Gerhard abandoned his studies. He returned to Koblenz and took a job with the World Church Service, an American Protestant organization engaged in international relief work. In this position he traveled widely. Gerhard became increasingly concerned with Germany's future when the government decided to rearm. As his work in Germany was coming to an end in 1952 and thinking that the United States offered more possibilities and greater security, Gerhard immigrated with his wife and two daughters in January 1953 with the help of World Church Service.

In the United States the family lived in New York and New Jersey where Gerhard continued to work for the World Church Service, providing disaster relief to people in eighty countries for eighteen more years. For Gerhard, who had been working for an American organization and who had traveled widely, the transition was easy ("ein reibungsloser Übergang"). He became an American citizen in 1958, and after his retirement in the late 1980s, the H.'s moved to Whitehall, Pennsylvania. When his wife died in 2008, Gerhard moved to Fredericksburg, Virginia, the home of one of his daughters.

Gerhard has many relatives in Germany, including a brother (another brother lives in France). He frequently visits Germany and France and at the time of the interview he told me that he was thinking of moving to France permanently.

Gerhard has visited Camp Crossville on several occasions and he enjoys giving presentations to students at local colleges.[36] Recently he was invited to give a talk at a naturalization ceremony in Knoxville, Tennessee. Like Rupert M., Rudolf T. and Heino E., Gerhard has published a memoir of his time as POW in America.[37]

Rupert M. returned to Germany in February 1948 (two years after leaving the United States), arriving in his hometown Bretzheim/Bad Kreuznach just in time for *Fassnacht* (carnival). He found his family alive and his home intact. Finally at home, Rupert spent a few weeks "living it up." Not having had a civilian occupation before he was drafted out of school, and having enjoyed his job as interpreter in the United States, in the spring of 1949 Rupert enrolled in interpreter college in Bad Kreuznach. There he met a fellow student, Almut, whose family had fled there from East Prussia. Bert and Almut married in 1950 when both graduated.

Rupert was eager to return to the United States. Soon after his return to Germany in 1949, he had contacted his friend Tom who had promised to sponsor him. Although Tom was now stationed in Germany as part of the U.S. forces, as an active member of the military, he was not eligible to act as a sponsor. Lacking relatives, this meant that Rupert had to put his desires to return to the United States on the back burner.

Using his excellent language skills, Rupert was able to get a job with the CIA interviewing German prisoners of war who were returning from Russia. He also "attended typing school." Not liking the CIA job, Rupert was able to get a job at the American hospital in Wiesbaden. At the hospital, he met a young American medical doctor, Merle Ingraham, and the two men soon became friends. When Dr. Ingraham, who was from Springfield, Massachusetts, offered to sponsor the young couple and their son, Rupert was finally able to realize his dream. The M.'s were able to get a visa in 1954. They arrived in New York on December 4, 1954, and were met by Ingraham and his wife. After a three-day tour of New York City, the two families drove to Greenfield, Massachusetts. In Greenfield they were able to move into their own apartment, after living with the Ingrahams for the first few weeks.

Rupert's first job was as a produce clerk at the Red and White supermarket. After working there for about four months, he saw an advertisement in the local newspaper for a proofreader at a printing company, Minnot Printing and Binding. The proofreading entailed reading price sheets, "a very boring task" (Metzroth, 143). Rupert gradually involved himself with art preparation and layouts. When the company changed to offset printing, Rupert was put in charge of the prep department. He enjoyed the work and also did some consulting work in layout and artwork for other printing places. Gradually the M.'s improved their economic position, and they were able to buy a house in 1959.

In Greenfield Bert and Almut had three more sons. In 1961 Almut took a job as a substitute teacher of German at the local high school. She liked the experience and decided to go back to school at the University of Massachusetts. She got a bachelor's degree in German, and the degree enabled her to get a permanent position teaching German. She eventually became chair of the Foreign Language Department at Greenfield High School. When Almut and Bert became citizens in 1961, they sponsored Almut's parents to come to the United States.

In the early 1970s when Minnot Printing declared bankruptcy, Rupert opened his own graphics and printing business. With their improved economic position, Rupert was able to fulfill his dream of owning a sailboat and the family spent summer vacations sailing in Maine. The M.'s had arrived in the American middle class. In 1989 Rupert and Almut retired and moved to Florida to "do some serious sailing."

Like the majority of my respondents, the M.'s did not experience anti–German sentiments. The family has visited Germany frequently and Almut regularly took her high school students for trips abroad, often accompanied by Bert who acted as chaperon for the male students. When their youngest son graduated from Marine Corps boot camp at Parris Island, South Carolina, Bert and Almut visited his old POW camp, Camp Blanding. Since then Bert has been in regular contact with Camp Blanding. In November 2010 he was invited to speak at the camp's 70th anniversary and Veterans' Day ceremonies. One of four speakers at this occasion (the other three were a National Guard general, the general of Camp Blanding, and an American veteran who was trained there in 1940), Rupert spoke of the many memories of his time at Camp Blanding.[38]

Josef G. returned to his native Saarbrücken in 1947. Although he had wanted to enter the diplomatic corps before he was drafted, in light of his experience working in the laboratory at Camp Atlanta, Joseph decided on a medical career. He was able to get a much-sought-after place to study medicine at the University of Göttingen, graduating in March 1953. During his internship, he decided to specialize in cardiology, and he spent three years in a country practice with his uncle near Saarbrücken.

At a conference in Frankfurt, Josef met his future wife, Caroline, an American doctor working for the U.S. forces, and they were married in 1958 in Portland, Maine. Josef had been interested in returning to the United States, and when he saw a program for additional U.S. medical training he decided to apply, and spent a year in Cleveland, Ohio. In 1958 Josef decided to immigrate permanently to the United States. Josef and Caroline settled in Arizona, where Caroline had grown up. Josef became a citizen in 1961. At the time of the interview they were still in practice together, she as an internist and he as a cardiologist.

The G.'s, who have four sons, travel widely, including to Germany. They frequently attend German American functions in Scottsdale and he never encountered any anti–German sentiments.

Harry H. returned to his home village, Kulmbach, on July 20, 1946, where he found his family alive and his home intact. Harry was thinking of studying chemistry, but he had already completed his *Vorphysikum* (pre-med) program in connection with his studies for the medical corps, so he decided to study medicine at the University of Heidelberg. Harry graduated with a medical degree and in 1950 and married Charlotte, a young woman he had met before the war (his parents did not approve and did not come to the wedding). Between 1951 and 1952 Harry worked at the American Hospital in Munich.

Harry had been eager to return to the United States and had wanted to immigrate as soon as immigration became possible in 1948. He "felt at home" in the United States; he admired American culture, in particular writers such as Upton Sinclair and Sinclair Lewis, and above all jazz. Although Harry had considerable contact with Americans while working in the fields in Wisconsin, these contacts were fleeting and did not produce a sponsor. Like several respondents, Harry was able to engage the family network of his spouse. Harry and Charlotte were sponsored by a relative of Charlotte's mother who resided in Philadelphia, and they were able to get a visa in 1952. On his transatlantic voyage, Harry met a young man, Bert who was from Chicago and who told him that Chicago was a far better place than Philadelphia, so the young couple took a Greyhound bus to Chicago.

After passing his state board examinations in medicine in 1954, Harry became eligible for military service. He served as a captain in the Medical Corps U.S. Army Reserve, from October 2, 1955 to October 1957, at various locations, including New York and Columbia, South Carolina. Harry became an American citizen in 1957.

Harry's wife died a few years ago and he remarried an American woman. Harry is not involved in German American clubs or organizations. He is active in a high school exchange program between Kenilworth High School and his hometown in Germany and he set up a foundation that sponsors two exchange students each year. (At the time of the interview an exchange student from Germany was living in his house.)

Although Harry's parents died in 1983 (father) and 1995 (mother), he visits Germany at least once a year and his many relatives come to visit him in the United States. At the time of the interview he was arranging an American trip with a cousin from Germany. Culturally, Harry is more American than German. Unlike several of the men I interviewed, he was not critical of his adopted country. On the contrary, he felt completely at home. "Americans," he said, "are great people."

Heinrich T. returned to Germany in 1947. Unable to return to his home in Silesia, Heinrich ended up in Völkersen (Kreis Verden, near Bremen), where his brother lived. His father had died in 1945; his mother, who had been forced from their home in Silesia, now lived in Plauen/Vogtland in the Soviet occupation zone.

After a brief visit with his mother in Plauen, Heinrich returned to Völkersen, where he was able to get work cleaning up rubble in nearby Bremen. He also began an apprenticeship as a bricklayer (*Umschulung*) in Bremen, which he completed in 1948. In Völkersen Heinrich met his future wife Elfriede. Elfriede's family were ethnic Germans from Rumania who had been resettled in Rarthegan, Poland, in 1940 as part of the Nazi attempt to "Germanize" newly acquired territories. In 1945, they had fled from the advancing Russian army and ended up in Völkersen.

When Heinrich and Elfriede were married in 1949, Efriede's parents and siblings were considering immigration. However, they did not know where to go and it was Heinrich who convinced them to go to the United States. Sponsored by the Church World Service, both families were able to immigrate in April 1952. Elfriede's parents ended up in Wisconsin, while Heinrich and Elfriede were settled in Chicago.

When they arrived in Chicago, the pastor who was supposed to meet them did not show up, but he left instructions that they should get a room at the YMCA. When he finally showed up a few days later he arranged a job for Heinrich on a chicken and rabbit farm in Barrington, Illinois. The pastor had no idea that Heinrich was married and had a child. When Heinrich rejected the job on the rabbit farm, the pastor took them back to Chicago. Fortunately Heinrich, who had completed an apprenticeship as a baker before the war, was able to get a job in a bakery, a job he held for seven years.

As the hours working in the bakery were difficult, Heinrich looked for a new job. Given his training, he found employment as a bricklayer. Three years later, responding to a newspaper advertisement, Heinrich was able to get a position as building material inspector, a position he held until he retired in 1986.

The T. family became American citizens in 1957. Heinrich built the house in Chicago where they lived at the time of the interview. The couple travels frequently, including to Australia and New Zealand, where Elfriede has many relatives. They also frequently return to Germany, and Heinrich has visited his childhood home in Poland. Unlike many of my respondents, Heinrich did not visit his former POW camp.

The T.'s are very involved in German American organizations, including the Lutheran church. Both do a lot of volunteer work, mowing lawns and raising money for the church, driving elderly people around. They are members of the Schwabenverein, Rheinischer Verein, DANK (Deutsch Amerikanischer National Kongress), and they subscribe to the *New Yorker Staats-Zeitung*.

Returning from France in June 1948, **Kurt P.**, could not return to his home in Silesia. He traveled to Königstein where he had met Emilie during the war. In Königstein, Kurt found work in a quarry making granite stones for buildings, and Kurt and Emilie were married later that year. Although he was married to a local woman, Kurt had difficulties getting a residence permit and the couple encountered difficulties finding a place to live. They ended up renting a room "at an exorbitant price."

Kurt had decided to immigrate almost immediately after his return. He was "homesick for the United States," where he perceived greater opportunities than in Germany. He felt rejected in Germany and "America gave me a new home." Although his new wife was not enthusiastic, she eventually agreed.

The farmer for whom he worked at Lodi had indicated that he was willing to sponsor the young couple, and after waiting for two years they finally received a visa in 1952. Unlike Willie S., who was also sponsored by a Wisconsin farmer, Kurt's return to the United States was difficult at first. It turned out that the farmer was in economic difficulty and had borrowed the money to bring Kurt and his wife to the United States to exploit them as cheap labor. He paid the young couple half of the going rate and kept half of Kurt's pay, allegedly to repay expenses associated with their travel and sponsorship. He also expected Emilie to work in the household without pay.

After nine months Kurt was able to find a new job through a salesman who sold insurance. When Kurt mentioned he was trained as a stonemason, the salesman recommended that Kurt seek out the local monument shop. He also offered them a cabin he owned as a free place to live. Kurt was hired in the shop and Emilie was able to get a job in a local bakery.

In 1971, Kurt started his own business, Pechmann Memorials, Inc. Since then the business has grown. Kurt credits his success to "using German quality work." Kurt became a citizen in 1959. He has retired from the business and his son Gerry is now in charge, but Kurt comes to the office almost every day.

Kurt is one of three men I interviewed who did not learn English in captivity (the other two are Oskar S. and Heinz K.). After arriving in the United States, Kurt and Emilie learned English in local night classes and decided to speak only English at home. Although Kurt does not have any surviving relatives in Germany, Emilie does. They have returned to visit many times, and he has traveled to his hometown to show his children and grandchildren where he grew up.

Kurt likes to attend the German American festival in Milwaukee. He is something of a local celebrity and has been interviewed numerous times by local newspapers and radio. He proudly displays a thick folder of newspaper clippings about him. Various letters and commendations line his office wall, including a Purple Heart he received for repairing a monument in Forrest Hill Cemetery in Madison which was damaged in 1986. He is also a member of U.S. veterans' groups. Kurt is clearly proud of his accomplishments and considers himself very American despite his strongly accented English.

The Westfrontgefangenen

When **Henry K.** finally returned to his home in Teltge in 1948, he found his family alive and well and his home intact. Henry was able to get a job as a street worker, "the only available job," laying mosaics and cobblestone. When he was offered the possibility of additional training to become a foreman, he declined because he would soon immigrate to the United States.

While a prisoner of war, Henry had corresponded with an uncle who had immigrated to the United States in 1923 and lived in Portland, Oregon. After returning to Germany, wanting to "get a new start," Henry "put his immigration in motion." He is one of eleven children. His mother encouraged him: "You are the man for it." Although his uncle sponsored him, it took him three years to get a visa. When he finally "got the message he could go, he was the happiest man."

Henry arrived in Portland in 1951 and was able to get a job in construction. With the help of his sister who immigrated a year later and worked as a nanny for the Philip Knight family, Henry was able to get a job as a gardener. Gerda, a young woman he had met soon after returning home, later joined him, and they were married in 1953. He became an American citizen in 1956.

Although Henry retired several years ago, he loved his job as a gardener. He appears to be on excellent terms with his boss, who sponsored him to run a marathon in Berlin a few years ago and continues to invite him as a "special friend" to many festivities. The K.'s continue to live in a small house owned by the Knight family. Like Kurt P. and Oskar S., Henry did not learn English when he was a POW. After immigration he took some night courses, and today his command of the spoken language is very good.

The K.'s frequently travel to Germany, where both have relatives. They are active in the German Society, and they love to dance, sometimes twice a week (both are in excellent physical shape). Henry did not encounter anti–German sentiments. They appear connected to their hometown. Henry never regretted having immigrated, but admits to a little *Heimweh* (homesickness), especially when thinking about "sturdy Westphalian peasants." Their house is filled with books about Westphalia.

Released to Germany in 1948, **Oskar S.** could not return to his home in East Prussia. His parents had fled from East Prussia and now lived in the Soviet occupation zone. Unable to join them, Oskar traveled to Göttingen, where his brother had moved after the war.

Oskar's apprenticeship as an electrician had been interrupted by his military service and he felt that it would be hopeless (*ausichtslos*) to finish it, given the situation in Germany. To support himself, Oskar worked as a truck driver. He met his future wife Lillie, who also worked for the owner of the company. Oskar and Lillie were married in 1951. Lillie and her family were Seventh-day Adventists who were preparing to immigrate to the United States with help from the church. Oskar didn't see much of a future in Germany, so his in-laws' immigration prompted him to think about returning to the United States. With the sponsorship of the Seventh-day Adventist Church, Oskar and Lillie arrived in Detroit in December 1954.

Unemployment was high at the time and Oskar had difficulties finding a job. Oskar did not have a trade and his English-language skills were limited. He was fired from his first job, delivering milk, because as a Seventh-day Adventist he was not allowed to work on Saturdays. He decided to try his luck in the in auto industry and luck was on his side. In an auto accident, Oskar was rear-ended by "a fairly high level GM executive" who helped Oskar get a low-level job as a sweeper and general *Laufbursche* (errand boy) at General Motors. After eight months on this job, Oskar was able to find another job in a tool factory, where he learned to run a tool-making machine.

Oskar liked the work and decided to take evening courses for three months to learn how to run other machines. When the company he worked for went bankrupt five years later, the foreman, who had started his own company, asked Oskar to join him. Five years later, inspired by his boss, Oskar started his own shop in his garage — O.S. Precision Machining, Inc.— while still working for his friend part time. In 1972 he was able to become totally independent. At the time of the interview in 2002, Oskar's son Ralph was running the business. Oskar was semi-retired, but he kept a hand in the business.

Oskar became an American citizen in 1959. What he likes most about the U.S. is "the boss-worker relationship," which he feels is more informal and less hierarchical than in Germany. Oskar's English is serviceable, but he prefers speaking German. Oskar and Lillie continue to speak mostly German with one another.

The S.'s visit Germany on regular basis, including the former GDR, as a brother lives in Leipzig. Oskar and Lillie also attended the *Rastenburger Treffen* (meeting of Rastenburgers) in Wesel, Germany, and later visited his hometown, which is now in Poland.

Oskar is involved in German American life in the Detroit area. He belongs to the German American Culture Center in Sterling Heights, where he is particularly fond of playing table-tennis, a sport he picked up when he was a POW.

Like Ernst F. and Harry H., Oskar has attended the yearly *Volkstrauertag* (day of people's mourning concerning those lost in wars) in Battle Creek, Michigan. Like Kurt P. and his wife Emilie, Oskar and Lillie were guest honorees at the gala opening of the Chandelier Ballroom in Hartford, Wisconsin, on May 1, 1998, the place that was his home as a POW.[39]

Ernst F. was discharged from Bolbec on April 4 and arrived on German soil two days later. Since his parents now lived in a small village at the Baltic Sea in the Soviet occupation zone, Ernst was discharged at Bad Aibling, south of Munich, where he was able to stay with friends who lived in Munich.

In Munich, Ernst found work as a janitor and orderly at an American military hospital. After only twelve days on the job, he quit and took a job as a potato peeler and kettle washer in an American barracks. An advantage of this job was that he had access to plenty of food. Meanwhile his parents had moved to the Soviet zone in Berlin, where his father worked as a dentist in a large hospital. In July 1946, Ernst received permission to join his parents in East Berlin.

Ernst's education had been interrupted by the war. In spring 1947 he applied to photography school in East Berlin, but due to a waiting period he was not admitted until 1948. After passing the journeymen's examination graduating in 1950, Ernst worked in East Berlin as a photographer. There he met his future wife, Barbara, a native of Pomerania who now lived in West Berlin. When they married in 1953, the young couple moved to West Berlin.

In West Berlin, Ernst worked as a photographer. After losing two jobs as a photographer in West Berlin, Ernst was able to get a third job because the person who had held the job was immigrating to the United States. Ernst had wanted to return to the United States, but he did not have a sponsor. When he found out that the man who held his job before him had immigrated with the sponsorship of the Episcopal Church, Hans applied. When he received a letter that he would have to take a job as a janitor in Long Island, New York, Ernst protested. He wanted to come to the Midwest, a place he knew from his time as a POW.

Ernst's dream came true when he, his wife and their four-month-old daughter arrived in New York on January 25, 1957. Their sponsor was the Episcopal Church in East Lansing, Michigan. From New York, they took the train to Lansing, as he had when he was a POW, and there they found a paid-for and fully equipped apartment. It took Ernst only four days to find work as a photographer. He worked for several photography studios in Lansing. In 1969 he opened his own studio in nearby Grand Ledge, specializing in industrial photographs.

Ernst, who became an American citizen in 1961, is well integrated into the Grand Ledge community, where he moved in 1960. He was president of the PTA in 1969, president of Band Boosters, and chair of the bicentennial celebrations. Ernst also belongs to the German American Club in Lansing and the F.'s always celebrate Oktoberfest. He was also a member of the Sachsen Club and the *Liederkranz* (song circle). He has been active in establishing international connections through the Blue Lake Fine Arts Camp, which brings artists and performers from Europe to Michigan. He recalls one anti–German experience, when a Jewish person asked for his business card and then tore it up and threw it in his face.

Ernst travels frequently. He attended the POW exhibit at the Las Cruces, New Mexico Farm and Ranch Heritage Museum in January 2002 and has returned to Las Cruces on several occasions. While there he usually stays with the grandson of one of the farmers he worked for. Ernst has frequently participated in the *Volkstrauertag* (Germany's national day of mourning at Fort Custer in Battle Creek (see also Kurt P., Elmar B. and Oskar S.), in honor of the twenty-six German POWs who died there during their captivity.[40] Like Peter E., Gerhard H., Heino E. and Hans W., Ernst is deeply engaged in talking to community groups about his life experiences.[41]

In addition to visiting Eureka in 1988, Ernst has visited Camp Hatch/Fort Bliss eight times since immigrating to the United States. He maintains a close friendship with the son and grandson and wife of Mr. Mundy, one of the farmers he worked for at Camp Hatch.

After disembarking in Cherbourg in August or September 1945, **Johannes (John) S.** was put on a train, this time a *Güterwagen* (freight wagon) hospital train which took him to Augsburg, where he spent another week in the hospital. He was released and given a ticket to Bremen. Still wearing his POW clothes, John got as far as Frankfurt, where he spent the night on the train platform. Luckily he was able to get a train to Bremen the next day. Arriving in his hometown, he found that his family home had been totally destroyed. His father had died shortly before the end of the war. In the street he ran into an acquaintance who took him to his mother.

John, who spoke excellent English, soon found work with the occupation forces. The Americans had confiscated the yacht club and needed someone to take people out on boats, especially American officers and their female friends, both American and German. He became the captain of one of the yachts. He recalls that they had "lots of food and whiskey and beer." This new job allowed him to practice and improve his English skills. Working at the yacht club for one year, he made connections that would lead to a job with the Allied Military Government, working in the transportation section. He was later transferred to the U.S. High Commissioner's staff as a Marshall Plan liaison aide. In 1950, Johannes was assigned the task of interviewing German manufacturers to help facilitate the country's export trade potential. When this program ended in July, he was transferred to the Public Safety Division, where he worked as a liaison officer assisting in a program aimed at reorienting German law enforcement officers. Assessing this job, John recalls that "the good part was that they served lunch."

John had made the decision to return to the United States when he left New York Harbor and saw the Statue of Liberty. "It was a beautiful day, all looked so peaceful," he remembered. When queried, John indicated that his main reason for immigrating was his belief that America would offer more opportunity. His education had been unfinished, and he felt that credentialism was of less importance in America. In short, he would be able to have a better career.

Sponsored by the deputy commissioner of the American Military Government, John was able to get a visa in 1951. His transportation to the United States was paid for by the American president of a shipping company whom he had met while working at the yacht club. He offered for John to take any of his ships to come to the United States. The whole trip cost him twenty-six dollars, mostly for wine and beer for the crew.

John arrived in Tampa the end of January 1952 "with $75, a suitcase and an accordion."[42] In Tampa his first job was a boat-building contract, but John wanted to race sailboats. Toward this goal he took an unpaid job as a navigator on a yacht. They sailed to Havana and stayed a week. John married an American woman, Bette, in 1954, but the marriage ended in divorce. In 1979 he married his second wife, Mary.

On a trip to New York he admired a boat in the harbor. The boat turned out to belong to a man who had a stevedore business. When he contacted the owner, he was told to see the treasurer of the company, who hired John as a payroll clerk. Eager to learn all about this business, John worked in several capacities, including as a timekeeper (responsible for everything built on the pier). When the company merged with another after two years, John became the office manager in the new company. He continued to work there for three years.

Meanwhile, his brother-in-law who was the Lufthansa manager for North America moved to North Carolina. (His sister had worked for Lufthansa and had met her husband there). When his brother-in-law started a building business, John agreed to join in the venture. John did not last long in this new position; he did not like North Carolina and could "not get used to the people there." He felt they were "too slow and never on time."

After a few months, John returned to New York, where he was able to get a job as treasurer in another company. Noting problems in the company's accounting system, he quit after two years. Following two and a half months of unemployment, John landed a new job as a comptroller in a life insurance company. The company, which had 500 agents and sixty-five people working in his office, had been losing money at the time he joined, but after one year John was able to turn the company around so that it was making money. He quit this job after two years. After a brief period of unemployment, he got a new job with another insurance company as internal auditor. When he transferred to Chicago to become regional auditor of the company's Midwest and eventually western regions, he took courses for auditors and eventually rose to vice president treasurer. When the company split up, John was asked to join "the data part." He became manager of southwestern marketing. He later moved to Dallas.

In the 1980s John moved again. He took a new job in Los Angeles, at a reinsurance company, where he was responsible for the data department. This was the time when he made "some good money." Between 1988 and 1989, when he was close to retirement, the company sent him to Germany to sell the data systems and software to German companies. John finally retired in 1991 and moved to Florida.

His sister died a few years ago, and now John has no close relatives in Germany. He never regretted immigrating; and he became particularly aware of how he preferred America when he lived in Germany in the late 1980s and noticed "the inflexibility of German system." He is convinced that he "could never have had the career in Germany" that he had in the United States.

John became an American citizen in 1956. He has traveled all over the United States and lived in several states. As he put it, "I visited forty-two states and fifty-four countries." John does not belong to German American organizations or subscribe to German newspapers. Since his retirement he volunteers for AARP, doing taxes for retired people, and he loves going on cruises. He confided that he spent about "three hundred days on cruises altogether" and could spend his entire time cruising, but apparently his wife is less enthusiastic.

Although **Heinz F.** could have returned to Germany in 1948, on the advice of his mother, who told him that "things were not too good in Germany," Heinz volunteered to stay in England an additional two years. Learning that his mother was sick, he returned to Germany around Christmas 1950. In England, he had been able to make some money raising chickens on the side, which allowed him to travel by plane from London to Hamburg to Berlin. He found his parents still living in the same apartment, which luckily had not been destroyed. His father worked for the power company in Berlin and was able to help him get a job with a cable company, making cables of rubber and plastic. In 1954 he married Gertrud.

The young couple was lucky as they were able to get an apartment through an acquaintance of his wife who owned a large apartment building. They were also looking for a *Heizer* (heating technician) and Heinz, who had experience working the boiler at his POW camp in Maine, got the job, which came with a free apartment. Gertrud was a professional cook who worked in a large hotel in Berlin.

Overall the F.'s were quite comfortable and Heinz had not really thought about immigrating, when an opportunity presented itself in 1960. A relative of his wife's girlfriend owned a German restaurant in Glendale, California, and offered Gertrud a job as a cook. Although Gertrud was hesitant, Heinz, who had positive memories of his stay in Maine, convinced her to take the offer. Sponsored by the relative, Heinz and Gertrud arrived in Glendale in 1961.

Heinz started out working as a dishwasher in the German restaurant, but he was soon able to find a job building conveyor belts in a food product factory. When the company was sold after a few years, Heinz was able to find a job in a small company making international medical systems, owned by Gunther, a German immigrant. There he was in charge of the machines. The company did well, growing from seven to 500 employees in four years. Heinz continued to work there until he retired in 1989. At that time when the F.'s sold the house in Los Angeles and moved to Oregon.

Like Elmar B. and unlike most of my respondents, Heinz lived in a German speaking environment. He and Gertrud worked with Germans, speaking German at work and with each other. After Gertrud died in 2003, Heinz sold the house in Oregon and he now lives in a small trailer on land owned by his friend Lilliane F. Heinz and Lilliane love to go ballroom dancing twice a week and they travel extensively; most recently they had gone on a thirty-day cruise to Australia and New Zealand. At the time of the interview they were planning to cruise the Mediterranean and were making plans to visit his old camp in Maine. In October 2008, Heinz and Lilliane visited the Houlton Historical Society and Heinz reminisced about his time as a POW.[43]

Ludwig N. returned to his native town of Rottenburg in May 1948, and after marrying Trudie in 1949, he decided that he wanted to leave Germany. Practically minded, he prepared by pursuing a new career, one that would be useful abroad. Rather than studying architecture as he had planned before the war, he completed an apprenticeship as an auto mechanic in 1951.

Ludwig summed up his POW time as a positive learning experience. "When I look back on my experiences, I learned that the world was larger than Germany. ... I was brought up in the narrow, traditional German way." Ludwig was eager to immigrate to the United States, and he had had friendly but fleeting contacts with farmers while working in sugar beets in Montana and as a lumberjack in Washington. However, Ludwig did not have a sponsor. In England he had met a British man who arranged from him to go to South Africa. He left in 1952, but returned to Germany one year later. South Africa turned out not to be the place for him.

Ludwig resumed working as an auto mechanic; at the same time he and his wife opened a small car rental business. Like Johann G. and his family, the N.'s were doing well economically and even owned a car. They did not actively pursue immigration.

Ludwig's desire to return to the United States was rekindled when a distant cousin of his wife was visiting from the United States in 1953. While visiting, the relative rented one of the N.'s cars and, hearing of Ludwig's desire to immigrate, he offered to act as a sponsor. Ludwig had improved his economic position and was now working at a car dealership in Baden-Baden where he was in charge of customer relations. However, he was eager to take advantage of this unexpected opportunity. The N.'s received their visas eight months later.

It turned out that the visa was easier to get than space on a transatlantic ship, but with the help of friends from England, Ludwig was able to book a passage on a ship from Bremerhaven. After "selling everything," the N.'s arrived in New York in November 1954. Traveling by Greyhound bus, they arrived in their sponsor's hometown, Detroit.

Their sponsor owned an apartment building, where the N.'s had an apartment in exchange for taking care of the building. Three years later, they were able to purchase their own home. Ludwig's career choice after the war paid off. He was able to find job with a Volkswagen dealership repairing cars. One of Ludwig's friends was working at Fisher Body and this allowed him to get a job in the engineering department. In 1972 Fisher Body closed shop and Ludwig and some 12,000 workers found themselves unemployed. Ludwig used the opportunity to go back to school at Wayne

State University. He then became a technician at GM Tech Center. He retired in 1982 as senior engineering technician. After his retirement the N.'s moved to northern Michigan, but, finding it too isolated, they moved to Big Rapids in 1985.

Ludwig "always lived among Americans," and he never joined any German American clubs or organizations. At the same time Ludwig and his wife kept their connections to the German language, subscribing to the *Nordamerikanische Wochenpost* and the *New Yorker Staats-Zeitung*. They travel to Germany frequently, and their daughter spent one year as a student at the Walddorfschule in Kassel.

Erwin H. returned to Germany toward the end of 1946. Unable to return to his hometown of Katowice, he ended up in Babenhausen (Hessen), where he felt like a stranger. Working on the large American military base there he befriended Captain Lonsky. One day in 1947, a jeep arrived with Captain Walter Niedermeyer, who asked if he could take Erwin to Stuttgart. As it turned out Niedermeyer, had been dating Erwin's sister Ilse, who had fled to nearby Ludwigsburg at the end of the war.

In Stuttgart, Niedermeyer, who "was one of the nicest persons," got Erwin a job working in the dry cleaning plant. He recalls that the PX was right around the corner. Erwin moved in with his sister in Ludwigsburg. Niedermeyer and Ilse were married in 1948 and moved to Niedermeyer's hometown, Richmond, Virginia. Erwin, who had acquired an affection for Americans, having never forgotten the kindness of people he met as a prisoner, and who spoke excellent English, had little incentive to stay in Germany. With Niedermeier's sponsorship he was able to get a visa in August 1949. He found transportation from Hamburg to Norfolk, Virginia, on a freighter, the Flying Enterprise.

In Richmond he rented a room for five dollars a week and worked a series of jobs — driving a taxi, working in a warehouse — that could sustain him. Soon after he arrived he was hospitalized for a collapsed lung, an event that would change his life. The doctor who treated him was impressed by the young German's many questions and asked Erwin if he wanted to be a doctor.

Erwin, who had no occupational training, had never considered becoming a doctor, but he was curious enough to inquire if it might be possible. He enrolled in Richmond Professional Institute (now Virginia Commonwealth University) and majored in chemistry. In 1957, he enrolled in the Medical College of Virginia, graduating with an MD in 1961. After completing his internship and residency in obstetrics and gynecology,

Erwin went into in private practice. He retired in 1989 but continued to volunteer in a clinic.

In 1951 he married a nurse, and he became an American citizen in 1952. He is the father of four children. After the marriage ended in divorce, he married his current wife, Esther, who is also a nurse.

Erwin considers his POW experience to be very important in giving him some idea of what it was like to live in the United States. He has visited Manford Lawrence, the farmer he had worked for, and he is good friends with the magistrate in Scotland Neck.

Erwin has traveled to Europe frequently, visiting Stuttgart and Ludwigsburg. In July 2010 he traveled to his hometown, where he visited the graves of his parents and wept. While he is not a member of any German American organization, he has many opportunities to, and enjoys, speaking German with acquaintances.

When **Johann G.** finally returned to Germany in May 1948, he was released in a camp near Bremen. Heading home to Gelsenkirchen, he found that his parents had survived the war. Johann was lucky to get a job at the same electric company where he had trained, and he married a young women, Gisela, in 1952. Although Johann and his family were doing quite well financially — they were able to buy a Volkswagen and traveled through Germany and Europe — Johann was determined to return to the United States.

"When I got back to Germany I had only one dream, to go back to the USA with all the wonderful people. I decided to go back in 1945; no one could have talked me out of it." During his stay in England and after returning to Germany, Johann had corresponded with Mr. Hansen, who had offered to sponsor him when he was still a prisoner of war. When Mr. Hansen could not guarantee a job to the young German as the jobs were filled by Americans, another contact, the farmer Mr. Moser, qualified as sponsor. Just as the immigration papers were ready, Johann and Gisela got married. Her inclusion required additional paperwork. "I did have to go through a lot of paperwork," Johann recalls. Finally, after four years, Johann was able to leave Germany behind.

The G.'s finally arrived in New York in 1953. With a Greyhound ticket from Mr. Moser they traveled to Idaho. In Idaho Johann worked on Mr. Moser's farm, planting and harvesting sugar beets. Johann soon discovered that farming was not his cup of tea, and when he had worked enough to reimburse Mr. Moser for his travel expenses, Johann decided to look for a job in his occupation. (See similar trajectories Kurt P. and Willie S.)

A skilled electrician, Johann was able to get a job at Ken's Electric Shop in Preston. When his job was terminated in 1955, Johann took a job at Cash Valley Electric in Logan, Utah. He worked at Cash Valley for thirteen years (1955 to 1968).

Johann and Gisela became American citizens in 1958, in part because the electric company had a government contract. In 1969, Johann and his family moved to Seattle (Auburn), but Seattle turned out to be too big for their tastes and after a brief stay they moved to Bellingham, Washington. In Bellingham, Johann worked for Mills Electric until he retired in 1989.

Since his retirement, Johann has remained active. He works with one of his sons who is a commercial fisherman. Johann and Gisela live in a house he built on the shores of a lake, which they expanded from a little cabin; they also own the lot across the street. His son and son-in-law have captain's licenses and own part of a barge, and Johann frequently joins them on fishing trips. Two of their children live nearby; a third lives in Portland, Oregon.

"I was lucky to come here," says Johann. The G.'s do not recall any anti–German experiences. On the contrary, they felt that "people were helpful." When they moved to Preston, their Mormon neighbors "came with all kinds of household goods," and although the neighbors tried unsuccessfully to convert them to the Mormon religion, Johann and Gisela made good friends. In Bellingham, the G.'s are members of the *Heimatkreis*, which has grown in recent years, and subscribe to a German paper, *Nordarmerikanische Wochenpost*.

Johann and Gisela visited Germany in 1961 and have returned on many occasions. In the 1970s, Johann's mother came to stay with them for a year. Although Johann's sister died a few years ago and he does not have close relatives in Germany any more, Gisela still has a sister in Germany, and another sister lives in Cairo (they traveled to Egypt as well). They have also traveled widely all over Europe and at the time of the interview they were planning a boat trip through the canals in the Netherlands. In 1992, like several former POWs, Johann visited the area where he had spent a defining year of his life. He is happy to tell people about his PW experience and says people are very interested.

Johann had never thought about America before he became a POW. "I would never have immigrated. I had no relatives, no interest." For Johann, America, or rather rural Idaho, was a revelation. He "loved the wide open spaces, the juxtaposition to Gelsenkirchen and its smokestacks. Completely different. You see the mountains."

Leaving Camp Bolbec, **Otto L.** was put on a train to Münster, where he was handed over to British occupation forces. In Münster he was loaded on a truck which took him to his nearby hometown, Osnabrück, where he arrived in April 1946. Although the city had sustained significant damage, his parents and numerous relatives had survived the war. After visiting all his relatives, Otto went to work for his father's office machines and supplies business. Otto wanted to return to the United States as soon as possible and applied for a visa in 1948. His sponsor was his buddy from Utah, Earl Jackson. It took three years till he received the visa.[44]

While waiting for the visa, Otto had several jobs. In fall 1946 he went back to work in the experimental institute (*Versuchsanstalt*) for small animals in Hamm and briefly worked on a farm in Schulte-Eickel. Following encouragement from his uncle, Otto, who was good at drawing, began a masonry apprenticeship in 1948–49, while also attending the *Berufsschule* (vocational school), requirements for a career as an architect. After less than a year, Otto decided that he did not want to become an architect and he returned to work in the field of small animal husbandry, running the poultry department on a farm in Hosel. He stayed there for a year until leaving for the United States.

Otto finally received the visa in 1951 and four days before leaving, on July 21, 1951, he married. Leaving his new wife behind, Otto arrived in New York and traveled to Utah by train, arriving in Ephraim, where his friend had started a feed business. Unbeknownst to Otto, by the time he arrived, the business had gone bankrupt, forcing Otto to take several odd jobs, including hauling and bagging grain, and laying brick.

Seeing no future in rural Utah, Otto contacted a German Catholic priest, Father Braun, whom he had met on the transatlantic journey and who was stationed in Utah. Father Braun was able to arrange a job at Holy Cross Hospital, a Catholic hospital in Salt Lake City. Otto began work in the hospital boiler room in fall 1951. Until his wife came to join him in 1952, he lived in a dormitory. Working at the hospital, Otto rose through the ranks. He worked long hours and took classes in hospital administration at the University of Utah. When he retired he had become the hospital administrator.

Otto became a citizen in 1959, as he tells it, somewhat reluctantly. He had applied in 1958 but did not want to answer in the affirmative that he was willing to fight for the United States. In 1959 he changed his mind "for the sake of convenience."

Otto's perceptions of the United States are entirely positive. As POW he had been much impressed with the U.S. Army, the clean quarters, the clothing (creases in the pants), the showers, the barracks, the generous food, the overall wealth, and the generosity and openness of the people he met. Otto did not encounter any anti–German sentiments, except for "some of the Jewish doctors at the hospital" who were not friendly toward him at first, but later warmed up to him and "even became friends."

In 1957 Otto and nine co-workers founded a successful federal credit union which has grown over the years with Otto serving as the chief executive officer. He retired from this position in 2011.

Otto visits Germany frequently and spends extended periods in his native country, where he has many old friends from his youth and friends of his wife, Elizabeth, who died in 1994. While he has friends in the United States, he feels that his American friends appreciate him mostly for his work, while his friends in Germany appreciate him for who he is.[45]

Henry R. returned to his native Braunschweig in November 1947. His father, who picked him up at the camp, did not recognize him. In Braunschweig Henry was able to get a job at Buessing, a bus and truck manufacturer, as a tool and die maker. He also was active in the black market. In 1948 Henry married a young woman whom he had much admired before the war. Her father, an instructor (*Oberlehrer*) at the *Kunstgewerbeschule* (crafts college), encouraged Henry to pursue a degree in photography at the school. Henry followed his advice, took the course, and graduated in 1953.

Henry wanted to return to the United States. Mr. Lykens had made a lasting impression on the young German, and like many of his compatriots who had read the novels of Karl May, he had fallen in love with the West, the openness of the country (especially compared to his native town of Braunschweig) and the friendliness of the people. He felt constrained and "wanted to get out."

Mr. Lykins would have been a natural sponsor for Henry, but, although Henry had his address, he was unable to contact him. (Even later, after he had immigrated and tried to track him down, he was unable to do so. Later someone who had read about Henry's futile quest in a local newspaper contacted him to inform him that Mr. Lykins and his sons had died.) Like many immigrants and several of my respondents, Henry was able to activate his wife's American network for sponsorship. An aunt, Mrs. Karl Fuehrer, who lived in New York was willing and able to sponsor the young couple, who arrived in New York in 1953.

Living in the Bronx, Henry had several jobs, including as a paper cutter, a job he did not like. Henry was ambitious; his goal was to work in a bank. To gather information about possible bank positions, Henry walked into several banks asking for a job. In this manner he was able to get a job at Hanover Bank (which later merged with Manufacturers Bank), where he was eventually promoted to foreign exchange expert. Henry became an American citizen in 1958.

One of the senior bank officers took an interest in the ambitious young German and encouraged Henry to get a master's degree in economics at New York University. When his friend moved to Montpelier, Vermont, Henry followed him there. In Montpelier, Henry opened a flower shop and started to work for a life insurance company as an investment analyst and portfolio manager. He rose to become executive vice president of the company and was instrumental in developing investment strategies and creating mutual funds. After he had three heart attacks in his late forties and early fifties, Henry retired with a "golden parachute" and moved to Charlottesville, Virginia. He also divorced his first wife and married an American woman, Charlie. Despite his health problems, Henry did not like retirement, and he started several business ventures, including an imports shop and an emu farm.

Henry was only seventeen years old when he became a POW on American soil. Coming from a provincial, conservative town in central Germany, Henry had been much impressed with the American countryside, and his chance meeting with Mr. Lykins had been a defining moment in his life.[46]

When **Erich K.** returned to Salzgitter in August 1946, he found his parents alive. Looking for a job, Erich went to the city hall, where he met Eleanor, whose family had been forced to flee to the West when her hometown became Polish. Erich and Eleanor married in December 1947 and Erich was able to get a job at a private railroad at the local steel works. Erich did not like the work, and he suffered a nervous breakdown. After that, Erich and Eleanor decided that they wanted to immigrate to the United States.

Erich had fond memories of his time in Ogden and wanted to go back to Utah. "When I came to Ogden I fell in love with the people and the scenery and decided then that I wanted to come back and live here someday" (*Standard Examiner*, June 16, 1952). The couple was able to find a sponsor in the Lutheran World Federation. They traveled from Bremerhaven, arriving in the United States on June 15, 1952. Unlike most German immigrants sponsored by churches, the K.'s did not want to settle in the Midwest, a place that was unfamiliar to Erich. To the surprise of their sponsors, they had specified that they wanted to be settled in Ogden. Luck-ily the small Lutheran church in Ogden was willing and able to take responsibility for the young German couple and their son. They arranged for a small basement apartment and Erich was able to find a job in repair services at Butler Plumbing and Electric Company. After three years on this job, Erich opened his own repair shop. When the repair shop turned out to be unsuccessful, Erich was able to get a job as a superintendent at a local school, a job he held for fourteen years until he retired at the age of sixty-two.

The K.'s have been active members of the Lutheran Church in Ogden and occasionally attend the local Oktoberfest. They became citizens in 1957. Although Erich has had his doubts about America, "depending on who is president" (Democrats are preferred), the K.'s consider themselves loyal Americans.

Peter E. had not had any news from his wife, Johanna, for one and a half years. Returning to his hometown, Munich, in 1946, he found that the house where they had lived with her parents after their marriage was the only one standing on the block. His mother-in-law opened the door.

Peter was able to get a job with the occupation forces. As a graduate of Fort Getty he "was received with open arms." He was in charge of organizing town meetings and helping to create order. He also reports writing a book, *From Military Government to State Department*, published by *Stars and Stripes* in 1948.[47]

Although Peter had wanted to return to the United States as soon as he returned to Germany, he was afraid that his wife would not agree and did not actively pursue immigration. An opportunity presented itself when his sister married a GI from Cleveland and moved to the United States in 1947. When she wrote that she was homesick and wanted her brother and his family to join her, Peter was able to convince Johanna. According to Peter, "the fact that I already knew America" was instrumental in his deci-sion to join his sister. Although his brother-in-law did not qualify as a sponsor, Peter, Johanna and their son were able to immigrate with the sponsorship of his sister's friend who was a vice president of Standard Oil, a man who wanted to remain incognito and refused to meet the E.'s after they arrived in 1953.

Crossing the Atlantic by ship, they were met in America by their brother-in-law, who drove them to his home in Parma, Ohio (a suburb of Cleveland). Johanna and Peter moved in with his sister and brother-in-law and Peter looked for a job. Given the recession of 1953, jobs were difficult to find. Eventually Peter was able to get a job reading blueprints at a steel partition company. Although he disliked the job, Peter continued to work there for two years while also taking courses in English and accounting.

Peter's ambition had always been to become a writer, and when he saw an advertisement for a writer in a local newspaper, he applied. Although Mr. Baker, the owner of the company that had placed the ad, a building materials firm with a mail order business, was not eager to hire a German immigrant who had no work experience in the field, Peter was able to convince him otherwise by writing an excellent test letter.

Peter made a career. After six years on the job, he was promoted to vice president for marketing, and eventually managed the export department. In charge of recruiting customers, Peter traveled widely, including to the Middle East. Johanna often accompanied him on his travels and sometimes would use the opportunity to visit her parents in Germany. Peter retired in 1988.

Over the years the E.'s and Bakers became good friends, attending each other's weddings and bar mitzvahs. Johanna, who was trained as a professional musician, ended up playing the violin for the Akron symphony. She retired at age sixty-two, but continued to play in churches.

The E.'s became American citizens in 1958. They continue to speak German with one another, but they are not involved in the German American community. They do not have surviving close family in Germany.[48]

Siegfried (Sig) K. was released from Camp Wings and returned to Germany in March 1946. Before Sig was drafted into the *Arbeitsdienst* and later the Wehrmacht, he had wanted to study agriculture and he had worked briefly on a farm in Pomerania. On his return he had changed his mind and now wanted to study veterinary medicine. His American certificates were recognized by the German authorities and he was able to complete a *Fachabitur*. But Sig's plans unraveled when he was unable to get a *Studienplatz* (a slot to study) at the University of Munich. At the time the limited positions were allocated on the bases of a priority list, starting with former concentration camp inmates, then anti–Nazis, then regular enlisted men, and then officers. Given that Sig had been an officer, he would have had to wait several years for a *Studienplatz*.

His dream for a university education put on hold, Sig took a temporary job in a *Sauerkrautfabrik* (sauerkraut factory) in Marktredwitz, 50 kilometers East of Bayreuth. He traveled to Stuttgart to visit a friend and to check out job possibilities there. He was able to get a job at the Rosenthal ceramics factory, where his friend's father worked. He worked at Rosenthal as a ceramic engineer for two years and married Beate.

In 1950 Sig changed jobs to work at a *Hochspannungswerk* (high voltage electricity company). Seven years later he took a job as *Betriebsleiter* (manager) in another firm, only to change jobs again three years later to work for a company that built factories in China. He worked there until 1963.

Unlike my other respondents, Sig did not deliberately immigrate. He came to the United States in 1968, as the North American representative of a ceramics company located in East Liverpool, Ohio. He worked there until 1975 when he started his own company to make pottery, primarily beer mugs (*Bierkrüge*). He also had a company that built agricultural machines to clean out manure from stables. He sold both companies when he turned sixty-five in 1988.

After two weeks of retirement Sig was "totally bored." He decided to go to China to export coffee cups that he decorated in Ohio. Working for Ceramic Corporation of America, he made about fifteen to sixteen trips to China between 1989 and 1993. In 1992 he also briefly worked for the *Treuhand*[49] to help privatize an East German lubrication company (he was interested in administration, not technology) which was bought by a West German investor. During this time he had two jobs and traveled frequently China and Germany.

At the time of the interview, Sig told me he had patents in lubrication and other interests. He had sold his house in Bonn and has lived more or less permanently in Sebring since 1976. Sig does not belong to German American organizations, but was a member of the Rotary Club. Considering himself a German businessman, Sig said, "As a German businessman you find first-class conditions in America."

Sig's move to the United States was primarily a business decision, and unlike my other respondents he never became an American citizen. His wife moved with him, but his children remained in Germany. Sig's POW experience seems to have had little or no impact on his return to the United States.

Summary and Analysis

My respondents returned to what was left of Germany between 1945 and 1950. The majority arrived between 1946 and 1948. While most were glad to return and find their families alive, the fact that they had spent between one and three and a half years on American soil, where they had been generally well treated and well fed, likely shaped their subjective experiences of the economic conditions they encountered as particularly difficult and negative. The contrast between life as a POW on American soil and life in Germany during the first two to three years after the war was perhaps more pronounced for the men who returned directly, arriving between 1945 and 1946, a time when there seemed little hope for a better future. Although 1947, which was marked by severe food shortages, turned out to be particularly difficult, the currency reform of 1948 and the founding of the Federal Republic provided some new hope for the population.

Independent of the timing of their return, the specific personal and socioeconomic conditions they found on their return differed considerably. The twenty-two respondents whose prewar homes were located in the Western occupation zones and Berlin, and the Austrian citizen, were able to return to their hometowns. Except for Josef G. whose hometown, Saarbrücken, was in the French zone, their homes were in the American and British zones.)[50] The physical destruction they found varied and was most pronounced in the large cities. Although family members had perished in the war, most were able to reconnect with their surviving families.

Although their hometowns (Munich and Kiel respectively) had suffered substantial damage, Peter E. and Heino E. were lucky. They found their prewar homes still standing and their families living. While Johannes S.'s home had been totally destroyed and his father had died before the end of the war, he was able to reunite with his mother in Bremen. Although Alfred M.'s parents had perished during the war, he was able to find refuge and lodging with his sister in Berlin. The immediate families of Josef G., Johannes G., Otto L. and Hermann B. had survived the war and its aftermath. The men from smaller towns (Rupert M., Ludwig N., Gerhard H., Harry H., and Henry K.) found that their hometowns had suffered relatively little physical destruction and that their immediate families (parents, one parent or spouses) had survived the war.

The respondents who had completed their education before joining the Wehrmacht were able to find work in their previous occupations. Hermann B. found employment as a printer in Stuttgart; Johann G. was able to find a job in the same electric company he had worked for before he was drafted; Otto L. found work on a farm raising small animals.

Several respondents who had not completed their education sought additional education and training. Two men, Harry H. and Josef G., who had completed the *Abitur* were able to enroll in medical school. Gerhard H. briefly studied languages but left school after a year. Rupert M. enrolled in interpreter school; Henry R. studied photography; Rudolf T. and Heinrich T. completed apprenticeships as bricklayers; Ludwig N. completed an apprenticeship as a mechanic. Siegfried K. was unable to get a *Studienplatz*, and ended up working as a ceramics maker.

Seven respondents, all of whom had learned English during their captivity, were able to find employment with British or American occupation forces. Their jobs ranged from unskilled work in hospitals and kitchens and driving a truck to skilled work as bookkeepers, liaison workers between the occupation forces and German authorities, policemen, interpreters, translators and accountants. Although it is impossible to assess their English language skills at the time and the role these might have played in their ability to get unskilled jobs, English skills were crucial for the more skilled jobs as interpreters, translators and liaison workers.

Wolf-Dieter Z. briefly worked for the American Occupation forces in Salzburg before joining his American wife in the United States, and Horst von O. worked as a liaison with the United States military government in Berlin. Alfred M. found work as a swim instructor and truck driver for the British occupation forces in Berlin, while Johannes S. found work with the Americans, first at the yacht club and later as a liaison in the transportation section in Bremen. Peter E. worked as a liaison between the occupation forces and the German population in Munich. Rudolf T. worked as an interpreter for the American forces in Giessen. After completing interpreter school, Rupert M. found employment in the American hospital in Wiesbaden.

The nine men from the eastern territories and the two men whose prewar homes were in the Soviet occupation zone were released in the American and British zones (as of 1947 a shared zone between the U.S. and Britain). Except for Heinz R. and Erwin H., the men from the eastern territories had spent additional time in forced labor in England or France and did not return to Germany until 1947 or 1948.

Most were able to reunite with members of their families who had fled to the West (Gunther K., Hermann F., Heinrich T. and Oskar S.). For example, Heinz R., who worked for the American Occupation Forces in Munich, was able to reunite with his wife and child who had been stranded in the Soviet occupation zone, with the help of his American employer. Two men found refuge with "friends" or relatives in the West — Horst U., Ernst F. After a brief stay with relatives in Munich, Ernst F. was able to join his parents, who were now living in East Berlin. Kurt P., whose parents had perished during the war, was able to join his fiancée in the West. Rudolf T. and Willie S., who did not have relatives or friends in the West, did not know where to turn. While Rudolf eventually discovered that his mother and sister had fled to Bavaria and briefly joined them there, seeking employment, Willie S. ended up in the Soviet occupation zone.

Except for Kurt P., who was able to find employment in his prewar occupation as a stonemason, the men from the eastern territories struggled to make a living. Gunther K., Oskar S., and Hermann F. worked in several unskilled jobs. Although Ernst F. was able to get training as a photographer, he had difficulties finding a secure position after graduation. After working in several unskilled jobs and some involvement in the black market, Rudolf T. found employment as an interpreter with the American occupation forces in Giessen. Erwin H. worked for the Americans in Babenhausen and Stuttgart.

The prewar homes of two respondents were now located in the Soviet occupation zone. Martin F. whose father had died during the war and whose mother now lived in Chemnitz, found refuge with an uncle in the West. As a trained engineer he did not have much trouble finding employment. Hans W.'s mother had fled her native Leipzig and now lived with her brother in Stuttgart, where Hans was able to join her and find employment as an interpreter with the Länderrat.

The objective push factors, destruction of home and family and job problems, were clearly magnified for the men from the eastern provinces of Silesia and Pomerania. Their surviving families had been scattered in the four occupation zones and they were now refugees in parts of Germany with which they were unfamiliar. In addition to their geographic displacement, most had not completed their education and they often encountered difficulties in finding secure employment.

Like their compatriots and thousands of German immigrants in the past, my respondents were drawn to the United States by the country's perceived high standard of living and greater perceived opportunity, an essential part of "the American way of life." While the images of America as the *Land der Unbegrenzten Möglichkeiten* (country of unlimited opportunities), knowledge of the country of wealth, modernity, technical knowhow and unbridled consumerism (Freund 2004, 98) was well ingrained among the German population. However, these images were based on secondhand information, on films, books and stories they had heard or read. In short, "Germans did not know about everyday life in America" (Freund 2004, 100; Rytlewski and Opp de Hipt 1987).

In contrast to their compatriots, my respondents had been able to observe and even participate in some aspects of American everyday life. To be sure, what they observed was a narrow slice of that life; it was mostly rural and small-town life. They had contacts and interactions with a variety of Americans from different occupations, farmers and their families, gas station owners, painters, GIs, guards, workers and supervisors in warehouses, physicians, laboratory workers and nurses, secretaries and other office workers, and military officers. For my respondents who had never met an American before, the personal contacts with Americans left an indelible imprint on their minds. With the exception of two men who reported poor treatment by farmers they worked for, my respondents were most taken by the people they encountered, especially their "kindness" and "friendliness."[51] Several respondents fondly recounted particular incidents of special treatment and encounters. Ernst F. was "sitting among GIs" waiting to be fitted for new glasses in New Mexico; Willie S. accompanied an officer to Chicago, where they ate in a German restaurant; Horst U. was taken to a picnic in Florida; Martin F. visited a circus; Henry R. learned to play Ping-Pong from Mr. Lykins; Heinz R. was taken fishing by his civilian employer. These are hardly the kinds of stories and experiences we associate with prisoners of war.

The interviews reveal considerable differences in the way the prisoner of war experience shaped their paths to immigration. Several respondents indicated that they had considered immigrating to the United States while they were still in captivity, or as soon as they returned to Germany. Finding only limited opportunities in their home country, others took a more gradual, and in some cases opportunistic, approach. At the same time, the strength of the desire to return to the United States was not necessarily correlated with the timing of their immigration. Several respondents who had been eager to immigrate had difficulties in securing the necessary visa.

As discussed above, until 1952 it was difficult to obtain a visa for the United States, as the available quota was filled with displaced persons and relatives of American citizens, and the majority of my respondents immigrated after 1951. This is hardly surprising, given prevailing American immigration policy, which gave preference to Displaced Persons and relatives of American citizens. Nonetheless, eight respondents were able to immigrate before 1952. Five of these early immigrants were sponsored by relatives, including the two men who were married to American women. Yet, among this group were two respondents (Alfred M., and Otto L.) who were sponsored by Americans whom they had befriended during their time as POWs, and one man (Johannes S.) who was sponsored by an American civilian member of the occupation forces whom he worked for after returning to Germany.

The majority of my respondents, 19 men, immigrated between 1952 and 1956, a four-year period when German immigration to the United States reached a postwar high. Among this group were several men who had been very eager to immigrate (Johannes G., Ernst F. and Horst U.), but whose quests for a visa were delayed by personal circumstances (Johannes G.) and difficulties of finding a sponsor (Ernst F. and Horst U). Four men opted to immigrate to Canada.

While the nine men from the eastern provinces were attracted by their previous American experience, as a group they experienced more significant push factors than the men who had been able to return to their prewar homes. After having spent several years in American captivity, and having few or no ties in western Germany, they saw America as "a second home," a place where they could begin a new life.

Although three respondents (Johann G., Heinz R., and Hans W.) expressed the firm conviction that they would not have considered immigrating to the United States had they not been prisoners of war, in most cases it is impossible to determine the precise role played by their captivity, or to disregard the pressures emanating from the economic and social conditions they found upon their return to Germany, and their particular personal and family circumstances.

4

Pathways to Immigration:
From German Prisoner of War
to American Citizen

Emigrants never represent a mirror image of a country's resident population. This was certainly the case for the thousands of individuals and families who were able to leave Germany in the fifteen years following the Second World War. Although they included single people, married couples and families with children, refugees and non-refugees, young as well as older people, members of diverse social strata, occupations and religions, city dwellers and rural populations, three relatively homogeneous categories dominated the exodus: young unmarried men and women; older families of expellees; and young non-refugee couples and families (Freund 2004, 44).[1]

German statistics on emigration to North America (the United States and Canada) available for the years 1953 and 1954 provide some information concerning the demographic and socioeconomic characteristics of German emigrants (Freund 2004, 398–403). They indicate that the age cohort between sixteen and forty-four was disproportionally represented among German emigrants; that two thirds of emigrants were families with children; and that refugees and expellees from east of the Oder Neisse Line and Eastern Europe, who made up nineteen percent of the resident population in West Germany, made up thirty-three percent of all emigrants. Furthermore, emigrants had lived predominantly in four states (Bavaria, Baden-Württemberg, Lower Saxony, and North-Rhine Westphalia), as well as the city-states of Bremen, Hamburg and Berlin.[2]

Information concerning the labor force status and occupation of German emigrants available for the years between 1953 and 1955 indicates that the majority of male emigrants were in the labor force and that their occupations were concentrated in the industrial/crafts sector (forty-five percent), including bricklayers, electricians, and metalworkers, followed by trade and restaurant occupations (seventeen percent), agriculture and animal husbandry (six percent) and technical occupations (three percent) (Freund 2004, 398–403). There are no data for professionals.

The former prisoners of war whom I interviewed for this study were born between 1916 and 1926, with the majority born in the early to mid-1920s. Most had been in their late teens and early twenties when they became prisoners of war on American soil and in their early and mid-twenties when they finally returned to Germany. Although five of the older respondents were married at the time of their captivity, the majority of the men were single. Except for three men who were single when they immigrated, all married shortly after their return to Germany and most had children before they immigrated.

Except for two men from east of the Oder Neisse Line who immigrated with their large extended families, my respondents were part of the stream of young couples and young families with children who were leaving Germany behind. As was the case for all German emigrants, former POWs hailing from east of the Oder Neisse Line were somewhat overrepresented among my respondents (i.e., thirty percent originally hailed from east of the Oder Neisse Line).

My respondents' educational and occupational backgrounds were diverse. As was the case for all German male emigrants at the time, almost half of the men (fourteen men, 42 percent) who had finished their education before their captivity or after returning to Germany had worked in the industrial and craft sector. My respondents also included two men with a strong agricultural background, two men with degrees in photography, two men in technical occupations, one man in business and five professional men (15 percent). With the possible exception of the professionals, the occupational distribution of my respondents roughly reflects that of all German emigrants at the time.

Like their compatriots, my respondents had to overcome the hurdles presented by exit visas, shortages of available overseas transportation, and, most important, American immigration policies. By the time immigration became possible for ordinary Germans, including former members of the Wehrmacht, exit restrictions had been lifted. Yet, given prevailing American immigration policies, the chances of getting a visa remained rather slim until 1952. Thus, while a total of 219,742 "Germans" immigrated to the United States between 1946 and 1950, only 95,118 (forty-three percent) were German citizens. The majority of immigrants were displaced persons who had come to Germany during the war, either voluntarily or forced, from the occupied territories of eastern and southeastern Europe. Between 1951 and 1955 the number of "German immigrants" increased to 282,014. Among them were 166,495 (fifty-nine percent) German citizens. In the following five years (1956 through 1960) the proportion of German citizens was ninety-one percent.[3]

Among the former POWs I interviewed for this study were eight men (and their families) who were able to immigrate between 1947 and 1951. All had returned directly to Germany, bypassing forced labor in England or France, and all were originally from what became the American or British occupation zones.

In addition to two men who were married to American women (Horst O. and Wolf-Dieter Z.), and were able to immigrate outside the quota system, these "early immigrants" included six men (Hermann B., Hans W., Alfred M., Hermann K., Otto L., and Erwin H.) who benefited from readily available sponsors, a fact that allowed them to pursue their quest for immigration without delay. For example, Hans W. and Hermann B. reported that they went to the American consulate in Stuttgart as soon as they heard that President Truman had opened immigration for ordinary Germans, and both men had relatives willing to sponsor them. They were probably among the first to apply and perhaps they were also lucky. Yet without access to the individual immigration files of my respondents it is impossible to determine the decision making process by consular officials in each case.

From Prisoner of War to Immigrant and American Citizen

The pathways to immigration taken by the former POWs reveal the complex and often circuitous processes involved in immigration. The interviews indicate that in terms of their demographic, social, and geographic characteristics, my respondents did not differ markedly from other German immigrants. They were among the thousands of young couples and families who sought a new life in the United States and like their compatriots, most immigrated between 1952 and 1956 when the pressure on the quota system had eased and sponsorship criteria were relaxed to include non-relatives.

As was the case for their compatriots, economic and occupational factors in Germany — push factors, economic insecurity, poor occupational outlook and fear of war — clearly played some, albeit perhaps a varying, role in their quest to return to the country of their captivity: a place where they had been safe, but also a place that promised better opportunities than those they perceived in Germany. Like their compatriots they were attracted to the United States as the land of opportunity and wealth, a place where they could make a living (pull factors). At the same time, the interviews suggest that their previous sojourn on American soil, their sense that they "knew the country," that they had been able "to observe the difference between Germany and the United States," that they had been much impressed by "the friendliness and generosity of the American people," and that they knew the language, added an important subjective and experiential dimension to their desire to return and a measure of confidence that they could begin a new life in the country of their previous captivity. While it is difficult to assess the precise role of these experiential factors in all cases, they were clearly important considerations for many of my respondents.[4]

Independent of the strength of their desire to return, all respondents confronted the challenges posed to the vast majority of German immigrants in obtaining a visa. Their pathways to getting a visa were diverse. As was the case for their compatriots, they included marriage, networks of American relatives, church sponsorship and *Etappenmigration* (step-by-step immigration) via Canada. For ten of my respondents (almost one third of my sample), captivity on American soil opened an additional pathway, one that was not available to their compatriots: the American networks of their captivity.

Marriage to an American Citizen

As discussed in the previous chapter, marriage to an American citizen represented the easiest and most reliable pathway to getting a visa, and this was particularly the case in the first four years after the war. Three respondents were able to immigrate on the "marriage pathway." Wolf-Dieter Z., who had been married to an American woman before he became a POW, was able to join his wife in 1947. Horst von O., who married his American wife after his return from captivity, in 1947, was able to immigrate one year later. Josef G., who met and married his American wife several years after the war, immigrated in 1958.[5] All three men were also highly educated professionals.

NETWORKS OF AMERICAN RELATIVES

American relatives willing and able to serve as sponsors represented the second most direct and promising avenue towards securing an American visa before 1952. Nine respondents were able to return to the United States with the help of their American relatives. In eight cases these were aunts or uncles of the respondent or his wife who had immigrated after the First World War. One man, Erwin H., was sponsored by his new American brother-in-law after his sister married an American soldier. Four of the nine men (Hermann B., Hans W. and Hermann K., Erwin H.) were able to secure the much-coveted visa before 1952; the other five arrived between 1952 and 1954. Except for Hermann F. and Erwin H., who hailed from Silesia, most were original residents of what had become the Federal Republic of Germany.

Hermann B., Hans W. and Erwin H. are good examples of this group. Hermann immigrated in 1949, three years after he returned to Germany and married Katie. Although Hermann found a job in his occupation as a printer, he felt that "things were very bad" in Germany and he was eager to return to the United States. Having used his time as a POW to learn English, he regularly listened to American Forces Network radio in Stuttgart and was well informed about American immigration policy. Having secured sponsorship from Katie's uncle in Niles, Michigan, he immediately rushed to the American consulate when he heard that immigration was reopened for ordinary German citizens in 1948, and he was placed at the top of the list.

Like Hermann, Hans W. had been able to improve his English skills while at Fort Robinson, Nebraska, and he returned to Germany eager to immigrate. Although he had considerable contacts with Americans at Fort Robinson, Hans was sponsored by an aunt who lived in Portland, Maine. Working as an interpreter for the *Länderrat* in Stuttgart, Hans had daily contact with Americans and, like Hermann, he was well informed about American policy, allowing him to secure a visa in 1949. A former resident of Silesia, Erwin H. did not "feel at home" in West Germany. Unlike Hermann and Hans, Erwin did not have American relatives. Luck was on his side when his sister married an American soldier who was willing and able to sponsor his new brother-in-law.

CHURCH SPONSORSHIP

Church sponsorship represented a major pathway to immigration for refugees and expellees from the eastern provinces. Five men and their families who originally hailed from the lost German territories in the East immigrated with the help of church sponsorship; a sixth man (Erich K.), who originally hailed from Rumania, but whose family had been resettled in Germany in the 1940s, also immigrated with the help of church sponsorship. As a group these men and their families immigrated between 1952 and 1956, somewhat later than the men who were sponsored by relatives.

Horst U. and Ernst F. reported having had excellent experiences and personal contacts with Americans and both were eager to return, but they struggled to find sponsors. It was not until 1954 that both men were able to secure church sponsorship. Erich K. was able to get a visa with the help of the Lutheran World Service in 1952. Heinrich T. and Oskar S. married women who were part of large refugee families from the eastern provinces who were already in the process of immigrating, allowing them to be included in the sponsorship. Heinrich and Oskar arrived in 1952 and 1954 respectively.

THE CANADIAN ESCAPE HATCH

Although Canada opened its doors to German immigration somewhat later than the United States, Canadian labor shortages in the early 1950s made it relatively easy to obtain a visa for Canada, providing a popular alternative for many German emigrants (Freund, 453–55). Among my respondents were four men who immigrated first to Canada. All four were able to move to the United States a few years later. Gunther K. arrived in Canada in 1951 and moved to California in 1958; Robert M. arrived in Canada in 1954 and moved to California in 1964; Heinz R. immigrated to Canada in 1954 and was able to move to Wisconsin in 1958; and Elmar B. arrived in Canada in 1951 and was able to move to Michigan in 1958.

POW CONNECTIONS

Although most of my respondents reported having had some contact with Americans during their captivity, only six men (eighteen percent) were able to immigrate with the sponsorship of Americans they befriended during their captivity. Three additional men were sponsored by Americans they worked for after returning to Germany. Among this group was one man who returned to Germany with the promise of sponsorship, but whose friend did not qualify as a sponsor.

The life stories of the six men who were sponsored by Americans they befriended during their captivity represent a broad spectrum of backgrounds and experiences. They include three members of the Afrika Korps who arrived on American soil in 1943 and three men captured in Italy and Normandy who arrived in 1944 and 1945, including one man who was captured in him hometown shortly before V-E Day. Although their numbers are relatively small, they most clearly demonstrate the connections between their prisoner of war experience and their immigration. As such, their cases merit more detailed analysis.

The six men had been interned in a variety of camps in different parts of the country. While three spent most of their captivity working in one or two camps or military bases, the three others, who worked primarily in agriculture, were moved frequently from camp to camp, spending only a few weeks in each camp. Leaving American soil at different times, three men returned directly to Germany, arriving in 1945 and 46, while the others spent additional time in England, arriving one or two years later.

Johann G.'s case best illustrates the direct pathway from POW to sponsorship. Johann was unambiguous when he stated that he "decided to go back in 1945." Only twenty years old when he became a POW at the end of the war, Johann was among the last cohort of prisoners to be transported to America in 1945. Although he did not know English when he arrived on American soil, he took advantage of his unanticipated situation. With the help of a comrade, he taught himself English and was able to get a job as a cook on the train from his first camp in Arizona to Camp Preston, Idaho. Despite his relatively short time (six months) in Idaho, Johann's experiences were transformative. In charge of procuring food for the camp, Johann had considerable freedom. He drove a jeep (albeit accompanied by a guard) through the Idaho countryside and had repeated and sustained contact with several American civilians, most notably a gas station owner and a farmer. Coming from the densely populated industrial Ruhr area of Germany, Johann was enchanted with the majesty and beauty of the rural Idaho countryside and "all the wonderful people."

Released from American captivity in February 1946, Johann spent two more years in forced labor in England. He returned to his native Gelsenkirchen in May 1948, one month after the currency reform, at a time when the economic situation in Germany was starting to improve. As a trained electrician, Johann was able to get a job with the same electric company where he had trained before the war. Yet, although Johann's personal situation was comparatively good, he was determined to return to the United States, and immediately started immigration procedures. Mr. Moser, the farmer whom he had befriended in Idaho, served as his sponsor. While waiting for the visa, Johann met a young woman, Gisela, and they married. He had to postpone his immigration so that she could be included on the visa. He recalls having to "go through a lot of paperwork." When they finally received their visa in 1953, the G.'s were doing well economically. They owned a car and had been able to travel extensively in Europe. Although their prospects for making a comfortable living in Germany were good, Johann had made up his mind and "no one could have talked me out of it." With his young wife, Johann returned to Preston, the very place where he had been a POW.

Like Johann, Alfred M. returned to Germany with the promise of sponsorship from his American friend, George Hughes. Alfred had spent almost three years in captivity, and unlike Johann, who was in a small side camp, Alfred was held at Camp Algona, Iowa, a large base camp. Although Alfred did not work outside the camp, his work in the cold storage facility at Camp Algona allowed him to have regular contact with Hughes.

Alfred returned directly to Germany and his hometown, Berlin, in 1946. He was able to find housing with his sister, but he discovered that his parents had perished during the war. Thanks to his knowledge of English acquired in Algona, he was able to find a job with the British Occupation Forces, but things did not look good and he longed to return to the peaceful setting of rural Iowa. With the help of his friend's father-in-law, Shorty Greiman, Alfred and his new wife, Edith, were able to immigrate in 1949. Like Johann, Alfred returned to the town where he had been a prisoner of war.

Like Johann and Alfred, Heinz E. and Otto L. struck up friendships with Americans while working in their respective POW camps. Unlike the former two, whose friends were civilians, Heinz and Otto befriended military personnel. Heinz, who was interned at Camp Campbell where he worked in the laboratory, befriended an American military physician. Otto, who worked in the pigeon loft at Fort Benning, struck up a close friendship with an American GI. Both men returned to Germany with the promise of sponsorship from their American friends, a promise they kept.

Unlike Johann and Alfred, Heinz and Otto did not return to the places where they had been prisoners of war. Instead they first settled in the hometowns of their sponsors. This meant that Otto found himself in rural Utah, a place quite unfamiliar to a German immigrant from an urban area. In addition, upon his arrival, Otto learned that his friend had gone bankrupt, leaving Otto without a job. Heinz's early American experience was considerably more pleasant. His sponsor, Dr. Brown, was a native of Cincinnati, Ohio, a place of historic German immigrant settlement, and he provided Heinz with a place to live and arranged for a first job.

Willie S. and Kurt P. had been interned in several camps in the Midwest. Working in agriculture and related industries, both men befriended American farmers who offered to sponsor them after the war. While both men kept their word, allowing Willie and Kurt to immigrate to the United States, their immigration experiences were different. Willie's sponsors were genuinely helpful and welcoming, while Kurt's sponsors seemed to be out to exploit the young German immigrant and his wife as cheap labor. Both men first settled near the small towns in Wisconsin where they had worked in the fields and the canning industry during their time as prisoners of war.

Rupert M. returned to Germany with a promise of sponsorship from an American GI. he had befriended on the ship crossing the Atlantic. After returning to Germany, Rupert contacted his friend, only to find out that the latter did not qualify as a sponsor. With his plan of returning to the United States as soon as possible on hold, Rupert enrolled in interpreter school to perfect the English he had learned during his POW time. After graduating, Rupert was able to use his English and typing skills to get a job with the American hospital in Wiesbaden. It is there that he met and befriended a young American physician, Dr. Ingraham, who offered to sponsor Rupert and his family. After arriving in the United States, they settled in Dr. Ingraham's hometown, Greenfield, Massachusetts.

Like Rupert, Johannes S. and Rudolf T. were sponsored by American civilians they befriended while working for the occupation forces after returning to Germany. While Rudolf made his way to Iowa, the home state of his sponsor, Johannes headed for Florida, a place he remembered fondly from his time as POW.

While the connection between the POW experience and their immigration is less tangible and more indirect for the six men sponsored by Americans they met after their return to Germany, the English skills they learned or perfected during their captivity helped them gain employment with American forces, putting them in daily contact with Americans and thus with potential sponsors.[6] While Heino E.'s pathway to immigration can be traced to his captivity on American soil, Heino's sponsor was not an American but a former POW comrade who had been able to immigrate relatively soon after the war and who had promised to sponsor his friend. When Heino immigrated he settled in his friend's adopted hometown, Minneapolis.

EMPLOYMENT AND PROFESSIONAL

Four respondents do not easily fit into these major categories. Siegfried K. immigrated late, in 1968. As a businessman who had been engaged in several business ventures in Germany and abroad, Sig was looking for new business opportunities in the United States. He is the only respondent who did not become an American citizen.

Heinz F., who immigrated in 1961, took advantage of an opportunity that presented itself when his wife was offered a job as a cook in California. Gerhard H. moved to the United States in 1953 and he continued to work for his American employer. Although Peter E. had been eager to return to the United States, he did not pursue immigration as his wife had wanted to stay in Germany. It was only when his sister married a GI. and asked her brother and sister-in-law to join her that Peter could convince Johanna to immigrate in 1953.

Life in the United States

As was the case for most German immigrants at the time, the majority of the returning POWs settled in or near the home cities and towns of their sponsors (Freund 2004, 481). Their destinations included traditional areas of German settlement in the Midwest — Chicago, Detroit, Michigan, Wisconsin, Iowa, Minnesota and Ohio. Three men settled in the New York area, five ended up in western states (California, Utah, Idaho, and Oregon) and two headed south to Florida and Virginia respectively.

While several men struggled initially to find meaningful and permanent work, others hit the ground running. This was particularly the case for the men who had completed an apprenticeship or profession in Germany: Martin F., Kurt P., Hermann B., Wolf-Dieter Z., Horst von O., Josef G., Harry H., Johann G., and Siegfried K.

Four men took advantage of available educational and professional opportunities in the United States. Although Heino E. initially struggled in a variety of temporary jobs, he was able to go back to school, eventually earning a master's degree in social work. With his second wife, Jean, Heino founded a successful international adoption agency. Rudolf T., whose first job in the United States was as a doorman at a hotel in Des Moines, was able to go to college and eventually earn a master's degree in history which enabled him to teach European history at a local college. After some initial struggles, Hans W. was able to go to college and on to medical school to become a practicing osteopathic physician. Like Hans, Erwin H. started out working in several unskilled jobs before he went to college and on to medical school. Neither Hans nor Erwin had planned a career in medicine.

Accidental meetings with Americans provided the impetus and encouragement for their career decisions.

Six respondents had successful careers in business. Rupert M., Kurt P., Oskar S., Heinz E. and Henry R. started their own small businesses after first working for employers. Siegfried K. was involved in several business ventures. All became successful members of a broad American middle class, and several men were able to have careers beyond those they were likely to have had in Germany.

Except for the men who immigrated first to Canada, moving to the United States a few years later, most of my respondents remained in the area of their initial settlement until their retirement. Only three men moved to other states during their professional lives. Heino E. moved from Minneapolis to Texas to escape the Minnesota winters; Heinz E. moved from Cincinnati to Florida to start a flower business; and Johannes S. moved frequently between several states in pursuit of his career in the insurance business. Like other Americans of their generation, several men who had settled in the Midwest moved to Florida or North Carolina after they retired: Horst U., Hermann B., Heinz E., Rupert M., and Martin F.

In many ways my respondents represent what used to be considered the ideal, traditional immigrant, individuals and families who left their country of origin with the intention of permanent settlement and becoming citizens of their adopted country. Only one man, Heino E., told me that he had briefly considered returning to Germany after he was divorced. Except for Siegfried K., who never became an American citizen, my respondents became American citizens as soon as legally possible, or soon thereafter. Most came to America and did not look back. Several men even made a conscious decision to speak English at home, and in most cases their children, including those born in Germany, lost their ability to speak the language of their parents.

Although they tried to acculturate quickly to their new country, most also kept some connections with their home country. They participated, albeit to varying degrees, in the German American community, reading German American newspapers, participating in German American organizations and attending local German cultural events, in particular the Oktoberfest. Most returned to Germany for several visits, and three respondents (Heinz. E., Rupert M., and Horst U.) also acted as sponsors for parents or brothers and sisters.

The men I interviewed did not attempt to hide the fact that they had once served in "Hitler's Army."[7] Three men, all members of the Afrika Korps, even proudly displayed their Wehrmacht insignia and medals in their home offices. Almost all respondents have visited their former camps and/or attended camp reunions, and several men have maintained contacts with the families they had befriended during their POW time (Ernst F., Willie S. Hans M., and Rupert M.). Others (Ernst F., Hans W., Kurt P., and Gerhard H.) regularly give informal talks about their experiences to high school and college students and civic groups.

Two men, Kurt P. and Gunther K. have so well assimilated that they have been recognized as patriotic Americans by their former enemies. Kurt has helped build, often at or below cost, several war memorials around Wisconsin. When the Veterans Memorial Monument at Forest Hill Cemetery was vandalized in 1986, Kurt volunteered to restore it. In 2007, when officials decided to memorialize an air force pilot who had sacrificed his life by crashing his disabled jet into Lake Monona, Kurt took on the job. Gunther K. received a certificate of appreciation from the Veterans of Foreign Wars of the United States. Harry H., who was drafted, ended up serving a second time, this time in the U.S. Army.[8]

5

Prisoners of War
and International Migration

In the context of more recent wars in Korea and Vietnam and the horrors of Guantánamo and Abu Ghraib, the events depicted in this book seem almost quaint, belonging to a different time and place. Yet, while they may appear unusual, they are not unique.

Although their numbers were considerably smaller, some of the 30,000 German POWs held in Canada also returned after the war. Of the 400,000 German POWs in Britain one year after the end of World War II, some 24,000 took advantage of an offer to remain as "civilian workers" after 1948.[1] Of these, an unknown number remained permanently, often marrying British women and becoming British citizens (Weber-Newth and Steinert 2006).[2] Similarly, of the 10,000 German former POWs who volunteered to stay in France as civilian workers after 1948, an unknown number remained permanently, most taking French citizenship and marrying French women.[3]

While students of international migration have recognized that war and the effects of war are major forces in international migration, they have focused primarily on civilian populations—refugees, asylum seekers, and displaced persons—not on combatants and more specifically prisoners of war. Yet, such migrations represent significant temporary population movements and, like all population movements, they engender some social contacts between migrants and the resident population, between enemy soldiers and civilians.

As our images of prisoners of war are increasingly dominated by the extreme isolation imposed on the prisoners at Guantánamo and Abu Ghraib, or the harsh treatment and isolation suffered by American POWs in Korea and Vietnam, it is important to remember that prisoners of war are not necessarily isolated from their surroundings. The degree of isolation varies considerably. The circumstances that defined the internment of German and Italian prisoners of war in the United States and Canada are examples of comparatively low degrees of isolation, whereas Guantánamo represents almost complete isolation.

Although this case study focuses on a relatively narrow slice of the prisoner of war experience — the postwar immigration of former prisoners to the country of their captivity — it touches on several issues that have informed current debates and perspectives on transnational migration: forced migration and forced labor, temporary labor and permanent settlement, networks and migration, tourism and return migration, and host country immigration policies and immigration control.

Prisoners of War, Forced Migration and Forced Labor

Forced migration, including refugee flows, asylum seekers and internal displacement of civilian populations, has accompanied modern warfare in the twentieth and twenty-first century and it has continued to grow in significance in the context of the disintegration of the former Soviet Union and Yugoslavia and ongoing wars in the Middle East, Africa and elsewhere (Gatrell 2007).[4] Although the migration and captivity of enemy soldiers on foreign soil represents a form of forced migration, it has received no attention in the migration literature.

There are multiple reasons for this omission. Compared to the increasingly massive and ongoing displacement of civilian populations and the social and political conflicts and human suffering they engender, the forced migration of prisoners of war lacks contemporary urgency and their overall numbers are considerably smaller.[5] In addition, the forced migration of enemy soldiers is considered an aspect of the "normal" operation of warfare. In the twentieth century it was sanctioned and regulated by international law, and it is presumed to be of temporary duration, as prisoners of war are to be returned to their home countries after the end of war.

This was certainly the case for the subjects of this study. As we have seen, the 1929 Geneva Convention on the Treatment of Prisoners of War legitimized the capture, transport and imprisonment of defeated enemy forces and outlined the legal conditions that defined their general treatment and employment. Most important, perhaps, the convention specified the temporary nature of migration and captivity, that prisoners of war were to be returned to their home countries as soon as possible after the war had ended.

Yet, as we have seen, this was not the case for most of the German POWs held in the United States.[6] Many remained on American soil for more than a year after the war had ended and even then many did not return directly to Germany, but spent between one and two years as forced labor in Britain and France. Although the conditions of their work were legally circumscribed by the Geneva Convention, most POWs were required to work (excluding officers and those too weak or sick) and they continued to work for their captors after the war was over. This represents a form of temporary forced labor.

Temporary Labor and Permanent Settlement

It has become a virtual truism that temporary labor programs have unintended consequences: they tend to become permanent.[7] Although the Provost Marshal General's Office was reluctant to give in to urgent demands by the War Manpower Commission to put their "Nazi" prisoners to work, once put in place, the work program grew rapidly and took on a life of its own. Functioning much like a temporary labor program, the POW labor program displayed the well-known tendency to become more permanent. Yet all POWs were returned by July 1946 to Europe, despite considerable pressures from growers who wanted to keep this source of temporary labor beyond the original legally prescribed time period, attempts by relatives to sponsor individual POWs to remain in the United States as permanent immigrants, and their own interests in remaining. In short, despite the pressures from employers and other interested parties, unlike other temporary labor programs, the POW labor program ultimately remained temporary. Responses to inquiries from employers and relatives who wanted to sponsor a POW to remain in the United States were met with the assertion that this would be against the Geneva Convention. At the same time, almost half of German POWs held on American soil ended up serving additional time as forced labor in Great Britain or France, representing a clear infraction of the Geneva Convention. The prisoners were renamed "disarmed enemy forces," a term reminiscent of the now familiar "enemy combatants" applied to the prisoners at Guantánamo.[8]

Why did the United States not permit some of its German POWs to remain after the war as was the case for Britain and France and why did it agree to send half of the men to serve additional time as forced labor in France and Britain, instead of returning them to Germany at the earliest time possible? The answers to these questions are complex and they involve American domestic considerations, poor social and economic conditions in Germany, and international and bilateral agreements made with the Allies before the end of the war.

On the domestic front, returning all POWs to Europe helped placate U.S. veterans organizations, patriotic organizations and perhaps most important, trade unions, which had long opposed the employment of POWs, fearing that this would undermine the wages of American workers. Their fears had been partially recognized when the Provost Marshal General's agreement with the War Manpower Commission stated that employers of POW labor had to pay the going wage rate for the labor requested and that POWs were predominantly employed in agriculture and related industries where unions were weak or nonexistent, and where native-born workers were difficult to find at a time of war. However, several thousand POWs also worked on railroad construction, foundries, open pit mines, and in meatpacking where unions were stronger. Indeed, during the war, the employment of POWs generated some conflicts in meatpacking, railroads and forestry and pulpwood (Krammer 1991, 94–96; Thompson 2008, 98–101; Springer 2010, 157–61). Not surprisingly, labor leaders were at the forefront of the American public demanding an immediate return of prisoners to Europe (Krammer 1991, 232). The continued open-ended employment of former POWs would only have fueled to an already contentious issue.

In addition, the former POWs would most certainly have provided an unwelcome competition for returning GIs who would flood the labor market and hardly needed competition from their former enemies. Unlike the other major form of agricultural labor during the Second World War, Mexican braceros, the vast majority of German POWs were not farm workers, but more or less skilled craftsmen and industrial workers. Had they had been permitted to stay as workers, they would not likely have remained in the menial jobs they had as prisoners of war.

Additional insight into this question can be gained by comparing the prisoner of war labor program with the bracero program, the bilateral agreement between the United States and Mexico concluded in 1942 that brought temporary Mexican workers to the United States and is largely credited for the origins of today's immigration from Mexico, both legal and undocumented (Heisler, B. 2007). Although billed as a strictly temporary labor program to be discontinued after the war ended, giving in to pressures from agricultural interest, the bracero program was extended several times.

In refusing to give in to the demands made by employers and individuals to allow some prisoners of war to remain in the United States, President Truman gave two reasons, one referring to labor market and economic concerns, the other to legal concerns. The former, used primarily when responding to pressure from agricultural interests, argued that extensions were not necessary and could not be justified in view of the fact that returning veterans would now be available to fill the jobs vacated by returning prisoners of war. The latter, used primarily when responding to individual inquiries by employers and relatives or POWs, referred to the Geneva Convention's mandate to repatriate prisoners as soon as possible after the war (Lewis and Mewha 1955, 173).[9]

Although the economic argument was also made when the American government sought to discontinue the bracero program, this "emergency labor program" was renewed several times until it was finally discontinued in 1964, almost twenty years after the end of the war. In their 99th meeting in July 1945, the War Manpower Commission's Labor Policy Management Committee noted that the War Department "will return to Europe at earliest practicable moment all German and Italian POWs" and instructed the discontinuance "of the uses of PWs in contract employment as soon as possible." The same minutes also noted that "arrangements were being made to cease further importation of Mexicans."[10] In the closing weeks of the war it appeared that the bracero program would indeed pass into history (Garcia y Griego 1981) and the State Department notified Mexico in November 1946 that it wanted to terminate the bracero program. In this case the fierce lobbying efforts by agricultural employers and businesses proved successful in insuring the continued recruitment and employment of Mexican braceros long beyond its original time frame (Galarza 1964, 48).

In light of the bracero decision, the economic argument not to permit some German POWs to remain in the United States hardly seems convincing. On the surface, the legal argument that the Geneva Convention mandated the return of prisoners appears to be on more solid ground. During the war, the United States had adhered rather closely to the rules of the convention and the government frequently referred to these rules to rebut accusations that prisoners were being coddled. Yet, once the war had ended and American prisoners in German hands had been freed, the convention ceased to be a prime concern and the American government began to interpret its rules more loosely.[11]

According to Article 75 of the Geneva Convention, "Repatriation of prisoners shall be effected with the least possible delay after the conclusion of peace." The fact that hostilities between the United States and Germany ended with the capitulation of the Wehrmacht on May 8, 1945, and no peace treaty had been signed served as a convenient legal excuse to delay the repatriation of German prisoners of war (Jung 1972, 241), extending the stay of many prisoners who were needed for continued labor in agriculture, lumber and pulpwood and certain military hospitals for up to an additional year after Germany's capitulation. In addition, the American Military Government in Germany warned that a rapid and immediate repatriation of "several hundred thousand combat veterans arriving in the newly-occupied enemy territory" (cited in Krammer 1991, 233) could only contribute to the precarious social and economic conditions in postwar Germany.

Notwithstanding these delays, the last German prisoners of war left American soil in July 1946.[12] From the point of view of the American population, which knew only that the prisoners had left American soil, the Geneva Convention ultimately served as a solid and for the most part convincing legitimation for resisting long-term pressures from employers or American relatives to allow some prisoners to remain in the United States.[13]

Yet, as we have seen, for almost half of the German POWs held on American soil, release from American captivity and return to Europe did not mean freedom, but an additional period of forced labor in France or England, a condition that was not in keeping with the Geneva Convention. The groundwork supporting the questionable decision to hand over to the Allies German prisoners kept on American soil was laid at the Yalta Conference in February 1945, when President Roosevelt inserted a mention into the final protocol that German labor should be used as labor reparations for the reconstruction of a war-devastated Europe (Jung 1972, 241). In addition, the French provisional government had sent a request for German POW labor to General Eisenhower's Allied military headquarters as early as September 1944, and an agreement signed on May 26, 1945, provided that a total of 1,750,000 German prisoners under American control were to be turned over to the French at the end of the war. While most of the men were from among the millions of captives held in Europe, their numbers were supplemented with 55,000 prisoners from America. British claims to some 130,000 "British-owned" German POWs held in America go back to the origins of the American prisoner of war program, namely the agreement between the United States and Britain to intern German prisoners of war taken in North Africa on American soil (Jung 1972, 243–44, 253).

Networks and Migration

In a recent article arguing for the need to consider forced migration "in their theoretical understandings of contemporary society," Stephen Castles notes that "forced migration needs to be analyzed as a social process in which human agency and social networks play a major part" (2003, 1). Although Castles did not consider prisoners of war among his examples of forced migration, this study provides evidence for the important role played by agency and networks.

The men I interviewed found themselves in an unusual and largely unexpected situation. Although their agency was limited by the fact that they were prisoners of war, they also had considerable opportunities to make the best of their situation. They were able to get a glimpse of the "American way of life"; they seized available opportunities to learn English and even to study other subjects. Most important, and perhaps most consequential, were their formal and informal contacts and interactions with Americans. Such interactions helped break down existing stereotypes that all Germans were Nazis and all Americans were "gangsters" or "superficial opportunists," making "enemies human" (Pabel 1955). They also created social networks of relationships that often continued after the last prisoners had left American soil.[14] While this study has focused primarily on networks that provided the impetus and support for later immigration, there is considerable anecdotal evidence for other types of postwar contacts and relationships, such as the sending of care packages and an active correspondence between former enemies.[15]

As we have seen, a third of my respondents immigrated with the support of networks they had been able to establish during their time as POWs, or indirectly after the war, by gaining employment with American forces in Germany. As we do not know how many former POWs immigrated to the United States, we do not know how many were able to immigrate with the help of such networks. In addition to the cases detailed in Chapters 3 and 4, I am aware of five additional men. All five men had died before I started this research. Although I do not have detailed knowledge about the experiences of these men, I was able to stitch together some basic information concerning their trajectories from German POWs to immigrant and American citizen.

William (Wilhelm) O., a native of Mühlheim, an industrial town in the Ruhr, was a member of the Afrika Korps. William arrived on American soil at the end of 1943. He was twenty-one years old. He was first interned in Camp Concordia, Kansas. In December he joined 250 POWs to help construct a new camp in Atlanta, Nebraska. During his time in Nebraska, he worked on several farms in the area, plucking chickens, harvesting potatoes, and picking apples and tomatoes. His last job was at Kimmel's apple and cherry orchard. Kimmel and William became friends and Kimmel offered William a job after the war. With Kimmel's sponsorship William returned to Nebraska in 1950 with his wife and young daughter and resumed work in the orchard. When Kimmel retired in 1965, William took over the farm (*Detroit News*, November 26, 1992; Oberdieck 1995; Thompson 1993).

Karl B., who was born in Branbauer, Westphalia, served on a submarine. He was captured in June 1944 in Normandy. After spending a few months in a POW camp in England, Karl was transferred to the United States, where he spent eight months at Camp Lyndhurst/Sherando Lake, Virginia. At Camp Lyndhurst Karl worked for a local farmer, Galen Heatwole, who sponsored Karl and his wife. Karl returned to Virginia in 1951. After working on the Heatwole farm to pay back the transatlantic passage, Karl worked as a toolmaker for the American Safety Razor Company in Verona, Virginia (Owen 1999).

Frederick W., who was born in Düsseldorf and drafted into the Wehrmacht at the age of 31, arrived in Hoboken, New Jersey. Frederick was interned in several camps, in Oklahoma, Texas, Arizona and California, ending up in Ogden, Utah, where he stayed from 1944 to 1946. While working at a local cannery, Frederick struck up a friendship with O.B. Hadlock, an Ogden schoolteacher who had been a Mormon missionary in Germany. Weber joined the Mormon Church before the war ended, and he left Ogden in 1946. Returning to Europe in 1946, he spent another year in England and when he returned to a destroyed Düsseldorf he and his wife Johanna joined the Mormon Church there. Sponsored by Hadlock, they immigrated in 1954 and settled in Salt Lake City. Weber, who had been a trained sculptor, found work doing marble repairs for a stone company, a job he kept until his retirement in 1976 (*Ogden Standard Examiner*, April 12, 1987).

Karl H., who was born in Berlin, was drafted in 1940. He became a POW in February 1944 in Italy. Transported to the United States, he disembarked in Norfolk, Virginia, from where he traveled by train to Fort Custer, Michigan. There he met and befriended Stella K., a civilian

employee for the War Department working in the Purchasing and Con-
tracting Department. When Karl ended up in England, he and Stella corresponded with each other. When Karl returned to Germany in March
1948, Stella was able to get a position as a secretary working in the headquarters of the American Occupation Forces in Berlin. Karl and Stella
married in Berlin on June 18, 1949. They returned to the United States
soon thereafter, and Karl worked for thirty-three years at the Ypsilanti
State Hospital in Ypsilanti, Michigan (Carlson 1997).

Although Karl D. did not immigrate, his case reveals the often important role played by personal and family considerations. Karl was interned
in camps in Wisconsin and New Mexico. While at Camp Roswell, New
Mexico, he worked for Morgan Nelson. Karl was in charge of a large group
of POW workers and was well liked by his employer who encouraged him
to return to the United States, offering to sponsor him after the war. After
returning to Germany, Karl worked as a domestic personnel manager at
the Oberpfaffenhofen Air Depot of the U.S. Army. While Karl was eager
to return to New Mexico and already had a visa, he made the difficult and
wrenching decision to remain in Germany when his parents found out in
1950 that his brother had been killed in Russia. As the only surviving son
he could not bring himself to leave his parents.[16]

Temporary Migrations, Networks and Immigration Policies

Although social networks play a central role in the process of migration, an ever-growing literature on networks has focused primarily on
networks of families, friends, neighbors and co-ethnics and has paid surprisingly little attention to the role played by the migrants' own previous
sojourns and experiences. A recent study of individuals who were granted
legal residence permits in the United States during July and August 1996
indicates that two thirds of these "newly arrived" immigrants had prior
experiences in the United States (Massey and Malone 2002). Based on data
from the New Immigrant Survey Pilot Study, the authors identified several
ways by which immigrants might have accumulated U.S. experience before
becoming a legal resident alien: crossing the border illegally, overstaying
a nonresident visa, coming and going as a tourist, entering as a temporary
worker, attending a U.S. college or university, or becoming a refugee or
asylum seeker.

Perhaps not surprisingly, illegal border crossing was the most common prior experience among the "newly arrived" immigrants (twenty-one percent of those with prior experience), followed by visa abusers (ten percent), and individuals who entered with valid visas but either over-stayed them or worked when the visa did not permit work. The most common among visa abusers were tourists who overstayed their visas (fifty-five percent of all visa abusers). Unfortunately this study did not investigate the role of previous experiences as illegal border crossers or visa abusers in becoming permanent residents.

In the age of easy travel and mass tourism, we tend to forget that for centuries war meant "travel" to foreign countries and contact with other cultures. As Leed has pointed out, the militarism of the first part of the 20th century represented "the only type of mass tourism" available (1991). Although tourism represents a form of temporary migration, the relationship between tourism and migration has remained relatively unexplored (Williams and Hall 2000). In particular there has been little research on how previous visits as tourists, students or other temporary sojourners might influence a later decision to return as immigrants. A study of Russian tourists who visited Israel suggests that while many of the tourists who returned to Israel as immigrants were influenced by economic factors, their perceptions of the friendliness of locals also played a role in their decision (Oigenblick and Kirschenbaum 2002). While recognizing that the former German POWs were hardly tourists in the traditional sense, for many of the men I interviewed for this study, it was "the friendliness of locals" that had impressed them most.

Finally, the experiences of my respondents serve to underline the important role played by political and social factors in the process of immigration, and the struggles of would-be immigrants to overcome existing hurdles. While the National Origins Quota Act of 1924 set a comparatively generous quota for Germans, this quota was insufficient to accommodate all those who desired to leave Germany behind.

The 1965 Immigration and Nationality Act, which abolished the national origins quota system, has been "revolutionary" (Barkan 2010). While the underpinnings of the law had been gradually eroding in the context of changing international migration pressures, especially the numbers of refugees, and the changes wrought by the civil rights movement, the new law basing immigration on family unification and employment had unanticipated consequences. It changed the face of America from a country of primarily European settlers to one with increasing populations drawn from Latin America and Asia. As Elliott Barkan correctly observed, the declining proportion of European immigrants was due less to the changes in the American law than to the remarkable economic and social changes in Europe. For the past forty years, immigration from Europe, including Germany, has continued to decline, representing an ever smaller proportion of newcomers to the United States. At the same time, European societies, including Germany, have become immigration countries in their own right. Indeed, at the very time when some of the men I interviewed arrived in the United States (in the early to mid–1950s), Germany had already embarked on a system of temporary worker recruitment. A largely unanticipated consequence of this decision has been that today Germany has become a significant immigration country.[17]

Chapter Notes

Introduction

1. Although German immigration to the United States reached its peak in the five decades between 1840 and 1980 — with a high between 1880 and 1899 — the 576,905 Germans who immigrated to the United States after the Second World War, between 1950 and 1959, represent the largest wave of German immigration in the twentieth century. United States Bureau of the Census, 1975, *Historical Statistics of the United States: Colonial Times to 1970* (Washington, DC: U.S. Government Printing Office), 105.

2. In addition to the 380,000 Germans, 50,000 Italians and 3,000 Japanese were interned on American soil.

3. See Arnold Krammer, 1991, *Nazi Prisoners of War in America* (Lanham, MD: Scarborough House), 266. Krammer refers to figures given to him by a former POW, John Schroer. When I contacted Mr. Schroer concerning the origin of his estimate, he responded that the estimate stems "from a remark made by an American employee of the State Department during lunch." (Letter from John Schroer to the author, March 30, 2009.) I suspect that the lack of reliable data may be one of the reasons that the POWs' return migration has not received any systematic attention.

4. The existing body of literature varies considerably in terms of its focus and intellectual rigor and includes books and journal articles, the latter mostly in local history journals. In addition to Arnold Krammer's informative historical overview, *Nazi Prisoners of War in America* (1991), Hermann Jung's 1972 volume *Die deutschen Kriegsgefangenen in amerikanischer Hand* (German Prisoners of War in American Hands), and most recently Antonio Thompson, *Men in German Uniform* (2010) the literature includes accounts of camps and camp life in particular states and regions (Bailey 2005, Billinger 2000, Billinger 2008, Buck 1998, Cowley 2002, Fiedler 2003, Gansberg 1977, Powell 1989, Simmons 2000) as well as individual camps (Geiger 1996, Koop 1988, Waters 2004), a growing number of experiential accounts and autobiographies (Erichson 2001, Gaertner 1985, Hennes 2008, Hörner and Powell 1991, Metzroth 2004, Pabel 1955, Schlauch 2003, Schmid 2005, Thill 2004), as well as popular history (Cook 2007) and even fiction (Fiedler 2011, Greene 1973, White 1995, Yarbrough 2003). Relevant journal articles, published predominantly in state and regional historical journals, are too numerous to list in this footnote. They will be referred to when appropriate.

5. In his seminal study of postwar German migration to the United States and Canada, Alexander Freund observed that in the migration literature dealing with the early period of the Federal Republic of Germany, migration overseas had not played a role. Instead the focus was on migration of refugees and expellees from the eastern provinces, as well as displaced persons and migrants from the Soviet occupation zone/German Democratic Republic and migration of guest workers into the Federal Republic. See Alexander Freund, 2004, *Aufbrüche nach dem Zusammenbruch: Die deutsche Nordamerika-Auswanderung nach dem Zweiten Weltkrieg* (Göttingen: V&R Unipress), 33–34.

6. My reference here is to the German civilian population, which was relatively isolated and compared to today did not travel much abroad. On the other hand, members of the

Wehrmacht did "travel" considerably, primarily within Europe. See Albrecht Lehman, 1984, "Krieg — Urlaub-Gastarbeiter," *Archiv für Sozialgeschichte*, no. 24: 457–80.

7. A survey of 150 randomly selected returning POWs in Baden-Württemberg conducted by the American Military Government's Information Control Division concludes that "the group had returned from the USA very impressed with America, ... especially (American) industrial development, standard of living and the urbanism of its culture," and noted that "several wished to return to the USA as soon as possible." Cited in Matthias Reiss, 2005, "The Nucleus of a New German Ideology? The Re-education of German Prisoners of War in the United States During World War II," in *Prisoners of War, Prisoners of Peace*, Bob Moore and Barbara Hately-Broad, eds., 99.

8. According to estimates, in spring 1947 one quarter of the resident population was considered "uprooted," including 10 million refugees and expellees, 3–4 million people who had been evacuated to the countryside and had not returned home and 5.2 million returning prisoners of war. Michael Krause, 1997, *Flucht vor dem Bobenkrieg: Umquartierung im Zweiten Weltkrieg und die Wiedereingliederung der Evakuierten in Deutschland. 1943–1963* (Düsseldorf: Droste Buchverlag). The population of 66 million included 8 million refugees from the former eastern provinces and Eastern Europe, 5.2 million former prisoners of war, an estimated 10 million people who had been evacuated to the countryside, and 250,000 displaced persons. See Freund, *Aufbrüche nach dem Zusammenbruch*, 56–57.

9. In a survey in March 1958, thirty-five percent of respondents said that "someone" in the family had immigrated to America "at some time." See Elisabeth Noelle and Erich Peter Neumann, eds. 1965. *Jahrbuch der öffentlichen Meinung 1958–64* (Allensbach/Bonn: Verlag für Demoskopie), 550.

10. With the unconditional German surrender on May 7 and 8, 1945, German state power ceased to exist and Allied military governments controlled all legislative and executive power, including migration. For more detailed discussion see Chapter 3.

11. This quota was relatively generous and the second largest after Great Britain and Ireland.

12. When the quota opened, large masses of people rushed to the American consulates (Reimers 1981, Freund 2004, 166–168). By June 5, 1949, American consulates in West Germany had received 500,000 applications (Nerger-Focke 1995, 253). Although the interest in emigration was equally high, residents of the Soviet occupation zone were excluded. *Der Spiegel*, September 3, 1948, "Quotenjäger" 39, 25. In a letter (undated) responding to an inquiry by Mrs. Buckholz of Batavia, New York, concerning her wish to sponsor a young German, G.L.C. Scott, Acting Staff Secretary of the American Military Government, informs her that the chances for getting a visa were very poor: "Half of the quota is reserved for emigration of German ethnic origin who come from east of the Oder-Neisse line, leaving 13,000 for the rest of Germany, one half of which are reserved for what are called preference cases (relatives of American citizens). That leaves 6500 for non-preference visas. The allocation of these is based on the order of their receipt." National Archives, OMGUS Record Group 260, Entry 181, Civil Administration Division, Displaced Persons.

13. The annual number of German immigrants increased substantially at this point. See Department of Justice, 1945–1947, *Annual Report of the Immigration and Naturalization Service* (Washington, DC: U.S. Government Printing Office).

14. Camp Ruston Archives, accessed 2004, www.latech.edu/tech/libary/campruston/slide167.

15. Given the age of this population, I assume that most of these individuals had died or were in a nursing home.

16. Given time to travel and expenses, it took me several years to conduct the interviews. I was well into writing the manuscript when I located three additional respondents in 2007, 2009 and 2010 respectively.

17. According to Bischof, about five to fifteen percent of prisoners of the Afrika Korps were hardcore Nazis; the majority were indifferent *Mitläufer* primarily interested in their personal survival. Hard-core Nazis were found mostly in the Waffen SS and among the paratroopers and tank infantry. He cites O.W. Thille, a POW who identified four categories: dangerous Nazis who intimidated others, those who went along, the lukewarm who sought to avoid conflict, and convinced anti–Nazis. Günter Bischof, 1999. "Einige Thesen zu einer Mentalitätsgescichte deutscher Kriegsgefangenschaft in amerikanischem Gewahrsam," *Kriegsgefangenschaft im Zweiten Weltkrieg: Eine Vergleichedne Perspektive*, in Günter Bischof and Rüdiger Overmans, eds. (Wien: Verlag Gerhard Höller), 175–212. While it is difficult to determine the degree to

which my respondents were supporters of the regime, I can tell with some confidence based on their history and their own account that about six respondents had not supported Hitler and two or three could be classified as "those who went along." Most of my respondents seemed to be opportunists or lukewarm supporters.

18. As a group the men captured in North Africa were somewhat older, including six men born in the second decade of the 20th century. All the others were born in the 1920s.

19. Based on interviews with German POWs captured on the western front in June 1944 and May 1945, the Psychological Warfare Division concluded that "with some exaggeration one could almost say that the average German P/W's [sic] ideas about America are a mixture of Karl May (extremely popular German writer of Wild West stories) and Josef Goebbels, with the whole picture overshadowed by a huge dollar sign. This idea is usually somewhat tempered by a certain realism due to the fact that very many German families have relatives or friends in the USA." *Summary Report on the Attitudes of German PWs* [sic] *towards the United States.* SHAEF, Psychological Warfare Division, as quoted in Matthias Reiss, 2002, *Die Schwarzen waren unsere Freunde: Deutsche Kriegsgefangene in der amerikanischen Gesellschaft 1942–1946* (Paderborn: Ferdinand Schöningh), 78.

20. They will be discussed in Chapter 3.

21. Billinger attributes the harsher treatment of Germans in France to the German occupation. Robert Billinger, 2008, *Nazi POWs in the Tar Heel State* (Gainesville: University of Florida Press), 172.

22. For a more detailed discussion of American immigration policy, see Chapter 3.

23. According to Freda Hawkins, 1988, *Canada and Immigration: Public Policy and Public Concern*, 2d edition (Montreal: McGill–Queen's University Press) *Etappenmigration* (migration in steps) was a common pattern in the post–World War II period. Getting a visa for the United States could take years, whereas a visa for Canada took less than a year. For additional examples see Freund, *Aufbrüche nach dem Zusammenbruch*, 454–455.

24. A similar situation existed in Canada, where some 40,000 Germans were interned. See David Carter, 1998, *POW Behind Canadian Barbed Wire: Aliens, Refugees and Prisoners of War in Canada, 1914–1946* (Calgary: Tumbleweed Press).

25. Half of my respondents did not return directly to Germany. They served additional time doing forced labor in England or France and did not return to Germany until 1947 and 1948.

Chapter 1

1. Estimates range from a high of 35 million to a minimum of 12 million. For details see Gerald Davis, 1977, "Prisoners of War in 20th Century War Economies." *Journal of Contemporary History* 12, no. 4: 623–634.

2. Germans held 95,000 Americans. See Helmut Hörner and Allan Powell, 1991. *A German Odyssey: The Journal of a German Prisoner of War* (Golden, CO: Fulcrum Publishing).

3. The North Africa Campaign produced many more prisoners than originally anticipated. While the Department of War had predicted that 10,000 would be captured, by May 1943 a total of 252,415 had been taken prisoner.

4. For detailed information on the convention and its signatories, see the International Committee of the Red Cross, www.icrc.org/IHL.NSF/FULL/305?OpenDocument.

5. A memorandum dated August 14, 1943 from the War Department to the commanding generals of the nine service commands outlines the need for a "firm general policy relative to the employment of prisoners of war so that the maximum use will be made of all available manpower in the United States." The memo clearly states that "safeguarding, housing and subsistence" come first, followed by employment on "the most essential and gainful work projects which are available." However, if the two conflict, "the safeguarding of the prisoners conformably to the requirements of internal security is considered paramount." National Archives, Provost Marshal General's Office, Record Group 389, Entry 439A. Prisoner of War Operations. Historical File, 1941–58.

6. Both the United States and Germany had signed the convention. Among the considerations for following the rules of the convention was to protect American POWs in German hands.

7. Due to previous German immigration to the United States, it was not uncommon that German POWs had close relatives who were American citizens.

8. For a discussion of escapes and captures, see Krammer, *Nazi Prisoners of War*, 115–46.

9. POWs referred to such nightly visits as "einen Deckenbesuch abstatten" (a blanket visit) or "der Heilige Geist" (the holy ghost). Author interview, Rudolf T., 2003.

10. For details, see Krammer, *Nazi Prisoners of War*, 170–73. See also Wilma Parnell, 1981, *The Killing of Corporal Kunze* (New York: Lyle Stuart). Kunze, who was 40 years old, was interned at Camp Tonkawa, Oklahoma. He had apparently provided information to the Americans. According to the Provost Marshal General's "A Brief History," there were four murders among the 477 deaths of German POWs on American soil. National Archives, Record Group 389, Entry439A, Historical File 1941–58. *PW Operations* Vols. I–III. This includes men who died of natural causes. Krammer lists five murders: Dreschler, Gunther, Kunze, Krauss, Menscher. Seven men who were convicted of murders of their fellow prisoners were interned at Fort Leavenworth, Kansas, and hanged on July 10, 1945. See Richard Whittingham, 1997, *Martial Justice: The Mass Execution in the United States* (Annapolis, MD: Naval Institute Press). In his autobiographical novel, former POW Hans-Werner Richter, who became one of Germany's best-known postwar authors, recounts the exchange between a new POW captured in Italy and an older Afrikaner, who called the newcomer "a deserter." When the former protested, he was severely beaten: "Pips was taken, what was left of him that is, to a hospital. We never saw him again." Hans-Werner Richter, *Die Geschlagenen*, 1994 (München: Verlag Kurt Desch), 145–146.

11. See also the title of a memoir by former POW Manfred Sonntag, *Im Goldenen Käfig* (In a Golden Cage), 1992 (Hamburg: Soldi Verlag). The Provost Marshal General's Office conducted over four weeks in December 1945 a non-representative survey of 22,153 departing POWs at Camp Shanks, New York, who were identified as "run of the mill prisoners detained in this country." The survey concludes that "approximately 74% of the German prisoners of war who were interned in this country left with an appreciation of the value of democracy and a friendly attitude toward their captors." Yet when asked what impressed them most about life in the United States, only forty-one percent reported having favorable impressions overall. The authors of the survey conclude they "were favorable in commenting on freedoms or unfavorable in pointing out our poverty, race discrimination, and illusions of democracy. The democratic relationship between officers and enlisted men drew many comments." The survey also indicates that even favorable answers were often accompanied by unfavorable comments, in particular concerning inequality and race issues. A typical answer might be, "I was impressed by the freedom of the press. I was dismayed to find the horrible housing conditions for the working classes. Provisions for old age pensions and health insurance are very poor." Or, "the American civilians know very little about democracy. They were unable to answer most of our questions. We PWs have learned about democracy in lectures. Why don't you do the same thing for the people here?" Forty-one percent responded favorably to question 12 in the survey, which asked, "From your contact with America and Americans through personal observation, newspapers, magazines, movies, books, radio, etc., what impressed you most about life in this country?" *Poll of German Prisoners of War Opinion*. National Archives. Provost Marshal General's Office, Record Group 389, Entry 439A, Historical File 1941–58. Prisoner of War Operations.

12. The decision was announced in a memorandum from the War Department to the commanding generals of the nine regional service commands dated August 24, 1943: "The War Department and the War Manpower Commission have agreed to cooperate, as set forth below, with regard to making contracts for use of PW labor by private employers and Federal, State and governmental agencies other than the War Department." The memorandum spells out "the basic features of the plan," namely that "requests for use of labor will be channeled to the military authorities through the War Manpower Commission, while contracts for the use of such labor will be executed and administered by the War Department." National Archives. Provost Marshal General's Office. Record Group 389, Entry 439A. Historical File 1941–58. Prisoner of War Operations.

13. The 1929 Geneva Convention on the Treatment of Prisoners of War spells out the rules and conditions for the treatment of prisoners, including their employment. Accordingly, only enlisted men can be required to work, noncommissioned officers can volunteer and officers can only volunteer and be employed in supervisory positions. Employment is limited to nonmilitary work (i.e., prisoners cannot be used to directly further the captor's war efforts), and work that is not dangerous by definition (e.g., work in mines is excluded, but forges and foundries were eventually declared within the bounds; so was the production of pulpwood, but not logging in general). Following the convention, which had been signed by both Germany

and the United States, the captured German soldiers were first employed in the camps (maintaining the camp site, preparing food, cleaning, repairing equipment). See "Enemy Prisoners of War — T.M. 19-500." July 7, 1943. National Archives, Provost Marshal General's Office. Record Group 398. Entry 467. POW Division Legal Branch.

14. According to Lewis and Mewha, there were only 100,000 available workers for 149,000 jobs. Although the majority of POWs contracted to private employers worked in agriculture, food processing, logging and lumbering (industries that were not unionized and where prisoners could work in relative isolation), prisoners were also contracted to work in railroad maintenance of way, in forges and foundries, and even in open pit mines, and were frequently delegated to emergency work projects, such as snow removal, flood control, storm clean-up and road construction. Lewis and Mewha, *History of Prisoner of War Utilization*, 140. See also Krammer, 1991, *Nazi Prisoners of War*, 84, 89. In November 1944, more prisoners were involved in agriculture than were working on military installations. More than 4,000 worked in foundries and 1,000 in quarries and open pit mines.

15. Indeed, the Army Service Forces became increasingly concerned with the effective utilization of all employable German prisoners of war. In April 1944, the War Department's POW Circular, issued on a regular basis, reminds all regional service commands of the general policy that every employable POW be employed in essential skilled and unskilled work of types permitted by Geneva Convention. See POW Circular, 24, April 24, 1944. National Archives, Secretary of War. Record Group 107. Entry 114. Records of the Legal Services, General Records 1942-45. Entry 114. A few days later, a memorandum from the Army Service Forces to the commanding generals (May 6, 1944) reminds them that "the manpower situation demands that every available prisoner of war must be employed in essential work," and urges that "maximum efficiency be obtained from every available man-hour," so that "the essential needs of agriculture and food processing industries for prisoners of war labor be satisfied to the greatest possible extent." POW Circular 26, Secretary of War. Records of the Legal Services, General Records, 1942-45. Entry 114.

16. For example, in Louisiana planters reacted to news of the American victory in Europe with foreboding. One county agent stated that POW repatriation would mean that the days of "free labor" on the plantations were a "thing of the past." Matthew Schott, 1995, "Prisoners Like Us: German POWs Encounter Louisiana's African Americans," *Louisiana History* 36: 277–90. An Arkansas congressman claimed that they were "absolutely dependent on" German POWs; planters in Mississippi claimed that Germans saved their cotton crop; similarly, the American Sugar League wondered how they could do without German POWs. In 1944 alone, prisoners had cut 246,000 acres of cane. A senator from Louisiana became the leading spokesperson for keeping German POWs in the United States. See Morton Sosna, 1991, "Stalag Dixie," *Stanford Humanities Review* 2, no. 1: 38–64.

17. In May 1944, the Tri-State Packers Association in Easton, Maryland, complained to the War Manpower Commission (WMC) that Illinois was allocated more prisoners than Maryland although "they do not yield as much processable food." Another memo, from the regional director of the WMC in Cleveland, Ohio, dated April 1945, complained to the Washington office concerning the scarcity of prison labor in Ohio and Michigan. (War Manpower Commission. Entry 155.) Thus, a memorandum from the Pennsylvania Forest Products Committee to the War Department, dated April 1945, refers to a previous petition to transfer an additional 100,000 German prisoners "from overseas for employment in urgent war production programs and agriculture." National Archives. War Manpower Commission. Record Group 211. Entry 155. Records of the Legal Services. General Records, 1942-45.

18. Although precise numbers are not available (as the Office of the Provost Marshal General and the Industrial Personnel Division seem to have kept no record of the exact number of prisoners at work at any given time), estimates indicate that the number of prisoners working in contract labor was substantial. In the same year and month, 58,000 Mexican braceros were working in agriculture and 62,000 on railways. See Ernesto Galarza, 1964, *Merchants of Labor: The Mexican Bracero Story* (Charlotte, NC: McNally and Loftin), 53. When employment of foreign labor peaked in 1945, the Office of Labor reported that in November of that year, 44,897 Mexicans, 11,499 Jamaicans, 4,248 Bahamians, 932 Newfoundlanders and 111,369 prisoners of war were employed in agriculture. See Walter Wilcox, 1947, *The Farmer in the Second World War* (Ames: Iowa State College), 95.

19. Although many of the prisoners were skilled workers, and often used their skills on the base, they could not be employed in these skills in contract labor positions. See the letter

withdrawing prisoners from the company because they had used them in skilled positions. This was seen as a gesture to organized labor. The cash value of German POW labor is estimated to have been $100 million. Terry Paul Wilson, 1974, "The Afrika Korps in Oklahoma: Fort Reno's Prisoner of War Compound," *Chronicles of Oklahoma* 52: 368–69.

20. In his detailed account of the history of World War II prisoner of war operations in the United States, Edward Pluth identified three phases. In phase one, the emphasis was placed on secure, isolated, large camps that could be guarded effectively. In phase two, the shift to engagement in work, demands for security were lowered and branch camps were established. In phase three, reeducation began in late 1944, but demand for prisoners as workers and difficulty in establishing a program stopped the implementation of a reeducation program. Pluth, "The American Operation of German Prisoner of War Camps in the United States During World War II." See also Powell, *Splinter of a Nation,* 76.

21. A map of distribution of base and branch camps as of August 1, 1943, indicates 71 camps with a high concentration in Texas and Oklahoma. Toward the end of the war, one fifth of all camps were located in the Midwest. On the geographic distribution and proliferation of camps over time, see Krammer, *Nazi Prisoners of War in America,* 26.

22. To further facilitate the optimal use of labor, the Provost Marshal General requested that a specific field representative of the War Manpower Commission be delegated to act as liaison with the commanding officer of each POW camp.

23. The 340 branch camps provided a new flexibility that allowed for optimal deployment of prisoner labor where it was most needed. For details, see speech titled "Enemy POWs in the United States" given by Brigadier General B.M. Bryan, Jr., Assistant Provost Marshal General, before the Military Affairs Committee, United States House of Representatives, April 26, 1945. See Maxwell McKnight, 1944, "The Employment of Prisoners of War in the United States," *International Labor Review* 50: 47–64.

24. Brigadier General B.M. Bryan, Assistant Provost Marshal General, voiced his irritation about overcautious camp commanders: "Our principal concern should be that of weighing work done against reasonable risk" (quoted in Krammer, *Nazi Prisoners of War in America* 1991, 39).

25. Only one percent of prisoners attempted to escape. Of these the vast majority were caught within days. For a more detailed discussion on escapes, see Arnold Krammer, *Nazi Prisoners of War,* Chapter 4.

26. National Archives, War Manpower Commission. Record Group 211, Entry 155, Records of the Legal Services, General Records. Field Instructions 69, October 19, 1943.

27. On Penal Division 999, see Charles Bardich, 1971, "Prisoners as Soldiers: The German 999th Penal Division," *Army Quarterly and Defense Journal* 102 (October): 65–69. -

28. It is important to note that not all members of the Wehrmacht were German citizens. For a detailed account see Antonio Thompson, 2010, *Men in German Uniform: POWs in America During World War II* (Knoxville: The University of Tennessee Press).

29. See photograph captioned "Do we pamper Nazi prisoners? Girl friends say good-bye to this trainload of Germans being transferred from California to New Mexico." *Newsweek,* February 26, 1945.

30. An early example took place in November 1943 in Lake Arthur, Louisiana, when, with the permission of the camp commander, a farmer invited ten POWs who had worked for him to a local restaurant for fish and beer. See Patrick O'Brien, Thomas Isern and Daniel Lumley, 1984, "Stalag Sunflower: German Prisoners of War in Kansas," *Kansas History* 7, no. 3: 194. Similar events were hardly unusual.

31. National Archives. War Manpower Commission. Record Group 211. Entry 11. POW Labor Program. Conference between WD and WMC, January 1944, Prisoner of War Labor 1944.

32. National Archives. Records of the Secretary of War. Record Group 107. Entry 180. POW Circular No. 3, January 4, 1944.

33. Matthias Reiss also notes that "quite a number of former German POWs report in their recollections that they or their comrade had intimate and sexual contact with female civilians in the United States." Matthias Reiss, 2005, "Bronzed Bodies behind Barbed Wire: Masculinity and the Treatment of German Prisoners of War in the United States," *The Journal of Military History* 69 (April): 496, footnote 108.

34. Not all Americans were sympathetic, and many felt that the German POWs were treated far too well, that they were coddled. Accusations of "coddling" eventually resulted in congressional investigation. See *Newsweek,* May 7, 1945, pp. 58–61. United States, Department

of the Army, Chief of Military History, Historical Services, History of Prisoner of War Operations of the Provost Marshal General's Office. National Archives, 286ff. And in some areas, the camps came to be known as "the Fritz Ritz" among the local population. Krammer, *Nazi Prisoners of War*, 28.

35. National Archives, Provost Marshal General's Office, Record Group 389. Entry 439A, Prisoner of War Operations, Historical File, 1941–58. Handbook for Work Supervisors of Prisoner of War Labor. Army Service Forces Manual M811, July 1945.

36. Officially created by an exchange of letters between Stimson and the secretary of state in April 1944. Provost Marshal General Allen Gullion was opposed to the reeducation program and argued that what Germans could observe during their work outside the compound would do much more to impress than "a teacher in a classroom or a lecturer from a platform." Quoted in Matthias Reiss, 2005, "The Nucleus of a German Ideology? The Re-education of German Prisoners of War in the United States During World War II," in *Prisoners of War, Prisoners of Peace*, Bob Moore and Barbara Hately-Broad, eds. (Oxford: Berg), 92.

37. Examples of such booklets are: *Kleiner Führer durch Amerika* (Small Guide through America) and *Eine Einführung in das Amerikanische Schulwesen* (An Introduction to the American System of Education).

38. Prisoners were selected by asking the nine service commands to submit names of their most cooperative anti–Nazi POWs. A total of 25,000 were selected. These were then asked to fill out a lengthy questionnaire, designed to reveal those who knew the most about Germany's liberal traditions. Among other things, they had to answer such questions as, "The German philosopher Fichte was the exponent of what ideas?" The questionnaires were screened by POW members of the Factory at Fort Kearney. On the basis of these reports and personal interviews and polygraph tests, they were divided into three categories: black, gray and white. Thirteen percent who were deemed black (Nazis) were eliminated; the grays, who represented most of the 25,000, were reevaluated and divided into black or white.

39. After the war the military government could find only 74 graduates of Fort Getty. The returning POW graduates were frequently ignored by the occupation forces. In general their experiences were negative. Reiss, "The Nucleus of a New German Ideology?," 97.

40. National Archives. War Manpower Commission. Record Group 211. Records of the Legal Services, General Records, 1942–45.

41. Interestingly, the men most likely to be returned early were those deemed less useful because they had been uncooperative. Those who had worked hard were deemed useful and remained in the United States longer.

42. For letters from relatives and farmers see Krammer, *Nazi Prisoners of War* and Reiss, *Die Schwarzen waren unsere Freunde*. See also letters from relatives in National Archives, Provost Marshal General's Office, Record Group 389. Entry 467. POW Division, Legal Branch.

43. Except for 134 men in hospitals and psychiatric wards, 25 escapees still at large and 141 men serving prison terms in penal institutions for crimes committed. See Billinger, *Hitler's Soldiers in the Sunshine State*, 170. www.mineaction.org/downloads/Emine Policy Pages/Geneva Conventions/Geneva Convention III.pdf.

44. www.mineaction.org/downloads/Emine Policy Pages/Geneva Conventions/Geneva Convention III.pdf.

45. Some may have ended up in Belgium and Luxembourg, most of these apparently were POWs held on European soil. In fact the United States transferred about 70,0,00 POWs held in Europe to France, 30,000 to Belgium and 50,000 to other European countries.

Chapter 2

1. Two of the officers I interviewed were selected to participate in the Special Projects Division Program at Fort Getty, where they spent three months before returning to Germany.

2. Author mail and telephone interview, 2007.

3. Author interview, January 23, 2003, Umatilla, Florida.

4. See also Robert Billinger, 2008, *Nazi POWs in the Tar Heel State* (Gainesville: University of Florida Press).

5. Author interview, October 6, 2002, Holiday Inn, Muscatine, Iowa.

6. For a detailed description of the history of Nazi domination and political activity at Camp Hearne see Michael Waters, 2004, *Lone Star Stalag: German Prisoners of War at Camp Hearne* (College Station: Texas A&M University Press), 110–34.

7. Corporal Hugo Kraus, 24, was born in Germany. Between 1928 and 1939 he lived in New York with his parents, who had become naturalized American citizens. Enamored with the Third Reich, he returned to Germany with the help of the German-American Bund and later joined the German army with which he served in Russia and North Africa. He was captured and transported to Texas, where his fluency in English allowed him to become an interpreter for the camp commander, which made him suspect in the eyes of his fellow prisoners. His naturalized parents in New York and the fact that he was critical of the German government while praising all things American further contributed to their suspicion that he was a spy. After the lights were out at 9 P.M. on December 17, 1943, from six to ten men entered his barracks and beat him to death while his comrades watched. No perpetrators were ever identified. See Krammer, *Nazi Prisoners of War*, 171.

8. According to Heino, German POWs did most of the work at the discharge center for American GIs at Fort Knox, where he acted as the interpreter between the Germans and Mr. Nall.

9. Author interview, June 25, 2004, Wood Dale, Illinois.

10. Camp White was established in 1941 as an army training base and deactivated in April 1946. For more on Camp White, see Robert Donnelly, 1992, "Reminiscence: John Fahey on Reeducating German Prisoners During WWII," *Oregon Historical Quarterly* 93: 368–393.

11. Author Interview, April 10, 2003, Darien, Illinois.

12. See also "German War Prisoner to Arrive to Assist with Pea Pack," *Marshfield News Herald*, July 10, 1945; Betty Cowley, 2000, *Stalag Wisconsin: Inside WW II Prisoner of War Camps* (Oregon, WI: Badger Press), 194–98.

13. Author interview, October 25, 2002, St. Clair Shores, Michigan.

14. *Der Ruf* was a sophisticated German-language journal published at the Factory and edited by a former publisher and novelist. The first issue appeared in canteens on March 6, 1946, priced at five cents. The reaction was mixed. At Camp Trinidad, seven officers were apprehended in the act of burning a batch of copies. At Camp Hulen, Texas, it was characterized as "Jewish propaganda." One of my respondents told me that he deliberately destroyed copies of the paper in his camp. In other camps prisoners were impressed. See Krammer, *Nazi Prisoners of War*; Milton Bailey, 2008, "Lessons in Democracy," *World War II*. (August/September): 52–59.

15. Author interview, February 22, 2003, Roseville, California.

16. The Luftlande-Sturm-Regiment 1 (also known as *Versuchsabteilung Friedrichshafen* or *Sturmabteilung Koch*) was a German air force parachute regiment which fought in Belgium, Crete and the eastern front.

17. He had requested the latter transfer because he found out that his brother was at Camp Trinidad, and depending on the commander of the camp, POWs could petition for transfers to camps where they had relatives, provided they paid for the transfer.

18. Author interview, September 21, 2002, Temecula, California.

19. Author interview, December 14, 2002, Arverne, New York.

20. The strike had national press coverage. For a detailed discussion see Billinger, *Hitler's Soldiers in the Sunshine State*, 133–39.

21. This was an extremely dangerous job. An estimated 1,800 were killed, and survivors are seeking compensation. See Georg Böhnisch, 2008, "Surviving German POWs Seek Compensation," *Der Spiegel Online International*, August 25. www.spiegel.de/international/europe/0,1518,574180,00.html

22. Author interview, February 28, 2004, Sun City, Florida.

23. POW Heinz Pfaeffle also reports visiting the Ringling Brothers circus in spring 1944. Wolfgang Schlauch, 2003, *In Amerikanischer Kriegsgefangenschaft: Berichte deutscher Soldaten aus dem Zweiten Weltkrieg* (Crailsheim: Baier Verlag), 142.

24. Based on the Geneva Convention, wounded prisoners were repatriated on five occasions between October 1943 and January 1945. Under the auspices of the Red Cross, prisoners were transported to Goteborg, Sweden. See Jung, *Die deutschen Kriegsgefangenen in amerikanischer Hand*, 244, 241.

25. The Hermann Göring Regiment was an elite Luftwaffe unit that saw action in Sicily, North Africa and on the eastern front. See Gordon Williamson and Stephen Andrees, 2003, *The Hermann Goering Division* (Oxford: Osprey Publishing).

26. Author interview, May 17, 2003, Georgetown, Maine.

27. The swing kids (*Swingjugend*) were a group of jazz and swing lovers in the 1930s. They were primarily 14- to 18-year-old boys and girls in high school, mostly middle- or upper-

class students, but there were also some apprentice workers. They copied the British and American way of life, defining themselves in swing music, and opposing the National Socialist ideology, especially the *Hitlerjugend*.

28. See Thomas Buecker, 2002, "Nazi Influence at Fort Robinson POW Camp During WWII," *Nebraska History* 73, no. 1: 39.

29. He does not remember the name of the camp; it was probably Camp Carson.

30. Author interview, December 13, 2003, Des Moines, Iowa.

31. Author telephone interview, December 2002. Follow-up interview in person with Edith M., September 13, 2003. Alfred had died in February 2003.

32. Author telephone interview, February 17, 2003.

33. There are other reports in the literature about POWs having dogs in camps.

34. In the interview Heinz said that he was "sent to Boston to be taught about democracy for two and a half months; there were about 700 PWs." However, there was no reeducation camp near Boston.

35. Author interview, February 20, 2004, his office at Tatexis Bleichroeder, New York, New York.

36. Author interview, February 6, 2004, Bethesda, Maryland.

37. Klaus Schenk von Stauffenberg was severely wounded in North Africa and became one of the leading officers involved in the July 20, 1944, failed attempt to assassinate Hitler. He was executed by firing squad on July 21, 1944 at the age of 37.

38. Author telephone interview, February 9, 2009, Fredericksburg, Virginia.

39. The Siegfried Line and the Westwall are the same thing. Germans called it Westwall whereas the Allies referred to it as the Siegfried Line (named after the original line constructed in World War I). It was a defensive line of bunkers, tunnels and tank traps which was 630 km long, stretching from north of the town of Klewe on the Dutch border to the southern town Weil am Rhein at the Swiss border. Hitler had planned the line in 1936 and it was built between 1938 and 1940.

40. Author interview January 24, 2003, Stuart, Florida.

41. For detail on Camp Blanding, see Jim Aston, Camp Blanding: The War Years. www.30thinfantry.org/blanding_history.shtml (June 2, 2008).

42. Author interview, September 19, 2002, Scottsdale, Arizona.

43. Interview, April 11, 2003, Kenilworth, Illinois.

44. He was a *Fahnenjunker*, the lowest rank for noncommissioned officers (*Unteroffizier*).

45. Author interview, June 25, 2004, Chicago, Illinois.

46. According to Krammer there were hundreds of minor work slowdowns and stoppages at camps across the country from 1943 until the end of the war. POW protests and work halts occurred very rarely in comparison with the total number of prisoners in camps across the country. See Krammer, *Nazi Prisoners of War*, 111–13.

47. Author interview, July 27, 2002, Madison, Wisconsin.

48. Author interview, February 25, 2003, Beaverton, Oregon.

49. Author interview, October 24, 2002, his office at O.S. Machining, Clinton Township, Michigan.

50. Oskar, who was from a small village in Pomerania, was a shy young man who had little experience with people.

51. Author interview, October 23, 2002, Grand Ledge, Michigan.

52. Author interview, February 28, 2004, Four Points Hotel, North Palm Harbor, Florida.

53. Author interview, November 14, 2007, Cottage Grove, Oregon.

54. Author interview, August 24, 2004, Big Rapids, Michigan.

55. Author telephone interview, December 12, 2010, Richmond, Virginia.

56. Author interview, April 28, 2003, Bellingham, Washington.

57. Author interview, September 23, 2002, Salt Lake City, Utah.

58. Author interview, February 2001, Charlottesville, Virginia.

59. Interview with wife Eleanor, March 10, 2006, Ogden, Utah. Erich had died a few weeks before I could make arrangements to travel to Utah for the interview. I had talked with him on the phone previously.

60. See Bundesministerium für Vertriebene, 2004, *Das Schicksal der Deutschen in Rumänien* (München: Deutscher Taschenbuch Verlag).

61. For details on this and other camps in Utah, see Allan Kent Powell, 1989, *Splinters of a Nation*.

62. A copy of the certificate is in the author's possession.

63. Author interview, September 26, 2003 Sheraton Hotel, Cuyahoga Falls, Ohio.

64. Author interview, October 27, 2002, Sebring, Ohio.

65. National Archives, Provost Marshal General. 1946. " Poll of PW Opinions," 36.

66. For example, a letter from the War Department to the Pennsylvania Forest Product Committee dated April 3, 1945, assures the latter that in answer to their previous request an additional 100,000 German POWs would be sent "from overseas for employment in urgent war production programs and agriculture. National Archives. Records of the War Manpower Commission. Record Group 211. Entry 175. General Records Relating to POWs 1944–45, Regions I–VII.

67. This explains why Elmar B., who was punished for destroying *Der Ruf* and hence classified as uncooperative, returned to Germany in August 1945. Similarly, Robert M., the Austrian citizen, returned directly to his native Austria.

68. Peter Lagrou, 2005, "Overview," in *Prisoners of War, Prisoners of Peace: Captivity, Homecoming and Memory in World War II*, Bob Moore and Barbara Hately-Broad, eds. (Oxford: Berg, 2005), 5.

69. National Archives. Provost Marshal General's Office. Record Group 389. "Poll of PW Opinions."

70. After he had immigrated to the United States, Henry made additional efforts to locate Mr. Lykins, but was unable to find him.

Chapter 3

1. The period between 1952 and 1967 that was characterized by high economic growth is generally referred to as the *Wirtschaftswunder*, the economic miracle.

2. The Allensbach Survey in 1954 indicated that seventy-two percent of West Germans (seventy-nine percent in big cities) did not feel safe from nuclear attacks. Cited by Frank Biess, "Cultural History Revisited," Democratization in Germany after 1945. Conference at Harvard Center of European Studies, November 5, 2007. www.ces.fas.harvard.edu/german_studies/berlin_archive/past_participants.htm.

3. EMNID-Institut, EMNID-Informationen. Bielfeld. 1957, 1961, 1970.

4. Beginning in 1950, the agency collected annual data based on data collected by the sixty *gemeinnützige Auswandererberatungsstellen* (non-profit emigration advice centers) throughout Germany.

5. A recent study of legal immigrants to the United States who acquired residence papers in 1996 found "that roughly two thirds of these newly arrived immigrants had prior experience in the United States within one of six basic categories: illegal border-crossers, visa abusers, non-resident visitors, non-resident workers, students or exchange visitors, and refugees/asylees. See Douglas Massey and Noland Malone, 2002, "Pathways to Legal Immigration," *Population Research and Policy Review* 21, no. 6: 473–594.

6. In view of these restrictions, there was considerable illegal emigration. For details, see Freund, *Aufbrüche nach dem Zusammenbruch*, 169–83.

7. Title of an article by Joachim Mohr in *Spiegel Special*, January 2006.

8. According to Roderich Ungern-Sternberg, twenty-five percent indicated the U.S., fourteen percent Australia, thirteen percent Canada and five percent South Africa. Roderich Ungern-Sternberg, 1992, "Die Wanderzüge Westeuropäer nach dem zweiten Weltkrieg," *Jahrbücher für Nationalökonomie und Statistik*. 165: 215–49.

9. This was a generous quota, second only to Great Britain, and followed by Ireland.

10. By June 5, 1949, American consulates in West Germany had received half a million applications. See Karin Nerger-Focke, 1995, *Die deutsche Amerikauswanderung nach 1945* (Stuttgart: Akademischer Verlag), 253. Although the interest in emigration was equally high, residents of the Soviet occupation zone were excluded. "Quoten-Jäger." *Der Spiegel* 25 (1948): 3.

11. Responding to an inquiry by Mrs. Buchholz of Batavia, New York, concerning her wanting to sponsor a young German, G.L.C. Scott, Acting Staff Secretary of the American Military Government, informed her that the chances for getting a visa were very poor: "Half of the quota is reserved for emigration of German ethnic origin who come from east of the Oder-Neisse line, leaving 13,00 for the rest of Germany, one half-of which are reserved for what are called preference cases (relatives of American citizens). That leaves 6500 for non-preference.

The allocation of these is based on the order of their receipt." National Archives. Record Group 260. Displaced Persons. Entry 181. Civil Administration Division.

12. The annual number of German immigrants increased substantially at this point. See Department of Justice, 1945–77, *Annual Report of the Immigration and Naturalization Service* (Washington, DC: Government Printing Office).

13. Although almost 1.5 million people emigrated from Germany between 1946 and 1961, only 780,000 (fifty-two percent) were German citizens. The rest were foreign citizens, most of whom were displaced persons. In May 1945 there were 4.5 million displaced persons in the western occupation zones. Almost three-fourths were repatriated, often forcefully. Of the 1.2 million displaced persons remaining, most were from Poland, Ukraine and the Baltic States and did not want to return to their home countries. Displaced persons made up ninety percent of emigrants until the end of 1951. It was not until 1951 that the number of German citizens increased among emigrants. After 1952 when the number of displaced persons declined significantly, the number of German citizens represented the largest contingent.

14. It is impossible to know how many former POWs wanted to return and were unable to do so. Letters written by former POWs to farmers they worked for indicate that the desire to immigrate was considerable. For examples, see Michael Luick-Thrames, ed., 2002, *Signs of Life: The Correspondence of German POWs at Camp Algona, Iowa* (Mason City, IA: Stoyles); Archives of the New Mexico Farm and Heritage Museum.

15. Camp Ruston Archives, accessed 2004, www.latech.edu/tech/libary/campruston/slide 167.

16. He was somewhat ambivalent about it, having had some bad experiences with health insurance that he was unwilling to discuss.

17. See Aliceville Museum, 2002, *Museum News*, Aliceville, Alabama. May.

18. "Prisoner returns with his family," *The Niles Daily Star*, October 24, 1949.

19. He believes it was due to the fact that he was in the Hitlerjugend.

20. Heino and Jean have co-authored a book about Heino's POW time. Heino Erichsen and Jean Nelson-Erichsen, 2001, *The Reluctant Warrior: Former German POW Finds Peace in Texas* (Austin, TX: Eakin).

21. Clarence Monisimth, "Former POW Returns with Family for Look in Area, *Chronicle-News*, August 21, 1963.

22. Several newspaper articles reported on the reunion. See Fred Baker, "The Friendly Invasion of Trinidad." *Empire Magazine*, May 31, 1964; "Group of Visitors Fulfill Long Wish, Climb Mesas Behind Fisher's Peak," *Chronicle News*, June 8, 1964; "Formal Welcome Is Given Visitors to Trinidad in Reception and Mayor's Talk," *Chronicle News*, June 8, 1984. Larry Pearson, "Ex-German PWs This Time Voluntarily Visit Colorado," *Rocky Mountain News*, June 7, 1964.

23. A copy of the certificate is in the author's possession.

24. A newspaper article reported on their visit, "Earlier Visit Here Was as POW," *Malborough Herald-Advocate*, May 9, 1994.

25. In 1957 they had a son, Harold. At the time of the interview, Hilde had Alzheimer's disease and Harold lived on the first floor of the house.

26. The German colonial plans concerning Africa in the era of National Socialism ascribed a central role to the sciences. Scientists of all possible fields launched into activities. Subjects which were directly related to the practice of colonial policies, such as African languages, ethnology, law, economic sciences, and medicine, were especially developed.

27. At the time of the interview Trudi was incapacitated by a stroke. Heinz died on Thanksgiving Day 2008.

28. German-American Citizens League of Greater Cincinnati. (www.gacl.org/schlar.html; http://www.schlaraffia.org)

29. See Paul Sauser, "Ex-German POWs Return: Their Memories of Fort Robinson Positive." *Star Herald*, August 22, 1987.

30. The Länderrat, 1945–49, represented a regular conference of Ministerpresidents of four states in the American occupation zone: Bayern, Nordwürttemberg/Nord-Baden, Hessen, Bremen (Meyers Lexikon Online). It was headquartered in Stuttgart and coordinated legislation within the U.S. zone.

31. Rudolf Thill, *Adrift in Stormy Times* (Decorah, IA: South Bear Press, 2004).

32. See copy of letter in the author's possession from George Hughes to Alfred Müller, dated October 28, 1948. The letter informs Alfred that his father-in-law "who is of German descent" will be "glad to help you in any way he can."

33. A copy is in author's possession. Unfortunately the name of the paper and the date were not recorded.

34. Alfred had not been aware of the nativity scene when he was a POW there.

35. Alfred and Edith have died since the interview.

36. A notice in the *Herald Citizen* (Cookeville, Tennessee) dated October 27, 1999, announced Hennes' presentation at Tennessee Tech University on October 28. The same newspaper, announcing a book signing, published a lengthy article on Hennes on November 12, 2004.

37. Gerhard Hennes, 2004, *The Barbed Wire* (Franklin, TN: Providence House Publishers).

38. At the time of the interview Rupert and Almut were writing separate autobiographies which have since been published. Rupert Metzroth, 2004, *Think for Yourself* (Stuart, FL: Black Yard Publishers); Almut Metzroth, 2007, *Thorns and Roses: A Life in the Context of History* (Fort Pierce, FL: Fiction Publishing).

38. The Schwartz Ballroom in Hartford was built in 1928 by the Schwartz Brewery Company. During the 1930s it was venue for big bands. It became a POW camp between 1944 and 1945. After World War II it featured mostly polka and rock and roll. Later it faced demolition. The Hartford Rotary Foundation acquired ownership of the ballroom in October 1997 and restored it to its former glory. Since 1998 it has been listed on the Wisconsin Historic Register.

40. Sixteen men died when a truck they were in was struck by a train as they were returning from work detail. The others died of natural causes. "Community Remembers German POWs," *POW-MIA InterNetwork*, November 22, 2003.

41. On May 9, 2012, Ernst was one of the speakers at the Federal Inter-Agency Holocaust Remembrance Commemoration in Washington, D.C.

42. See article: "Ex-POW Chooses Tampa for Home," *Tampa Daily Times*, January 14, 1952.

43. "Return to Camp Houlton Sparks German POW's Memories," *Houlton Pioneer Times*, October 8, 2008.

44. Otto thinks the delay was due to his membership in the *Hitlerjugend* and the fact that he was born in East Germany (but the reason was most likely the quota system).

45. During my visit, Otto made several calls to Germany about German election results.

46. Like Gunther K. and Alfred M., Heinz proudly displays his Afrika Korps memorabilia in his study.

47. The book was later published under his pseudonym, Peter Christen: *From Military Government to State Department: How a German Employee Sees the Work of the US Military Government and State Department in a Small Bavarian Town, Its Successes and Its Handicaps* (Erding, Germany: A.P. Wagner, 1950).

48. Peter's wife Johanna died in 2004. Peter remains active, giving talks to a variety of organizations about his experiences growing up in Nazi Germany and his experiences as a prisoner of war in the United States.

49. The *Treuhandanstalt* (trust agency) was the agency that privatized the East German enterprises, owned as public property. Created by the *Volkskammer*, the unicameral legislature of the German Democratic Republic, on June 17, 1990, it oversaw the restructuring and selling of about 8,500 firms with initially over 4 million employees. At that time it was the world's largest industrial enterprise, controlling everything from steelworks to the Babelsberg Film Studios.

50. After World War I and World War II, the Saarland was forcibly made a protectorate by the victorious Allies as part of a policy of "industrial disarmament." The protectorate, which was administered by France, was short-lived, lasting from 1947 to 1956 when the region was fully integrated as a state into the Federal Republic of Germany.

51. Several men also commented positively on the more open and fluid class structure, the lack of "credentialism," and the "can-do attitude" that had attracted them.

Chapter 4

1. Freund's categories are based on German documents and his own oral history interviews with 60 men and women who immigrated to the United States and Canada.

2. Many were not prewar residents of these states.

3. See Wolfgang Köllmann and Peter Marschalck, 1973, "German Emigration to the United States," in *Studies of American History Vol. VII. Dislocation and Emigration*, Donald Fleming and Bernard Bailyn, eds. (Harvard University: Charles Warren Center), 551–52 and Table XV, p. 552. See also RG 260 OMGUS Report, Report Displaced Persons Branch Entry 181; *Der Spiegel*, "Quotenjäger."

4. Johann G.'s story provides perhaps the clearest example of the central role played by his first American experience. While John's sojourn on American soil was short, he had thoroughly enjoyed his time in Idaho. Although he was able to get a good job as an electrician after he returned to Germany, and he and his family were comfortable, even owning a car, from the start he was determined to return to the place "with all the friendly people."

5. In his book *In Amerikanischer Kriegsgefangenschaft*, Schlauch reports on another German former POW, Heinz Pfaeffle, who was interned in Louisiana and Texas and who married an American woman he met while working for the military in Heidelberg. Pfaeffle was able to immigrate in 1949. Unfortunately, he had died by the time I began this research.

6. Many Germans who had not been POWs on American soil also worked for the occupation forces and doubtless some of these individuals were able to immigrate.

7. Glenn Thompson reports that he found several former POWs who had been at Camp Atlanta, Nebraska, who preferred not to be identified, "fearing reprisals from Jews." Glenn Thompson, 1993, *Prisoners on the Plains: German POWs in America* (Holdrege, NE: Phelps County Historical Society).

8. All young male immigrants at the time were subject to the draft. As a medical doctor Harry was high on the list. For other examples see Freund, *Aufbrüche nach dem Zusammenbruch*, 298.

Chapter 5

1. See James Richards, "Life in Britain for German Prisoners of War." http://www.bbc.co.uk/history/british/britain_wwtwo/german_pows_01.shtml

2. Among those staying on in the United Kingdom was Bert Trautmann, who become a celebrated soccer goalkeeper for Manchester City. Most married British women. See James Richards, "Life in Britain for German Prisoners of War," http://www.bbc.co.uk/history/british/britain_wwtwo/german_pows_01.shtml; Luke Salkeld, "Love Across Enemy Lines: First 'Traitor' Bride and Her German POW Mark Diamond Wedding." www.dailymail.co.uk/news/article-475365; Helen Weathers, "Sleeping with the Enemy: The British Women Who Fell for German POWs." www.dailymail.co.ul/femail/article-476097/.

3. See François Cochet, 1995, "France 1945: Le dossier controversé des prisonniers de guerre allemands," *L'Histoire* 191: 44–48. Cochet mentions a former prisoner, Wolfgang Lucki, who remained in France and married a French woman. He was a native of what became the Soviet occupation zone and did not want to return there. See also my respondent Hermann F., who contemplated staying in France, but did return to Germany.

4. On the aftermath of World War II, see the articles in *Contemporary European History* 16, no. 4. On population displacements during World War I, see the collection of articles in *Captivity, Forced Labour and Forced Migration in Europe During the First World War*, Matthew Stibbe, ed., 2009 (London: Routledge).

5. For example Morawska estimated that 80 million Eastern Europeans were forcibly displaced during the twentieth century. Ewa Morawska, 2000, "Intended and Unintended Consequences of Forced Migration: A Neglected Aspect of East Europe's Twentieth Century History." *International Migration Review* 30, no. 4: 1049–1087.

6. Except for the Soviet Union, which was not a signatory of the Geneva Convention and did not return the last POWs until 1956, the Allies returned all German POWs by 1948. For an excellent account of German POWs in the Soviet Union, see Frank Biess, 2006, *Homecomings: Returning POWs and the Legacy of Defeat in Postwar Germany* (Princeton: Princeton University Press).

7. This lesson was learned by European countries when they imported temporary workers in the 1960s. On this subject see W.R. Böhning, 1972, *The Migration of Workers in the United Kingdom and the European Community* (Oxford: Oxford University).

8. See Günter Bischof, 2004, "Is the Abuse of POW's under American Control Unprece-

dented?" George Mason University History News Network, May 10. Bischof concludes this short article with the following paragraph: "The abuse of POWs in Baghdad and the legal no man's land constructed for the Guantánamo "enemy combatants" is nothing new, then, in the annals of American warfare. It is rare though that we get to see such explicit pictures of abused prisoners so soon after their maltreatment. It is also unique among the American public to have such a widespread suspicion that something is very fishy with the Guantánamo "enemy combatants" being denied any legal protections for over two years now — now under review by the Supreme Court. German 'DEFs' during World War II were only left in such legal limbo for a few chaotic postwar weeks, before the vast majority of them were released and sent home."

9. When the official repatriation plans were made public, agricultural employers wrote letters and besieged their Congressmen. The first 60,000 men were returned in December 1945, an additional 70,000 in January 1946, another 70,000 in February, 83,000 in March and 43,000 in April 1946.

10. National Archives. War Manpower Commission, Record Group 211. Records of Legal Services. Records of the Legal Services, General Records, 1942–45. In the 99th meeting of the Labor Management Policy Committee, the intention was stated "to withdraw as early as possible PW and foreign labor as free labor becomes available" and mentions that arrangements are made to cease further importation of Mexicans. In the following meeting, on August 19, 1945, the minutes report that a telegram will be sent to all regions, saying that "the War Department will return to Europe at earliest practicable moment all German and Italian PWs. You are instructed to discontinue the uses of PW in contract employment as soon as possible."

11. In spring 1945, to conserve food, the government drastically reduced the food rations for German POWs, a move that was interpreted by some as a violation of the Geneva Convention which mandated that prisoners of war receive rations equal in nutritional value to those of the captor's troops. For a detailed discussion, see Krammer, 240–43.

12. Left behind were 134 men in hospitals or psychiatric wards, 25 escapees still at large and 141 men serving prison terms for crimes committed during their stay.

13. This brings to mind more recent scholarly debates concerning the possibility of an "international governance of migration" (Betts 2011, Hansen 2010, Hatton 2007) to regulate and set standards for different types of migration, most of which are negotiated and regulated at the level of the nation-state, bilaterally or regionally, such as in the European Union. While most scholars agree that a global migration governance regime for voluntary migration (similar to the United Nations High Commissioner for Refugees for forced migration) is not likely to become a reality in the near future, an international agreement guiding the uses of temporary workers could have helped add legitimation to the termination of the bracero program which was favored by the Mexican government. The bracero program was based on a bilateral agreement between unequal partners (Mexico and the United States).

14. Some examples of answers to question 13 (What is the most important single idea you have learned during your internment in America?) in the Provost Marshal General's poll of departing German POWs at Fort Shanks indicate that thirty-four percent of the "run-of-the-mill prisoners," ninety percent of the Fort Eustis prisoners and seventy-eight percent of Camp Atlanta prisoners had "favorable reactions" concerning their internment. Although some of the answers were negative (i.e., "Americans drink too much. Americans don't like to work, and cheat their government"), positive answers include the following: "We expected to find mostly gangsters but we found out the Americans are no different from the Germans"; "I have come to know the land, of which the Nazis gave a distorted picture through their lying propaganda"; "I have learned that the little man in America is not so very different from the little man in Germany." Provost Marshal General's Office, Record Group 389. Entry 438A Historical File 1941–58. Poll of PW Opinion: 22–25.

15. For letters between former prisoners and their American friends see Luick-Thomas, *Signs of Life.* and the collection of letters in the New Mexico Farm and Heritage Museum.

16. Karl Drescher, letters to the Nelson family dated November 16, 1948, and January 25, 1949. New Mexico Farm and Heritage Museum Archives.

17. There is a large literature on immigration to Europe and in particular to Germany. For one of the earlier overviews, see Martin Heisler and Barbara Schmitter Heisler, eds., 1986, "From Foreign Workers to Settlers? Transnational Migration and the Emergence of New Minorities." *Annals of the American Academy of Political and Social Science* 485 (May).

Bibliography

Andersch, Alfred. 1946. "Die Kriegsgefangenen, Licht und Schatten — eine Bilanz." *Der Ruf* October 15: 6–7.

Auerbach, Frank. 1952. "Who Are Our New Immigrants?" Department of Justice, Immigration and Naturalization, *I&N Reporter* 1: 4–6.

Bade, Klaus, ed. 1992. *Deutsche im Ausland — Fremde in Deutschland: Migration in Geschichte und Gegenwart.* München: Beck.

Bailey, Milton. 2005. *Behind Barbed Wire: POWs in Houlton, Maine During World War II.* Presque Isle, ME: Printworks.

Bailey, Ronald. 2008. "Lessons in Democracy." *World War II* (August/September): 52–59.

_____, and the Editors of Time-Life Books. 1981. *Prisoners of War.* New York: Time-Life.

Barclay, David, and Elisabeth Glaser-Schmidt, eds. 1997. *Transatlantic Images and Perspectives: Germany and America Since 1776.* Washington, DC, and Cambridge: German Historical Institute and Cambridge University Press.

Bardich, Charles. 1971. "Prisoners as Soldiers: The German 999th Penal Division." *Army Quarterly and Defense Journal* 102 (October): 65–69.

Barkan, Elliot. 2010. "Crossing the Atlantic Rim: European Immigration to the United States After World War I." In *Leaving Home: Migration Yesterday and Today*, Diethelm Knauf and Barry Moreno, eds. Bremen: Edition Temmen, 2010: 167–207.

Bartov, Omar. 1991. *Hitler's Army: Soldiers, Nazis and the War.* New York: Oxford University Press.

Bessel, Richard. 2009. *Germany 1945: From War to Peace.* New York: HarperCollins.

Betts, Alexander, ed. 2011. *Global Migration Governance.* Oxford: Oxford University Press.

Biess, Frank. 2006. *Homecomings: Returning POWs and the Legacies of Defeat in Postwar Germany.* Princeton: Princeton University Press.

_____. 2007. "Cultural History Revisited: Democratization in Germany." Paper presented at Harvard University, Center for European Studies. November 5.

Billigmeier, Robert. 1982. "Recent German Immigration to America." In *Contemporary American Immigration: Interpretive Essays*, edited by Dennis Laurence. Boston: Twayne.

Billinger, Robert. 1977. "Hitler's Wehrmacht in Virginia." *Virginia Magazine* 85 no. 3: 259–73.

_____. 2000. *Hitler's Soldiers in the Sunshine State: German POWs in Florida*, Gainesville: University Press of Florida.

_____. 2008. *Nazi POWs in the Tar Heel State.* Gainesville: University Press of Florida.

Bischof, Günter. 1999. "Einige Thesen zu einer Mentalitätsgeschichte deutscher Kriegsgefangenschaft in amerikanischem Gewahrsam." In *Kriegsgefangenschaft im Zweiten Weltkrieg: Eine Vergleichenede Perspektive*, edited by Günter Bischof and Rüdiger Overmans, 175–212. Wien: Verlag Gerhard Höller.

_____, and Rüdiger Overmans, eds. 1999. *Kriegsgefagenschaft im Zweiten Weltkrieg: Eine Vergleichenede Perspective.* Wien: Verlag Gerhard Höller.

_____, Stefan Karner, and Barbara Stelzl-Marx, eds. 2005. *Kriegsgefangene des Zweiten Weltkrieges: Gefangennahme-Lagerleben-Rückkehr.* Wien: Oldenburg Verlag.

Blum, John Morton. 1976. *V Was for Victory. Politics and American Culture During World War II*. New York: Harcourt Brace Jovanovich.

Böhme, Kurt. 1972. Die *Deutschen Kriegsgefangenen in amerikanischer Hand*. Wissenschaftliche Kommission für deutsche Kriegsgefangenengeschichte. Vol. 10, part 2. München: Ernst und Werner Gieseking.

Böhning, W.R. 1972. *The Migration of Workers in the United Kingdom and the European Community*. Oxford: Oxford University Press.

Böhnisch, Georg. 2008. "Surviving POWs Seek Compensation." *Der Spiegel Online International*. www.spiegel.de/international/europe/0,1518,574180,00.html.

Boyd, Monica. 1989. "Family and Personal Networks in Migration." *International Migration Review* 23, no. 3: 638–70.

Buck, Anita. 1998. *Behind Barbed Wire: German POW Camps in Minnesota*. St. Cloud, MN: North Star Press.

Buecker, Thomas. 1992. "Nazi Influence at the Fort Robison POW Camp During WWII." *Nebraska History* 73, no. 1 (1992): 32–41.

_____. 2006. *Fort Robinson and the American Century 1900–1948*. Tulsa: University of Oklahoma Press.

Bundesministerium für Vertriebene. 2004. *Das Schicksal der Deutschen in Rumänien*. München: Deutscher Taschenbuch Verlag.

Busco, Ralph, and Douglas Alder. 1971. "German and Italian Prisoners of War in Utah and Idaho." *Utah Historical Quarterly* 39, no. 1: 55–72.

Butler, Joseph. 1973. "Prisoner of War Labor in the Sugar Cane Fields of Lafourche Parish, Louisiana, 1943–44." *Louisiana History* 14, no. 3: 283–96.

Carlson, Lewis. 1997. *We Were Each Other's Prisoners: An Oral History of World War II American and German Prisoners of War*. New York: Basic Books.

Carter, David. 1980. *POW behind Canadian Barbed Wire: Aliens, Refugees and Prisoners of War in Canada, 1914–1946*. Calgary: Tumbleweed Press.

Castles, Stephen. 2003. "Toward a Sociology of Forced Migration." *Sociology* 37, no. 2: 13–34.

Choate, Mark. 1989. *Nazis in the Pineywoods*. Lufkin, TX: Best of East Texas Publishers.

Christen, Peter. 1950. *From Military Government to State Department: How a German Employee Sees the Work of the US Military Government and State Department in a Small Bavarian Town, Its Successes and Its Handicaps*. Erding, Germany: A.P. Wagner.

Clark, Penny. 1988. "Farm Work and Friendship: The German Prisoner of War Camp at Lake Wabaunsee." *The Emporia State Research Studies* 36, no. 3 (1988): 5–43.

Cochet, François. 1995. "France 1945: Le dossier controversé des prisonniers allemands." *L'Histoire* no. 191 (September): 44–48.

Coker, Kathy Roe. 1992. "World War II Prisoners of War in Georgia: German Memories of Camp Gordon, 1943–1945." *The Georgia Historical Quarterly* 76 no. 4: 837–61.

Cook, Ruth Beaumont. 2006. *Guests Behind the Barbed Wire*. Birmingham, AL: Crane Hill.

Coles, David. 1994. "'Hell-by-the Sea': Florida's Camp Gordon Johnston in World War II." *The Florida Historical Quarterly* 64 no.1: 1–22.

Cowley, Betty. 2002. *Stalag Wisconsin: Inside WW II Prisoner of War Camps*. Oregon, WI: Badger.

Daniel, Peter, 1990. "Going Among Strangers: Southern Reactions to World War II." *The Journal of American History* 77, no. 3: 886–911.

Davis, Gerald. 1977. "Prisoners of War in Twentieth-Century War Economies." *Journal of Contemporary History* 12, no. 4: 626–34.

Donnelly, Robert. 1992. "Reminiscence: John Fahey on Reeducating German Prisoners During WW II." *Oregon Historical Quarterly* 93: 368–393.

Doyle, Frederick. 1978. "German POWs in the Southwest U.S. During WWII: An Oral History." Ph.D. Thesis. University of Denver, Department of History.

Doyle, Robert. 2010. *The Enemy in Our Hands: America's Treatment of Enemy Prisoners of War from the Revolution to the War on Terror*. Lexington: University of Kentucky Press.

EMNID-Institut: EMNID-Informationen. Bielefeld. 1957, 1961, 1970.

Enssle, Manfred. 1987. "The Hard Discipline of Food Scarcity in Stuttgart, 1945–1948." *German Studies Review* 10, no. 3: 481–502.

Erichsen, Heino, and Jean Nelson-Erichsen. 2001. *The Reluctant Warrior: Former German POW Finds Peace in Texas*. Austin, TX: Eakin.

Ermath, Michael, ed. 1993. *America and the Shaping of German Society 1945–1953*. Providence, RI: Berg.

Fairchild, Byron, and Jonathan Grossman. 1959. *The Army and Industrial Manpower*. Washington, DC: Office of the Chief of Military History, Department of the Army.

Fawcett, James. 1989. "Networks, Linkages and Migration Systems." *International Migration Review* 23, no. 3: 671–80.

Fay, Sidney, 1945. "German Prisoners of War." *Current History* 8 (March 1945): 193.

Fickle, James, and Donald Ellis. 1990. "POWs in the Piney Woods: German Prisoners in the Southern Lumber Industry, 1943–1945." *Journal of Southern History* 56 no. 4: 695–724.

Fiedler, David. 2003. *The Enemy Among US: POWs in Missouri During World War II*. St. Louis: Missouri Historical Society Press.

_____. 2011. *My Enemy, My Love*. St. Louis, MO: D.W. Fiedler.

Fincher, Jack. 1995. "By Convention, the Enemy Within Never Did Without." *Smithsonian Magazine* 26 no. 3: 126–43.

Freund, Alexander. 2004. *Aufbrüche nach dem Zusammenbruch. Die deutsche Nordamerika Auswanderung nach dem Zweiten Weltkrieg*. Göttingen: V&R Unipress GmbH.

Gaertner, George. 1985. *Hitler's Last Soldier in America*. New York: Stein and Day.

Galarza, Ernesto. 1964. *Merchants of Labor: The Mexican Bracero Story*. Charlotte, NC: McNally and Loftin.

Gansberg, Judith. 1997. *Stalag USA: The Remarkable Story of German POWs in America*. New York: Thomas Crowell.

Garcia y Griego, Manuel. 1981. "The Importation of Mexican Contract Laborers to the United States, 1942–1964: Antecedents, Operation and Legacy." Working Papers in U.S.–Mexican Studies II. La Jolla. Program in United States–Mexican Studies. University of California, San Diego.

Gassert, Philip. 1997. *Amerika im Dritten Reich*. Stuttgart: Franz Steinert Verlag.

Gatrell, Peter. 2007. "Introduction: World Wars and Population Displacement in Europe in the Twentieth Century." *Contemporary European History* 16, no. 4: 414–26.

Geiger, Jeffrey. 1996. *German Prisoners of War at Camp Cooke, California: Personal Accounts of 14 Soldiers, 1944–1946*. Jefferson, NC: McFarland & Co.

Greene, Bette. 1973. *Summer of My German Soldier*. New York: The Dial Press.

Grothe, Hugo. 1959. "Europäische Auswandrung nach dem Zweiten Weltkrieg," *Geographische Rundschau* 11: 253–61.

Hahn, Lauren. 2000–01. "Germans in the Orchards: Post–World War II Letters from Ex-POW Agricultural Workers to a Midwestern Farmer." *The Journal of the Midwest Language Association* 33, no. 3 (Fall/Winter): 170–78.

Hansen, Randall. 2010. "The Future of Migration: Governance and Regional Consultative Processes." Background Paper WMR. Geneva: International Organization for Migration.

Hardach, Karl. 1984. "Germany Under Western Occupation, 1945–1949." In *Contemporary Germany: Politics and Culture*, edited by Charles Burdick, Hans-Adolf Jacobsen, Winfried Kudszus, 66–76. Boulder, CO: Westview Press.

Hatton, T.J. 2007. "Should We Have a WTO for International Migration?" *Economic Policy* 22, no. 50: 339–83.

Hawkins, Freda. 1988. *Canada and Immigration: Public Policy and Public Concern*. Kingston, ON: McGill University Press.

Heintz, Julie. 1998. "The War at Home: Prisoner of War Camps in Iowa During World War II." MA Thesis. University of Northern Iowa.

Heisler, Barbara Schmitter. 2007. "The 'Other Braceros': Temporary Labor and German Prisoners of War in the United States, 1943–1946." *Social Science History* 31, no. 2 : 239–71.

Heisler, Martin, and Barbara Schmitter Heisler, eds. 1986. "From Foreign Workers to Settlers?: Transnational Migration and the Emergence of New Minorities." *The Annals of the American Academy of Political and Social Science* 485 (May).

Hennes, Gerhard. 2004. *The Barbed Wire: POW in the USA*. Franklin, TN: Providence House.

Hörner, Helmut, and Allan Kent Powell. 1991. *A German Odyssey: The Journal of a German Prisoner of War*. Golden, CO: Fulcrum.

Hohn, Uta. 1991. *Die Zerstörung deutscher Städte in Zweiten Weltkrieg 1940–45: Regionale Unterschiede*. Dortmund: Dortmunder Vertrieb für Bau- und Planungsliteratur.

Hutchinson, E. 1949. "Immigration Policy Since World War I." *Annals of the American Academy of Political and Social Sciences* 262 (March): 15–21.

Jaehn, Tomas. 2000. "Unlikely Harvesters: German Prisoners of War as Agricultural Workers in the Northwest." *Montana: The Magazine of Western History* 50, no. 3 :46–57.

Jarausch, Konrad. *2006. After Hitler: Recivilizing Germans.* New York: Oxford.
Jarausch, Konrad, and Michael Geyer, eds. 2003. *Shattered Past: Reconstructing German Histories.* Princeton: Princeton University Press.
Jung, Hermann. 1972. *Die deutschen Kriegsgefangenen in amerikanischer Hand: USA.* München: Gieseking.
Junker, Detlev. 1997. "German Views of America 1933–1945." In *Transatlantic Images and Perceptions,* edited by D. Barclay and E. Glaser-Schmidt, 213–64. Washington, DC, and Cambridge: German Historical Institute and Cambridge University Press.
Kampfhoefner, Walter, and Wolfgang Helbich, eds. 2003. *German American Immigration and Ethnicity in Comparative Perspective.* Madison: University of Wisconsin Press.
Keefer, Louis. 1992. *Italian POWs in America. Captives or Allies.* 1942–1946. New York: Praeger.
Kelley, Ninette, and Michael Trebilcock. 1998. *Making of the Mosaic.* Toronto: University of Toronto Press.
Klessmann, Christoph. 1991. *Die doppelte Staatsgründung: Deutsche Geschichte 1945–1955.* Bonn: Bundeszentrale für Politische Bildung.
Köllmann, Wolfgang, and Peter Marschalck. 1973. "German Emigration to the United States." In *Studies of American History, Vol. VII: Dislocation and Emigration,* edited by Donald Fleming and Bernard Bailyn, 499–554. Cambridge, MA: Charles Warren Center, Harvard University.
Koop, Allen. 1988. *Stark Decency: German Prisoners of War in a New England Village.* Hanover, NH: University Press of New England.
Kramer, Alan. 1991. *The West German Economy 1945–1955.* New York: Berg.
Krammer, Arnold. 1991. *Nazi Prisoners of War in America.* Chelsea, MI: Scarborough House.
Krause, Michael. 1997. *Flucht vor dem Bobenkrieg: Umquartierung im Zweiten Weltkrieg und die Widereingliederung der Evakuierten in Deutschland. 1943–1963.* Düsseldorf: Droste Buchverlag.
Lagrou, Pieter. "Overview." 2005. In *Prisoners of War, Prisoners of Peace,* edited by Bob Moore and Barbara Hately-Broad, 3–10. Oxford: Berg.
Landsberger, Kurt. 2007. *Prisoners of War at Camp Trinidad, Colorado, 1943–46.* Ramsey, NJ: Arbor Books.
Laney, Monique. 2008. "Wernher von Braun and Arthur Rudolph: Negotiating the Past in Huntsville." *German Diasporic Experiences,* edited by Mathias Schulze, et al., 443–54. Waterloo, ON: Wilfrid Laurier University Press.
Lasby, Clarence. 1971. *Project Paperclip: German Scientists and the Cold War.* New York: Atheneum.
Leed, Eric J. 1991. *The Mind of the Traveler: From Gilgamesch to Global Tourism.* New York: Basic Books.
Lehmann, Albrecht. 1984. "Krieg — Urlaub — Gastarbeiter. " *Archiv für Sozialgeschichte* 24: 457–80.
Levie, Howard, 1973. "The Employment of Prisoners of War." *The American Journal of International Law* 57, no. 2 (1973): 318–353.
Lewis, George, and John Mewha. 1955. *History of Prisoner of War Utilization by the United States Army, 1776–1945.* Washington, DC: Office of the Chief of Military History, Department of the Army.
Lowe Kunzig, Robert. 1946. "360,000 P.W.'s: The Hope of Germany." *American Magazine.* November.
Luebke, Frederick. 1990. "Three Centuries of Germans in America." In *Germans in the New World: Essays in the History of Immigration,* 157–190. Urbana: University of Illinois Press.
Luick-Thrams, Michael, ed. 2002. *Signs of Life: the Correspondence of German POWs at Camp Algona, Iowa, 1943–46.* Mason City, IA: Stoyles.
MacKenzie, Simon Paul. 1994. "The Treatment of Prisoners of War in World War II." *The Journal of Modern History* 6, no. 3 (1994): 487–520.
Maschke, Erich. 1974. *Die deutschen Kriegsgefangenen des Zweiten Weltkrieges: Eine Zusammenfassung.* München: Ernst und Werner Gieseking.
Massey, Douglas, and Nolan Malone. 2002. "Pathways to Legal Immigration." *Population Research and Policy Review* 2, no.6: 473–594.
May, Lowell. 1995. *Camp Concordia: German POWs in the Midwest.* Manhattan, KS: Sunflower University Press.
Mayer, Karl Ulrich. 1998. "German Survivors of World War II: The Impact on the Life Course

of the Collective Experiences of Birth Cohorts." In *German Sociology*, edited by Ute Gerhardt, 207–221. New York: Continuum.

Mazuzan, George, and Nancy Walker. 1978. "Restricted Areas: German Prisoner of War Camps in Western New York, 1944–1946." *New York History* (January): 55–72.

McKnight, Maxwell. 1944. "The Employment of Prisoners of War in the United States." *International Labour Review* 50 (July): 47–64.

Metzroth, Almut. 2007. *Thorns and Roses: A Life in the Context of History*. Ft. Pierce, FL: Fiction Publishing.

Metzroth, Rupert. 2004. *Think for Yourself*. Stuart, FL: Black Yard.

Mohr, Joachim. 2006. "Traumland Amerika" *Spiegel Special* 1: 46–49.

Moore, Bob. 2005. "Foreword." In *Prisoners of War, Prisoners Peace*, edited by Bob Moore and Barbara Hateley Broad, Oxford: Berg.

_____, and Barbara Hateley Broad, eds. 2005. *Prisoners of War, Prisoners of Peace*. Oxford: Berg.

_____, and Kent Fedorowich, eds. 1996. *Prisoners of War and Their Captors in World War II*. Oxford: Berg.

Moore, John Hammond. 1977. "Hitler's Wehrmacht in Virginia, 1943–1946." *The Virginia Magazine of History and Biography* 85, no. 3: 259–73.

Moore, John Hammond. 1978. *The Faustball Tunnel: German POWs in America and Their Great Escape*. New York: Random House.

Morawska, Ewa. 2000. "Intended and Unintended Consequences of Forced Migrations: A Neglected Aspect of Eastern Europe." *International Migration Review* 34, no.4: 1049–1087.

_____. 2007. "International Migration: Its Various Mechanisms and Different Theories That Try to Explain It." IMER. Malmo, Sweden. Willy Brandt Series of Working Papers in International Migration and Ethnic Relations.

Nerger-Focke, Karin. 1995. *Die deutsche Amerikaauswanderung nach 1945*. Stuttgart: Akademischer Verlag.

Noelle-Neumann, Elisabeth, and Erich Peter, eds. 1956. *Jahrbuch der öffentlichen Meinung 1947–55*. Allensbach/Bonn: Verlag für Demoskopie.

Noles, James. 2002. *Camp Rucker During World War II*. Charleston, SC: Arcadia Publishing.

Oberdieck, William. 1995. *America's Prisoner of War 1943–1946*. New York: Carlton Press.

O'Brien, Patrick, Thomas Isern, and Daniel Lumley, 1984. "Stalag Sunflower: German Prisoners of War in Kansas." *Kansas History* 7, no. 3: 225–47.

Overmans, Rüdiger. 1995. "Die Rheinwiesenlager." In *Ende des 3. Reiches — Endes des Zweiten Weltkrieges*, edited by Hans Erich Volkmann. München: Militärischen Forschungsamt, 1995.

_____. 1999. "Ein untergeordneter Eingang im Leidesbuch der jüngeren Geschichte? Die Rheinwiesenlager 1945." In *Kriegsgefangenschaft im Zweiten Weltkrieg: eine vergleichenede Perspective*, edited by Günter Bischof and Rüdiger Overmans, 233–64. Ternitz-Pottschach: Verlag Gerhard Höller.

_____, ed. 1999. *In der Hand des Feindes: Kriegsgefangenschaft von der Antike bis zum Zweiten Weltkrieg*. Köln: Bohlau Verlag.

_____. 2000. *Soldaten hinter Stacheldraht; Deutsche Kriegsgefangene des zweiten Weltkriegs*. Berlin: Econ Ullstein List Verlag.

Owen, Gregory. 1999. Interview with Mr. Karl Baumann, March 13. Special Collections Internship. James Madison University. Spring.

Pabel, Reinhold. 1995. *Enemies Are Human*. Philadelphia: Winston.

Parnell, Wilma. 1981. *The Killing of Corporal Kunze*. New York: Lyle Stuart.

Pelz, Edwin. 1985. "A German Prisoner of War in the South: The Memoir of Edwin Pelz," edited by William Shea. *Arkansas Historical Quarterly*, 44, no. 1: 42–55.

Pluth, Edward John. 1970. "The Administration and Operation of German Prisoner of War Camps in the United States During World War II." Ph.D. Thesis. Ball State University.

_____. 1975. "Prisoner of War Employment in Minnesota During World War II." *Minnesota History* 44, no. 8: 290–303.

Portes, Alejandro. 1995. *Economic Sociology of Immigration: Essays on Networks, Ethnicity*. New York: Russell Sage Foundation.

_____. 1997. "Immigration Theory for a New Century: Some Problems and Opportunities." *International Migration Review* 31, no. 4: 799–825.

Portes, Alejandro, and Josef Börösz. 1989. "Contemporary Immigration: Theoretical Perspectives on Its Determinants." *International Migration Review* 23, no. 3: 606–30.

Powell, Allen Kent. 1989. *Splinter of a Nation: German Prisoner of War in Utah.* Salt Lake City: University of Utah Press.
Pritchett, Merrill, and William Shea. 1978. "The Africa Korps in Arkansas 1943–1946." *Arkansas Historical Quarterly* 37 (Spring): 3–22.
_____. 1979. "The Enemy in Mississippi (1943–1946)." *The Journal of Mississippi History* 1, no. 4 : 351–371.
_____. 1982. "The Wehrmacht in Louisiana." *Louisiana History* 23, no. 1 (Winter): 5–19.
Reimers, David. 1981. "Post–World War II Immigration to the United States: America's Latest Newcomers," *Annals of the American Academy of Political and Social Science 454* (March): 1–12.
Reiss, Matthias. 2002. *Die Schwarzen waren unsere Freunde: Deutsche Kriegsgefangene in der amerkinischen Gesellschaft 1942–146.* Paderborn: Ferdiand Schöningh.
_____. 2004. "Icons of Insult: German and Italian Prisoners of War in African American Letters During World War II." *Amerikastudien.* 49, no. 4: 539–562.
_____. 2005. "Bronzed Bodies Behind Barbed Wire: Masculinity and the Treatment of German Prisoners of War in the United States During World War II." *The Journal of Military History* 69 (April): 475–504.
_____. 2005. "The Nucleus of a New German Ideology? The Re-education of German Prisoners of War in the United States During World War II." In *Prisoners of War, Prisoners of Peace,* edited by Bob Moore and Barbara Hately-Broad, 91–104. Oxford. Berg.
Richter, Anthony. 1983. "A German POW in Illinois." *Journal of the Illinois State Historical Society* 76, no. 1: 62–70.
Richter, Hans-Werner. 1993. *Die Geschlagenen.* München: Deutscher Taschenbuch Verlag.
Robin, Ron. 1995. *The Barbed-Wire College: Reeducating German POWs in the United States During World War II.* Princeton: Princeton University Press.
Rössler, Horst. 1992. "Massenexodus: die Neue Welt des 19. Jahrhunderts." In *Deutsche im Ausland — Fremde in Deutschland. Migration in Geschichte und Gegenwart,* edited by Klaus Bade, 148–56. München: Beck.
Rumbaut, Ruben. 1994. "Origins and Destinies: Immigration to the United States Since World War II," *Sociological Forum* 9, no. 4: 583–621.
Rytlewski, Ralf, and Manfred Opp de Hipt. 1987. *Die Bundesrepublik in Zahlen 1945/49–1980: Ein Sozialgeschichtliches Arbeitsbuch.* München: Beck.
Sauer, Angelika. 1993. "A Matter of Domestic Policy? Canadian Immigration Policy and the Admission of Germans, 1945–50." *Canadian Historical Review* 74, no. 2: 226–63.
_____. 1996. "Christian Charity, Government Policy and German Immigration to Canada and Australia, 1947 to 1952," *Canadian Issues* 18: 159–80.
Schlauch, Wolfgang. 2003. *In amerikanischer Kriegsgefangenschaft: Berichte deutscher Soldaten aus dem Zweiten Weltkrieges.* Crailsheim, Germany: Baier.
Schmid, Walter. 2005. *A German POW in New Mexico.* Albuquerque: University of New Mexico Press.
Schott, Matthew. 1995. "Prisoner Like Us: German POWs Encounter Louisiana's African Americans." *Louisiana History* 36, no. 3: 277–90.
Schroer, John. Letter to the author. March 30, 2009.
Schulz, Robert. 1996. *Triologie hinter Stacheldraht. Als deutscher Kriegsgefangener in den Lagern der Alliierten auf drei Kontinenten 1943–194,* Hildesheim: Scultetus Verlag.
Shea, William. 1985. "A German Prisoner of War in the South: The Memoir of Edwin Pelz." *Arkansas Historical Quarterly* 1 (Spring): 42–55.
Simmons, Dean. 2000. *Swords into Plowshares: Minnesota's POW Camps During World War II.* St. Paul, MN: Cathedral Hill Books.
Smith, Arthur, Jr. 1996. *The War for the German Mind: Reeducating Hitler's Soldiers.* Providence, RI: Berghahn.
Smith, Beverly. 1943. "Nazi Supermen Hit the Dirt." *American Magazine.* 140: 45–61.
Sonntag, Manfred. 1992. *Im Goldenen Käfig. Freiheit hinter Stacheldraht.* Hamburg: Soldi Verlag.
Sosna, Morton. 1991. "Stalag Dixie." *Stanford Humanities Review* 2, no. 1: 38–64.
Speier, Hans. 1981. *From the Ashes of Disgrace.* Amherst: University of Massachusetts Press.
Spidle, Jake. 1974. "Axis Invasion of the American West: POWs in New Mexico, 1942–1946." *New Mexico Historical Review* 49, no. 2: 93–133.
Springer, Paul. 2010. *America's Captives: Treatment of POWs from the Revolutionary War to the War on Terror.* Lawrence: University Press of Kansas.

Steelman, Danny. 1983. "German Prisoners of War in Oklahoma: Oklahoma's Prisoner of War Operations During World War II." *The Oklahoma State Historical Review* 4 (Spring): 1–13.

Steinert, Johannes-Dieter. 1995. *Migration und Politik. Westdeutschland-Europa-Übersee 1945–1961.* Osnabrück: secolo Verlag.

Steinert, Johannes-Dieter and Inge Weber-Newth. 2003. *European Immigrants in Britain 1933–1950.* Munich: Saur.

Stern, Fritz. 2006. *Five Germanys I Have Known.* New York: Farrar, Straus and Giroux.

Stibbe, Matthew, ed. 2009. *Captivity, Forced Labour and Forced Migration in Europe During the First World War.* London: Routledge.

Taeuber, Irene. 1949. "Postwar Emigration from Germany and Italy." *Annals of the American Academy of Political and Social Science* 262 (March): 82–91.

Thill, Rudolf. 2004. *Adrift in Stormy Times.* Decorah, IA: South Bear Press.

Thompson, Antonio. 2008. *German Jackboots on Kentucky Blue Grass.* Clarksville, TN: Diversion Press.

_____. 2010. *Men in German Uniform: POWs in America During World War II.* Knoxville: University of Tennessee Press.

Thompson, Glenn. 1993. *Prisoners on the Plains: German POWs in America.* Holdrege, NE: Phelps County Historical Society.

Tilly, Charles 1990. 'Transplanted Networks." In *Immigration Reconsidered: History, Sociology, and Politics,* edited by Virginia Yans-McLaughlin. 79–95. New York: Oxford University Press.

Tissing, Robert, Jr. 1973. "Utilization of Prisoners of War in the United States During World War II: Texas, a Case Study." MA thesis. Baylor University.

_____. 1976. "Stalag Texas." *Military History of Texas and the Southwest* 13: 24–34.

Uhse, Horst. 2004. "Life Behind Barbed Wire." *Museum News* 11, Issue 2 (May). Aliceville Museum.

Ungern-Sternberg, Roderich. 1952. "Die Wanderzüge Westeuropäer nach dem zweiten Weltkrieg." *Jahrbücher für Nationalökonomie und Statistik.* 165: 215–249.

United States Department of Justice. *Annual Report of the Immigration and Naturalization Service,* Washington, DC, 1945–1977.

United States Bureau of the Census. 1975. *Historical Statistics of the United States: Colonial Times to 1970.* Washington, DC: Government Press.

Wagner, Jonathan. 2006. *A History of Migration from Germany to Canada.* Vancouver: University of British Columbia Press.

Walker, Richard. 2001. *The Lone Star and the Swastika: German POWs in Texas.* Austin, TX: Eakin Press.

Ward, Leslie. 1982. *History of the Concordia Prisoner of War Camp.* Concordia, KS: Kansan Printing House.

Warner, Richard. 1986. "Barbed Wire and Nazilagers: PW Camps in Oklahoma." *The Chronicles of Oklahoma.* 64 (Spring): 37–67.

Waters, Michael. 2004. *Lone Star Stalag: German Prisoners of War at Camp Hearne.* College Station: Texas A&M University Press.

Weber-Newt, Inge, and Johannes Dieter Steinert. 2006. *German Migrants in Postwar Britain.* London: Routledge.

Wedekind, Volker. 2006. *Der Nullpunkt.* Stuttgart: J.B. Metzlersche Verlagsbuchhandlung.

Wehler, Hans-Ullrich. 2003. *Deutsche Gesellschaftsgeschichte. vol. 4: Vom Beginn des Ersten Weltkriegs bis zur Gründung der beiden deutschen Staaten, 1914–1949.* München: Verlag C.H. Beck.

White, Michael. 1996. *A Brother's Blood.* New York: Cliff Street Books.

Whittingham, Richard. 1997. *Martial Justice: The Last Mass Execution in the United States.* Annapolis, MD: Naval Institute Press.

Wilcox, Walter. 1947. *The Farmer in the Second World War.* Ames: Iowa State College Press.

Williamson, Gordon, and Stephen Andrew. 2003. *The Hermann Göring Division.* Oxford: Osprey Publishing.

Wilson, Terry Paul. 1974. "The Afrika Korps in Oklahoma: Fort Reno's Prisoner of War Compound." *Chronicles of Oklahoma.* 52: 360–69.

Yarbrough, Steve. 2003. *Prisoners of War.* New York: Alfred A. Knopf.

Websites

www.bbc.co.uk/history
www.bbc.co.uk/history/british/britain_wwtwo/german_pows_01.shtml
www.ces.fas.harvard.edu/german_studies/berlin_archive/past_participants.htm.
www.claytoday.biz/content/2834_1.php
www.dailymail.co.uk/news/article-475365/
www.dailymail.co.ul/femail/article-476097/
www.gacl.org/schlar.html
www.icrc.org/IHL.NSF/FULL/305?OpenDocument
www.latech.edu/tech/library/campruston/slide167
www.mineaction.org/downloads/Emine Policy Pages/Geneva Conventions/Geneva Convention
     III.pdf.
www.schlaraffia.org
www.spiegel.de/international/europe/0,1518,574180,00.html
www.30thinfantry.org/blanding_hiaorey.ahrmL

Newspaper and Magazine Articles

Andersen, Carol. "POW Visits Algona Creche." *The Algona* (Des Moines), November 10, 1994.
Austin, Gloria. "Return to Camp Houlton Sparks German POW's Memories." *Houlton Pioneer Times*, October 8, 2008.
Baker, Fred. "The Friendly Invasion of Trinidad." *Empire Magazine*, May 31, 1964.
"Banquet Ends Reunion After Five Hectic Days for Germans Trinidad, Colorado." *Chronicle-News*, June 11, 1964.
Bright, David. "Former POW to Help Indians." *Bangor Daily News*, May 12, 2008.
Cairns, Becky. "Utah's POWs." *Standard-Examiner* (Ogden, UT), April 12, 1987.
"Camp Aliceville Reunion to Be Held April 4–7." *The Lamar Democrat and Sulligent*, April 4, 2007.
"Death and Treason." *Newsweek*, February 5, 1945, 47–48.
Dell'Angela, Tracy. "German Fondly Revisits POW Site in Des Plaines." *Chicago Tribune*, June 5, 1996.
"Earlier Visit Here Was as POW." *Malborough Herald-Advocate*, May 9, 1994.
Erman, Lynn. 2004. "Learning Freedom in Captivity." *The Washington Post Magazine*. January 18.
"Ex-POW Chooses Tampa for Home." *Tampa Times*, January 14, 1952.
"Ex-POW Is Back to Make Home in Area." *The Marshfield New-Herald*, March 6, 1956.
Farquhar, Michael. "Enemies Among US: German POWs in America." *The Washington Post*, September 10, 1997.
"Former POW Here Returns to Start His Life Anew." *Standard Examiner*, June 16, 1952.
"Former POW Memories." *The Chardon Record*, August 25, 1987.
"Freedom Improves Germans' View of Nebraska." *Omaha World Herald*, August 27, 1987.
"German Atrocities Raise Question: Are Nazi POWs 'Coddled' Here." *Newsweek*, May 7, 1945, 60–61.
"German Couple Will Settle in the Land of the Enemy." *Garner Leader Signal*, December 28, 1949.
"German War Prisoner to Arrive to Assist with Pea Pack." *Marshfield News Herald*, July 10, 1945.
"Group of Visitors Fulfill Long Wish, Climb Mesas Behind Fisher's Peak." *Chronicle News*, June 9, 1996.
Herald Citizen, Cookeville, TN, October 27, 1999.
Hessleberg, George. "Kurt Pechmann Died Sunday; His Time in Wisconsin as POW Was Life-Changing." *Wisconsin State Journal*, June 30, 2009.
"The Kriegsmarine Escape." *Newsweek*, January 8, 1945, 33–34.
Little, W.T. "Ex-Nazi POWs Get VIP Care in Trinidad, Denver." *Rocky Mountain News*, June 8, 1964, 5–6.
Mayer, Cynthia. "German Ex-POWs Returning to U.S." *Detroit News*, November 26, 1992.
Moor, Joachim. "Traumland Amerika." *Spiegel Spezial* January 2006.
Norris, Tim. "Prisoner in a Free Land." *Milwaukee Journal Sentinel*, October 1, 1995.

Pachal, Allan. "The Enemy in Colorado: German Prisoners of War 1943–1946." *Colorado Magazine*, Summer/Fall 1979, 119–42.
"Prisoner Returns with His Family." *Niles Daily Star*, October 24, 1949.
"Quoten-Jäger." *Der Spiegel*, September, 25, 1948.
Reiner, Ed. "German POW Pays Nostalgic Visit." *The Gettysburg Times*, July 16, 2001.
Sauser, Paul. "Ex-German POWs Return: Their Memories of Fort Robinson Positive." *Star Herald*, August 22, 1987.
"Swastika Over Arizona." *Newsweek*, February 26, 1945.
"Town's Fond Memories of the Enemy." *The New York Times*, March 17, 2002.
Wiegman, Carl. 1945. "Nazi Prisoners Learn It Isn't So About U.S.: Decadent? 300,000 Are Changing Minds." *The Chicago Tribune*, April 6.

Archival Sources

Entry 11. POW Labor Program. Conference between WD and WMC, January 1944, Prisoner of War Labor — 1944.
Entry 155. Records of the Legal Services. General Records, 1942–45.
Entry 155. Records of the Legal Services, General Records. Field Instructions 69, October 19, 1943.
Entry 175. General Records Relating to POWs 1944–45, Regions I–VII.
Entry 180. Security-Classified Correspondence, 1941–45. POW Circular No. 3, January 4, 1944.
Entry 181. Report, Displaced Persons Branch, Civil Administration Division, Displaced Persons.
Entry 458. POW Division, Legal Branch. Report from William Molton. Division of Modern Languages Cornell University to Office of Military Government for Germany. "Former Special Prisoners of War." June 26, 1947.
Entry 439A. Prisoner of War Operations. Historical File, 1941–58. "Poll of German Prisoners of War Opinion." 1946.
Entry 439A. Memorandum from Armed Forces Office to commanding generals, nine service divisions, March 24, 1944.
Entry 439A. Prisoners of War Operations, Historical File, 1941–58. Memorandum from Armed Forces Office to commanding generals, nine service divisions, February 17, 1944.
Entry 439A. Prisoner of War Operations Historical File 1941–58. Memorandum from Armed Forces Office to commanding generals, nine service divisions, March 24, 1944
Entry 439A. Prisoner of War Operations Historical File 1941–58. Handbook for Work Supervisors of Prisoner of War Labor. Army Service Forces Manual M811. July 1945.
Entry 439A. Prisoner of War Operations Historical File 1941–58. Office of the Chief of Military History, Department of the Army, Washington, D.C. "Prisoner of War Operations." 4 vols. August 31, 1945.
Entry 467. POW Division, Legal Branch. Letters by employers and relatives of German prisoners of war inquiring to sponsor a POW, a nephew, cousin or brother.
Entry 467. POW Division, Legal Branch. Memorandum from War Department, the Adjutant General's Office, Washington, to Commanding Generals, First, Second, Third, Fourth, Fifth, Sixth, Seventh, Eighth and Ninth Service Command. Subject: "Employment of Prisoners of War off Reservations." August 24, 1943.
Entry 467. POW Division, Legal Branch. Memorandum from Headquarters Army Service Forces. Washington, D.C., to Commanding Generals, Fifth to Ninth Service Commands. Subject: "Violations of Prisoner of War Regulations." February 17, 1944.
Entry 467. POW Division, Legal Branch. Memorandum from Army Service Forces. Office of the Commanding General. Washington, D.C. to Commanding General. Subject: "Employment of Prisoners of War During Peak Agricultural and Food Processing Season." May 6, 1944.
New Mexico Farm and Ranch Heritage Museum. Las Cruces, NM.
NMF and RHM Oral History Program. Prisoners of War in New Mexico Agriculture. archives. nmsu.edu/rghc/index/pow/categories.html.
National Archives, College Park, Maryland
Record Group 260. Office of Military Government
Record Group 389. Office of the Provost Marshal General

Record Group 211 War Manpower Commission
Record Group 107. Records of the Secretary of War

Interviews (in the order in which they appear in the text)

Horst U., author mail and telephone interview, Spring Hill, FL, January 2007, and email follow-ups, 2009–10
Hermann B., author interview, Umatilla, FL, January, 23, 2003
Heino E., author interview, Holiday Inn, Muscatine, IA, October 6, 2002
Martin F., author interview, Wood Dale, IL, June 25, 2004
Willie, S., author interview, Darien, Il, April 10, 2003
Elmar B., author interview, Clair Shores, MI, October 25, 2002
Gunther K., author interview, Roseville, CA, February 22, 2003
Robert M., author interview, Temecula, CA, September 21, 2002
Hermann F., author interview, Averne, NY, December 14, 2002
Heinz E., author interview, Sun City, FL, February 28, 2004
Hans W., author interview, Georgetown, ME, May 17, 2003
Rudolf T., author interview, Des Moines, IA, December 13, 2003
Alfred M., author interview, December 13, 2002, follow-up interview with Edith M., Faribault, MN, September 13, 2003
Heinz R., telephone interview, Milwaukee, WI, February 17, 2003,
Wolf-Dieter Z., author interview at Tatexis Bleichroeder, New York, NY, February 20, 2004
Horst von O., author interview, Bethesda, MD, February 6, 2004
Gerhard H., author telephone interview, Fredericksburg, VA, February 9, 2009
Rupert M., author interview, Stuart, FL, January 24, 2003
Josef G., author interview, Scottsdale, AZ, September 19, 2002
Harry H., author interview, Kenilworth, IL, April 11, 2003
Heinrich T., author interview, Chicago, IL, June 25, 2004
Kurt P., author interview, Madison, WI, July 27, 2002
Henry K., author interview, Beaverton, OR, February 25, 2003
Oskar S., author interview at O.S. Machining, Clinton Township, MI, October 14, 2002
Ernst F., author interview, Grand Ledge, MI, October 23, 2002
Johannes (John) S., author interview at Four Points Hotel, North Palm Harbor, FL, February 28, 2004
Heinz F., author interview, Cottage Grove, OR, November 17, 2007
Ludwig N., author interview, Big Rapids, MI, August 24, 2004
Erwin H., telephone interview, Richmond, VA, December 12, 2010
Johann G., author interview, Bellingham, WA, April 28, 2003
Otto L., author interview, Salt Lake City, UT, September 23, 2002
Henry R., author interview, Charlottesville, VA, February 2001
Erich K., telephone interview, Ogden, UT February, 23, 2003, follow-up interview with Eleanor K., March 10, 2006.
Peter E., author interview, Cuyahoga Falls, OH, September 26, 2003
Siegfried K., author interview, Sebring, OH, October 27, 2002

Index